Globalization Unmasked

Globalization Unmasked
Imperialism in the 21st Century

James Petras and Henry Veltmeyer

Fernwood Publishing • Zed Books

Editing: Douglas Beall
Design and production: Beverley Rach
Printed and bound in Canada by Hignell Printing Limited

Published in Canada by Fernwood Publishing Ltd.
Box 9409, Station A
Halifax, Nova Scotia, B3K 5S3

Published in the rest of the world by Zed Books Ltd.
7 Cynthia Street, London NI 9JF, UK
and Room 400, 175 Fifth Avenue,
New York, 10010, USA
Distributed in the USA exclusively by Palgrave,
a division of St. Martins Press, LLC, 175 Fifth Ave., New York, 10010, USA.

Zed Books
ISBN   1 85649 939 1 Paper
ISBN   1 85649 938 3 Cloth

British CIP available from the British Library
American CIP has been applied for.

Fernwood Publishing Company Limited gratefully acknowledges the financial support of the Department of Canadian Heritage and the Canada Council for the Arts for our publishing program.

Le Conseil des Arts   The Canada Council
du Canada   for the Arts

First printing: April 2001
Second printing: May 2002

Canadian Cataloguing in Publication Data

Petras, James F., 1937-

Globalization unmasked: imperialism in the 21st century

Includes bibliographical references and index.
ISBN 1-55266-048-6 (bound). —ISBN 1-55266-049-4 (pbk.)

1. Globalization. 2. International economic relations. 3. Capitalism—Political aspects. I. Veltmeyer, Henry. II. Title.

JZ1318.P48 2201   337   C00-901779-8

Contents

Introduction

Currently the term "globalization" enjoys immense popularity. It is a key word in not only the dominant theoretical and political discourse but also in everyday language. As both a description of widespread, epoch-defining developments and a prescription for action, it has achieved a virtual hegemony and so is presented with an air of inevitability that disarms the imagination and prevents thought of and action towards a systemic alternative—towards another, more just social and economic order.

Chapters 1 to 3 of this book explore the ideological dimensions of "globalization," exposing the class project behind it—the attempt to obfuscate rather than accurately describe what is going on worldwide, the attempt to throw an ideological veil over the economic interests of an emerging class of transnational capitalists. In these interests, the existing world economic order is in the process of being renovated so as to create optimal conditions for the free play of greed, class interest and profit-making. In the same interests, this New World Order is portrayed as both inevitable and necessary, the driving force of the development process and harbinger of future prosperity. It is presented as the only road available.

Chapter 4 brings into focus an alternative term—"imperialism"—which the authors see as having much greater descriptive and analytical use for understanding what is going on. The term is rescued from a Marxist-informed discourse that has been abandoned by many intellectuals on the Left in the ideological war of words that has been unleashed in the wake of the collapse, in 1989, of socialism as it had taken form in the Soviet Union and Eastern Europe. It is ironic that, precisely when the conditions so well described and explained by the concept of "imperialism" have become truly global, it has been abandoned as a tool for understanding what is going on and informing political practice.

This book is offered as a modest contribution towards the rehabilitation of this notion of imperialism and its associated discourse. The "inevitability" of globalization and the adjustment or submission of peoples all over the world to free market capitalism depend on the capacity of the dominant and ruling classes to bend people to their will and make them see the interests of capital as their own. It also depends on the capacity of these dominant classes and their ideologues to undermine the growing resistance to their model of free market capitalism—or, for that matter, capitalism in any form.

We hope that this book will support and advance the intellectual and political opposition to the system being put into place everywhere. It will likely be a long and hard struggle, but the construction of a new, more just world that is truly emancipatory requires the forging of a new understanding, a set of intellectual tools and weapons that can be used in this struggle. "Imperialism" is one such tool, a weapon that can be turned against the advocates of "globalization" and the propagators and guardians of the world economic order.

Chapter 4 examines the imperialist project as it has been put into practice in Latin America. The focus of the chapter is on the machinations of Euro-American imperialism in the current context—at the beginning of a new millennium.

In Chapter 5, our focus shifts towards privatization, a key component of the neoliberal program of structural reforms and policies designed to create optimal conditions for global capital, freed from the restrictions and regulations under which it has operated to date. As of the 1950s and into the 1970s global capital had to contend with conditions generated by an economic model that was protective of domestic markets, promoted the nationalization of strategic industries and involved the regulation of the transnational corporations and banks, restrictions on foreign direct investment, and state intervention in the economy. The 1973 military coup against the democratically elected socialist regime of Salvador Allende in Chile set in motion forces of reaction and counter-revolution throughout the continent and beyond. Within a decade, a new economic model was put into place, creating widespread conditions for a New World Order that entrenched private ownership of the means of production, seeing the world market as the "engine of growth" and the private sector as its chauffeur. Chapter 5 examines some of the pitfalls of this form of development, with specific reference to privatization, a policy put on the political agendas of many countries across the system, North and South.

Chapter 6 turns towards the political dimension of neoliberal capitalism and its imperialist project. Until the 1980s, it was widely assumed by the advocates of and apologists for capitalist development that it required economic but not political liberalization (liberalism); the authoritarian state was viewed as a better political form of capitalist development than the liberal democratic state. In the 1980s, however, the whole issue was recast with an emphasis on *political liberalization* and the democratization of the state as an essential precondition, or inevitable consequence, of the *economic* liberalization process. In this intellectual and political context the long but uneasy relationship between capitalism and democracy was put into question. Chapter 6 examines the issues involved.

Chapters 7 and 8 focus on widespread efforts to give the structural adjustment (and globalization) process a social dimension and human face: a more equitable form of community-based and participatory "development" based on the decentralization of government, the strengthening of "civil society," and the agency of non-governmental organizations (NGOs). At issue here are three modalities of economic development: via (1) *process insertion*—electoral, globalization, modernization, development, etc.—by the state; (2)

project implementation by non-governmental organizations, in partnership with central governments and international development and financial institutions; and (3) *anti-systemic struggle* by social movements. These two chapters review the dynamics of thought and practice associated with each of these alternative approaches and expose the hidden agenda behind the community-based and local forms of "participatory development" that constitute the "new paradigm" of development. In this context we provide a critique of non-governmental organizations, widely viewed today by the social (versus political) Left, as well as governments and proponents of "another development," as the most appropriate and effective agency of economic change. As we see it, the agency of the NGOs reflects the World Bank's "cooperation for development" and partnership strategy, exposing thereby the local face of imperialism.

Chapters 9 and 10 go beyond the battle lines drawn by the forces of imperialism to examine some of the complex political dynamics involved in the implementation of their project. Once again, Latin America provides the context for this analysis, illuminating as it does a process that takes different forms in different parts of the world.

In the concluding chapter we provide a socialist perspective on the globalization project and the imperialist designs of capitalists in the U.S. and Europe. At issue here is the neoliberal model of capitalist development and, across the threshold of a new millennium, the need to reconstruct a socialist alternative. The possible conditions required for a socialist project in an age of imperialism are briefly reviewed.

Chapter 1

"Globalization" or "Imperialism"?

Posing the Problem

Globalization is at the centre of diverse intellectual and political agendas, raising crucial questions about what is widely considered to be the fundamental dynamic of our time—an epoch-defining set of changes that is radically transforming social and economic relations and institutions in the 21st century.

Globalization is both a description and a prescription, and as such it serves as both an explanation—a poor one, it has to be said—and an ideology that currently dominates thinking, policy-making and political practice. As a *description*, "globalization" refers to the widening and deepening of the international flows of trade, capital, technology and information within a single integrated global market. Like terms such as "the global village," it identifies a complex of changes produced by the dynamics of capitalist development as well as the diffusion of values and cultural practices associated with this development (UNRISD 1995; Watkins 1995; WCCD 1995). In this context, reference is often made to changes in the capitalist organization of production and society, extensions of a process of capital accumulation hitherto played out largely at the national level and restricted to the confines (and regulatory powers) of the state. As a *prescription*, "globalization" involves the liberalization of national and global markets in the belief that free flows of trade, capital and information will produce the best outcome for growth and human welfare (UNDP 1992). When the term "globalization" is used, whether to describe or prescribe, it is usually presented with an air of inevitability and overwhelming conviction, betraying its ideological roots.

How the before-mentioned epoch-defining developments and changes are interpreted depends in part on how "globalization" is conceived. Most scholars see it as a set of interrelated processes inscribed within the structures of the operating system based on capitalist modes of global production. Others, however, conceive of it not in structural terms but as the outcome of a consciously pursued strategy, the political project of a transnational capitalist class, and formed on the basis of an institutional structure set up to serve and advance the interests of this class.

We have here a major divide in analysis and theoretical perspective. On the one hand, those who view globalization as a set of interrelated processes tend to see it as inevitable, something to which necessary adjustments can and should be made. This is even the case for analysts like Keith Griffin (1995) on the left of a well-defined ideological divide within the field of development studies, a well-known proponent of "human development" as defined by the United Nations Development Program (UNDP) and a declared advocate of radical change or social transformation. From the inevitability-of-globalization perspective, the issue is how a particular country, or group of countries, can adjust to changes in the world economy and insert themselves into the globalization process under the most favourable conditions. Griffin, for one, believes that such integration and adjustment is both necessary and possible. The issue, he argues, is how the forces driving the globalization process can be harnessed to serve the requirements of human development (Griffin and Khan 1992).

On the other hand, those who view globalization as a class project rather than as an inevitable process tend to see the changes associated with it differently. In the first place, "globalization" is regarded as not a particularly useful term for describing the dynamics of the project. It is seen, rather, as we do—as an ideological tool used for prescription rather than accurate description. In this context it can be counterposed with a term that has considerably greater descriptive value and explanatory power: *imperialism*.

Using this concept, the network of institutions that define the structure of the new global economic system is viewed not in structural terms, but as intentional and contingent, subject to the control of individuals who represent and seek to advance the interests of a new international capitalist class. This class, it is argued, is formed on the basis of institutions that include a complex of some 37,000 transnational corporations (TNCs), the operating units of global capitalism, the bearers of capital and technology and the major agents of the new imperial order. These TNCs are not the only organizational bases of this order, which also include the World Bank, the International Monetary Fund (IMF) and other international financial institutions (IFIs) that constitute the self-styled "international financial community," or what Barnet and Cavenagh (1994) prefer to call "the global financial network." In addition, the New World Order is made up of a host of global strategic planning and policy forums such as the Group of Seven (G-7), the Trilateral Commission (TC) and the World Economic Forum (WEF); and the state apparatuses in countries at the centre of the system that have been restructured so as to serve and respond to the interests of global capital. All of these institutions form an integral part of the new imperialism—the new system of "global governance."

From this alternative perspective, "globalization" is neither inevitable nor necessary. Like the projects of capitalist development that preceded it—modernization, industrialization, colonialism and development—the new imperialism is fraught with contradictions that generate forces of opposition and resistance and that can, and under certain conditions will, undermine the capital accumulation process as well as the system on which it depends. The recent crisis of the Asian economies (of Indonesia, South Korea, Thailand, Malaysia, etc.) was deeply rooted in their integration into the world's financial markets and the highly volatile movement of international capital.

Globalists emphasize the constraints placed on government policy or the action of social groups, the strategies pursued by diverse social organizations and the possibility of significant or substantial (systemic) change. Critics of globalization, on the other hand, emphasize the opportunities and emergence of social forces for change provoked by the social contradictions of the imperialist system—developments that chronically disrupt all areas of life under capitalism. At issue in this controversy are the conflicting interests at play, the forces of opposition and resistance generated, and the practical political possibilities for mobilizing these forces.

The "inevitability" of globalization is a critical issue. But a more critical issue, perhaps, is what the discourse on globalization is designed to hide and obfuscate: the form taken by imperialism in the current, increasingly worldwide capitalist system for organizing economic production and society. (Chapter 3 explores some critical dimensions of this issue in Latin America, on the periphery of what has been termed the "world capitalist system.")

The Dynamics of Change: World Capitalism Today

There is little question that capitalism has undergone profound changes in its national and global forms of development in the post-World War II period. This is particularly obvious in view of the deep systemic crisis that beset the system in the late 1960s. Nor is there much argument about the capitalist nature of the organization that has been put into place. That this organization has increasingly taken a global form is also not disputed. In fact, this is the defining characteristic of the epochal shift that has occurred. What is disputed, however, is the significance and meaning of these changes, and the question of whether globalization represents a qualitatively new phenomenon or yet another phase in a long historical process of imperialist expansion.

Whatever view is taken on this point—and it is hotly disputed—it is possible to identify within the history of capitalist development a series of long waves, each of which is associated with a protracted period of crisis in the conditions of capital accumulation and a subsequent restructuring of the whole system. The last of these waves extended roughly from the 1920s to the 1970s. By drawing on diverse perspectives on this development, we can identify some key structures of the system put into place.

1. The concentration and centralization of capital that ensued in the last decades of the 19th century, in the context of a system-wide crisis in the late 1870s, resulted in the merging of large industrial and financial forms of capital, the growth of corporate monopolies, the territorial division of the world into colonies, the export of capital, and the worldwide extension of the market based on a division of labour between countries specializing in the production of manufactured goods and those oriented towards the production of raw materials and commodities.

2. The adoption of a Fordist regime of accumulation and mode of regulation resulted in a system of mass production and the scientific management of labour at the point of production within diverse formations of the nation-state.

3. Under pressure from labour unions and Left parties, a series of state-led

economic and social reforms created the political conditions for a capital-labour accord on the share of labour in productivity gains, the social redistribution of market-generated income, and the legitimacy of a capitalist state based on the provision of social programs (welfare, health and education) and the guarantee of full employment. In the pre-World War II context, these reforms were designed to save the capitalist system from its contradictory features and its propensity towards crisis. In addition, the representatives of the capitalist class accepted welfare reforms to compete with the new Communist welfare states for the allegiance and loyalties of the working class in Europe, Asia and the rest of the Third World. These welfare reforms did not put an end to the class struggle but did push it into reformist channels. These reforms, which in effect responded to the demands made by Marx in the *Communist Manifesto*, resulted in what Patel (1993) has termed "the taming of capitalism." In the post-war context, the deepening of social reforms temporarily instituted a social democratic form of state capitalism, a state-led capitalist development that expanded production on both a national and global scale.

4. In the post-World War II context of an East-West division of the world, the hegemony of the U.S. within the world economic system, a major decolonization process and the resolve (at Bretton Woods) to impose a liberal world economic order created the framework for twenty-five to thirty years of continuously rapid rates of economic growth and capitalist development—the "Golden Age of Capitalism" (Marglin and Schor 1990). Within the institutional framework and economic structure of this world order, and through the agency of the nation-state, a large part of the developing world—countries organized as the Group of 77 within the United Nations system—were incorporated into the development process, initiating what Patel (1992) has termed the "Golden Age of the South," characterized by high rates of economic growth and major advances in social development.

5. The state in many instances was converted into the major agency for national development, implementing an economic model based on nationalism, industrialization and modernization, the protection of domestic industry, and the deepening and extension of the domestic market to incorporate sectors of the working class and direct producers.

By the end of the 1960s this system experienced cracks in its foundations and began to fall apart under conditions of stagnant production, declining productivity, and intensified class conflict over higher wages, greater social benefits and better working conditions. These conditions created a profit-crunch on invested capital (Davis 1984). In this context, two schools of political economy emerged, one emphasizing the inherent tendency of capitalism towards crisis and the social contradictions that chronically disrupt all areas of capitalist life, the other laying stress and focusing on various forms and levels of response to systemic crisis. It is possible to identify several strategic responses:

1. *Diverse efforts of the U.S. administration to offset world market pressures on its production apparatus that had been reflected in a rapid deterioration in its trade*

balance and the loss of market share to the economies of Germany and Japan. These efforts took a number of forms, including the unilateral abrogation of the Bretton Woods agreement on the value and exchange rate of the U.S. dollar (with a fixed gold standard) and the manipulation by the Federal Reserve Board of exchange and interest rates (Aglietta 1982).

2. *Relocation by TNCs of their labour-intensive industrial operations in the search for cheaper labour.* In the process, there emerged a new international division of labour (NIDOL) characterized by the growth of a new global production system based on the operations of the TNCs and their affiliates, now estimated by the United Nations Conference on Trade and Development (UNCTAD 1994) to number some 206,000. By 1980 the world's top five hundred TNCs had an annual turnover exceeding $3 trillion (U.S. dollars), equivalent to almost 30 percent of gross world production and an estimated 70 percent of international trade (UNCTAD 1994: 93). According to UNCTAD, 50 percent of these operations, in terms of their market value, did not involve the world market but consisted of intra-firm transfers.

3. *The internationalization of capital in both productive forms (investment to extend trade and expand production) and unproductive or speculative forms.* The driving force behind this process was a policy of liberalization and deregulation. This strategy was designed and fostered by economists associated with the IFIs and was adopted all over the world by governments that were either dominated by transnational capital or subject to its dictates. The first form of capital to be internationalized and to escape the regulatory powers of the state involved the formation of offshore capital markets based on portfolio investments centred on speculation on foreign currency exchange rates. From the mid-1970s to the early 1990s the daily turnover of the foreign-exchange markets climbed from $1 billion to $1.2 trillion a day, close to twenty times the value of daily trade in goods and services (UNCTAD 1994; McMichael 1996). Joel Kurtzman, editor of the *Harvard Business Review*, estimates that for every U.S. dollar circulating in the real economy, $25–50 circulates in the world of pure finance (Sau 1996). Less than five percent of circulating capital has any productive function whatsoever (*Third World Guide 95/96*: 48).

On the heels of these globalizing and ballooning money markets, defined by the United Nations Conference on Trade and Development (UNCTAD 1994: 83) as "less visible but infinitely more powerful" than other capital flows, a number of banks in the 1970s began to internationalize their operations, resulting in a large-scale debt financing of government operations and development projects in countries all over the developing world. This was particularly the case for Mexico, Argentina and Brazil, countries that collectively received by volume over 50 percent of all such loans. In 1972 the estimated value of the overseas loans extended by these banks was $2 billion (Strange 1994: 112). The value of such loans peaked in 1981 at $90 billion ($58 billion for Latin America), falling to $50 billion in 1995 in the wake of a major region-wide debt crisis.

In the late 1980s, these forms of capital, used to finance government operations or development projects, increasingly gave way to foreign direct investment (FDI). This has become the capital of choice, estimated to represent up to 60 percent of the new capital extended to the developing world in the 1990s (UNIDO 1996). In 1990 the flow of FDI to Latin America and Asia, the two regions of the world that consumed the bulk of development finance or investment capital, was valued at only $2.6 billion, less than a twentieth of the international loans made that year. By 1995 the flow of FDI to Latin America had increased to $20.9 billion, more than 25 percent of the total loans extended to these two regions and close to one-half of all official transfers. Though most FDI goes to the Organization for Economic Co-operation and Development (OECD) countries, the higher rates of return on productive and speculative investments in developing countries and the opening up of privatization programs to the TNCs have resulted in a rapid expansion of FDI in this direction (UNCTAD 1994). By 1993, according to UNCTAD, developing countries attracted a record $80 billion in FDI, double the flow of 1991 and equal to the total level of FDI in the world in 1986. As a result, the share of these countries in the global flow of FDI, the largest component of new resource transfers to developing countries, grew from 20 percent in the mid-1980s to 40 percent by 1993 (UNCTAD 1994: xix, 3). One of the major consequences of developing countries' dependency on foreign financing is the growing vulnerability and volatility of their economies and financial markets as evidenced by the Mexican crash of 1994/95 and the near collapse of the economies of South Korea, Indonesia and Thailand in 1997. Massive foreign financing provides an immediate spur to growth, followed by a resounding economic crisis of overaccumulation, huge debt payments and collapse.

4. *The creation and growth of an integrated production system based on a new international division of labour, the global operations and strategies of the TNCs, a new enabling policy framework and new technologies.* These factors have dramatically shortened and lowered the costs of the transportation and communication circuits of capital in the production process and revolutionized the internal structure of production (see UNCTAD 1994: 123). By the end of the 1980s, entire lines of production and industries were technologically converted, and transformed in the process, dramatically raising the productivity of labour and shedding large numbers of workers and employees. This trend towards technological conversion and transformation has been associated with a shift in the structure of production and generated profound changes in labour markets and class structures all over the world.

5. *The adoption of new, flexible production methods based on a post-Fordist regime of accumulation and mode (or social structure) of regulation of both capital and labour.* These production methods were predicated on what has been termed a new "social structure of accumulation," a structure that requires a radical change in the relation of capital to labour. The conditions for such a change have been generated in different contexts through a protracted political process

based on an ongoing struggle between capital and labour which, according to Robinson (1996), has taken on the dimensions of another world war. The campaigns and battles in this war can be traced out at the national and the global level in political terms, and structurally in the reduced share of labour (wages) in the benefits of economic growth (income). Since the widespread implementation of neoliberal programs of structural adjustment in the 1980s, the share of labour in national income has been drastically reduced—from 48 percent to 38 percent in Chile, 41 percent to 25 percent in Argentina and 38 percent to 27 percent in Mexico (Veltmeyer 1999a). In terms of a tendency towards wage dispersal (deviation from the average), the fall in the real value of wages and the share of wages in value added to production, the situation is even worse. In Latin America, conditions of structural adjustment have exaggerated disparities in income and wealth that were already the worst in the world.

6. *In the 1980s and 1990s, capital launched a direct assault on labour in terms of its wages, conditions and benefits, as well as its capacity to organize and negotiate contracts.* This offensive has taken numerous forms and is reflected in empirical evidence of a reduced capacity and level of labour organization, the compression and polarized spread of wages, the fall of wages as a share of national income, widely observed changes in the structure of labour markets all over the world and associated conditions of employment and unemployment (Veltmeyer 1999a).

The International Labour Organization (ILO) (1996) argues that this system-wide decline in the value of wages and the dramatic expansion of jobs at the low end of the wage spectrum result in part from changes in the structure of production (the shift towards services, etc.), the introduction of new technologies and changes in the global economy. However, it adds, with reference to the U.S., that at least 20 percent of the variance can be attributed directly to a weakening of labour's capacity to negotiate collective agreements, which is directly associated with declines in organizational capacity and level of unionization and with the decentralization of negotiations (from the sectoral to the firm level)—all consequences of a protracted political struggle with capital.

It is evident that labour has borne the brunt of the restructuring and adjustment process. In the global context it is estimated by UNCTAD (*Third World Guide 95/96*: 28) that up to 120 million workers are now officially unemployed (35 million in the European Community alone) and another 700 million are seriously underemployed, separated from their means of production and eking out a bare existence in what the ILO defines as the unstructured or informal sector, accounting for over 50 percent of the developing world's labour force (ILO 1996; McMichael 1996). In addition to this reservoir of surplus labour, it is estimated by the authors that a mobile labour force of 80 million expatriate labourers has formed to constitute a new world labour market.

7. *The creation of a New World Order found expression in the founding of the*

IMF and the World Bank, which established an institutional framework for a process of capitalist development and free international trade. Initially, in the 1940s, protectionist forces in the U.S. prevented the institution of a third element of this world economic order, namely the International Trade Organization (ITO). In a compromise solution, the institution of the General Agreement on Tariffs and Trade (GATT), a forum designed to liberalize trade through various rounds of negotiation, cleared the way for a world market with low tariffs and the elimination of other barriers to free trade in goods and services. It was not until 1994, fifty years later, that the original design was completed in the form of the World Trade Organization (WTO), instituted as part of an ongoing effort to renovate the existing world economic order and establish what ex-president Bush and the Heritage Foundation, a Washington-based right-wing policy forum, termed the "New World Order."

The pursuit of the New World Order and the widespread adoption of structural adjustment programs (SAPs) led to a new enabling policy framework for a global free trade regime and the constitution of a new imperial economy. Its one missing element was a general agreement governing the free flow of investment capital. It is to this end that the political representatives of imperial capital designed the Multilateral Agreement on Investment (MAI), at first behind the closed doors of the OECD, the club of the world's richest and most powerful nations, and then the World Trade Organization, its latest and one of its most effective institutional weapons. The MAI and GATT, as well as the WTO itself have been criticized by, *inter alia*, the South Commission (South Centre 1997a). The Commission argued that the imperial arrangements pressed for by the GATT and to be facilitated by the MAI were not in the interest of the South. For one thing, "a fully liberalized regime ... would not necessarily promote widespread growth and development or take account of developing countries' preoccupations" (1997a: 2). On the contrary, the Commission notes, the worldwide implementation of liberalization, deregulation and privatization measures since the mid-1980s has resulted in a significant deterioration of socio-economic conditions for a large part of the world's population and a widening of the North-South gap in market-generated wealth and income. In addition, these measures have seriously eroded the capacity of developing countries to pursue and advance their national interests, not to mention to control their own destiny. Echoing the conclusions of the UNDP, a recent statement by the South Commission was that "[globalization] is proceeding largely for the benefit of the dynamic and powerful countries" (1997a: 82).

The UNDP's conclusion was derived from its analysis of the anticipated results of a process unleashed by the implementation of agreements negotiated at the GATT Uruguay Round. At the time, the UNDP (1992) calculated that these agreements would lead to an increase of $212–510 billion in global income— anticipated gains from greater efficiency, higher rates of return on capital, and expansion of trade. But the least developed countries, it argued, as a group would lose up to $60 million a year. Sub-Sahara Africa, containing a group of countries that could least afford losses and their associated social costs, would lose $1.2 billion a year (UNDP 1992: 82).

The loss for the least developed countries that would result from the GATT-induced growth in global incomes—and from their unequal access to trade, labour and capital—was estimated by the UNDP at $500 billion a year, ten times what they receive annually in the form of foreign assistance (1992: 87). In this context, the UNDP added, the notion that the benefits of increased free trade on a global scale would necessarily trickle down to the poorest "seem far-fetched" to say the least. Subsequent developments have confirmed this worst-case scenario.

8. *The restructuring of the capitalist state to serve the imperial project.* For Aglietta (1982) and other regulationists, the world economy is theorized as a system of intersecting national social formations, which is to say, nation-states that have been able to resist what Petras and Brill (1985) have termed "the tyranny of Globalization." As Lipietz (1987: 24–25), a companion-in-theory of Aglietta, has put it: "A system must not be seen as an intentional structure or inevitable destiny [simply] because of its coherence.... Its coherence is simply the effect of the interaction between several relatively autonomous processes, of the provisionally stabilized complementarity and antagonism that exists between various national regimes of accumulation." These regimes, Lipietz (1987: 14) notes, are identifiable at the level of the nation-state and are designed to secure "the long term stabilization of the allocation of social production between consumption and accumulation." The same applies to the corresponding "mode of regulation," which "describes a set of internalized rules and social procedures for ensuring the unity of a given regime of accumulation" (Lipietz 1987: 14). In this view, the nation-state remains the major agency of the capital accumulation process even under conditions of its globalization.

Notwithstanding considerable evidence of the state's continued prominence and agency within the global development process, it is just as clear that under the present widespread structural and political conditions, the powers of the nation-state have been significantly eroded, giving way to the influence of international institutions. A closer look at these IFIs (the World Bank, IMF, Inter-American Development Bank [IDB], etc.) reveals that within their internal composition and mode of selection of key policy-makers and beneficiaries, a distinct set of nation-states are dominant, namely the advanced capitalist, or imperialist, states of North America, Europe and Asia. This was already well recognized in the 1970s when the sheer size and economic clout of the biggest TNCs, as well as their relative international mobility, was seen as a major pressure on national sovereignty—on the capacity of the state to regulate the operations of capital or make national policy. In the 1980s, under the conditions of the New World Order, the powers of the state have been drastically reduced relative to those of TNCs and other global organizations. Political economists such as Manfred Bienefeld (1995), formed in an earlier mould, deplore this fact and search for conditions that might restore to the nation-state its sovereign powers or policy-making capacity. Others, Keith Griffin (1995) among them, argue that globalization and reduced power for the state are inevitable. From this perspective, the view and efforts of scholars such as Bienefeld, who is oriented towards a Keynesian welfare state or a strong developmentalist state able to determine national policy over vital areas of economic and social life, are somewhat quixotic and highly anachronistic.

Cutting across this debate is a view of the new role of the state in a context of globalization, whereby the real issue is seen to be not the reduction of the size and powers of the state, the loss of national sovereignty or the hollowing out of state responsibilities and functions, but the realignment of the state towards the interests of the transnational capitalist class.

The Economic Benefits of Globalization and Their Distribution

Another major issue is whether world inequalities and the North-South gap in the distribution of economic resources and income is growing, as supporters of the imperialism thesis argue, or, as globalization theorists argue, conditions are maturing for a reduction of these disparities. This issue would seem to be easily settled by examination of relevant facts and statistics. However, the question is by no means clear or settled. It has been widely recognized or conceded that market-led or market-friendly developments associated with globalization have exacerbated existing global inequalities or generated new ones. Social inequalities in the distribution of economic or productive resources, and income, are widely seen to be on the increase. Many studies along these lines take a critical approach towards neoliberal capitalism and global development. However, even a number of advocates and apologists for globalization have come to the same view. The UNDP, for example, in its 1992 *Human Development* report determined that from 1960 to 1989 those countries with the richest 20 percent of the world's population saw their share of global output (income) rise from 70.2 percent to 82.7 percent while the share of those with the poorest 20 percent shrank from 2.3 percent to 1.4 percent. The United Nations Industrial Development Organization (UNIDO 1997) has argued the same point on the basis of more recent data.

Similarly, the World Bank and the International Monetary Fund have acknowledged that a large number of countries have regressed in the conditions of their development, in many cases to levels achieved in 1980 or even 1970. These countries have clearly failed to share in the fruits of recent development or to participate in what is seen by the World Bank (1995: 9) as a "trend towards prosperity." In the case of sub-Saharan Africa, it is estimated by the World Bank (2000) that per capita incomes since 1987 have fallen by 25 percent. The World Bank explains this failure in terms of wrong-headedness or policy mistakes, to an inability or unwillingness of certain countries to draw the necessary lessons from the development record or consistently pursue prescribed policies and adopt the institutional changes required. The Bank takes the position that, on the basis of correct policies, the gap in global incomes can be closed and more and more countries can share in the "trend towards prosperity."

Advocates of globalization have not been especially concerned about the identified increase in global social inequalities. With reference to a theory that has been converted into a doctrine, growing inequalities are generally taken to be the inevitable *short-term* effect of the market-led growth process, based as it is on an increase in the national savings rate and an increased propensity to invest these savings. The reason for this is that necessary conditions for an increase in the rate of savings and investment include a larger share of capital in national income and, ergo, a decline in the share of income available for consumption, that is, distributed in the form of wages or salaries. A trend in this direction has been identified at the national level in diverse contexts, particularly in Latin America, but it also exists at the global level. Indeed, global disparities in income have reached such a point that some scholars are drawing attention to them as a problem that could reach crisis proportions. The political dimensions of these global social inequalities have been subject to considerable analysis and, at the national level, to corrective policy. The problem is that the social discontent generated by these inequalities is liable to be mobilized into movements of opposition and resistance, giving the adjustment process the potential to destabilize political regimes committed to them (on this point see chapters 4 and 5).

Despite broad agreement among advocates and opponents of globalization that global inequalities in economic resources and income can be assumed or shown to be on the increase since the mid-1980s, there are some who argue the contrary—that the North-South gap is closing. Interestingly (or oddly) enough, this point has been made by, *inter alia*, Griffin (1995), a recognized opponent of market-led development and an advocate of state regulation of the operations of capital in the market. As Griffin sees it, and argues in a heated debate with Bienefeld, the empirical evidence clearly suggests that the North-South income gap is closing rather than growing. Griffin also argues that global income inequality has begun to diminish in recent years. There has occurred, he notes, "a remarkable change in the distribution of the world's income," with average global incomes rising, resulting in many of the poor becoming less poor.

Is this an empirical or conceptual issue? How can Griffin's view be reconciled with the argument advanced by Bienefeld and many others that the North-South gap in wealth and income has been growing and has accelerated under conditions of structural adjustment and globalization? The UNDP, for example, has documented a dramatic worsening of the disparity in income distribution between the richest and poorest segments of the world's population along North-South lines. According to the UNDP (1992), since 1980, the disparity between the poorest and richest 20 percent of the world's population has increased from 11:1 to 17:1. UNIDO, which makes reference to an earlier study by Griffin and Khan (1992), makes the same point in different terms, citing the obvious fact (also noted by the UNDP) that globalization has clear winners and losers, and that the developing countries are clearly the losers. A part of the discrepancy in viewpoint and analysis lies in the assumption made by Griffin and others that with the rise of average global incomes the poor are relatively better off. However, as Bienefeld (1995) points out, most of the world's poor do not have access to income-generating productive resources. And with the explosive growth of the world's informal sectors and low-income activities or forms of employment, as well as the sharp decline of real wages and wage incomes in many parts of the world, a significant part of the world's population is worse off today than in the mid-1980s. Quite apart from the growth of average incomes at the global level, this deterioration in socio-economic conditions is reflected in the persistent growth in numbers of those in poverty, whether measured in absolute numbers or as a percentage of population.

The dynamics of this process might take the form of structural forces (or that is how they appear to many economists), but they relate to actions by organizations and capitalist enterprises clearly taken in their own interests. This was the point—one not well understood or ignored by many economists—made by the prime minister of Malaysia in his critical remarks on a global economic system that allows "traders [to] take billions of dollars of profits and pay absolutely no taxes to the countries they impoverish" (South Centre 1997a: 7). Michel Chossudovsky (1997) documents the working of this process on a global scale. He views the process in the same way as did the delegates at the April 2000 Conference of the Group of 77 (now 133)—as the globalization of poverty.

The "globalist view" that describes the world market as made up of integrated and interdependent national economies was totally demolished by the events leading to and following the collapse of the Asian economies, when insolvent loans led to massive bankruptcies among of banks and enterprises. Asian regimes putting out the begging bowl to the big banks of Europe, North America and Japan highlighted the nature of imperial relations in the so-called globalized economy. U.S. and European TNC buyouts of large Asian corporations for a fraction of their previous value, under the dictates by U.S. and European leaders of the terms of refinancing, further highlight the imperial nature of interstate relations in the world economy. The outcome of the Asian and Latin American crises in which the former lose and the imperial financiers win describes not "integration" and interdependence but rather subordination and imperialism. The inequalities and exploitation that define the interstate system illustrate the utility of the imperial over the globalist conceptual framework.

The Political Dimension of Globalization: The Question of Governance

One of the political arguments of globalization theorists has been that a diffusion of democratic institutions or the democratization of existing institutions accompanies the growth of "free markets." This process has unfolded at various levels. One has been a widespread trend towards decentralization of government that for the most part can be traced back to initiatives "from above and within" the state apparatus. In theory, if not in practice, this process has created some of the mechanisms and conditions (local power) for popular participation in public decision-making (Veltmeyer 1999a). However, the critics of "decentralization" point to the lack of control by local authorities over the allocation of funds and the design of macroeconomic policy, and to the undemocratic nature of the selection of local officials. Another dimension of the "(re)democratization" process has been a shift away from military regimes and unconstitutional governments and towards civilian regimes formed within the institutional framework of liberal democracy. (Chapter 5 expands on this theme and identifies the associated or lack of dynamics of change.)

These trends have been so pervasive and concomitant with the institution of market-friendly economic reforms and structural adjustment policies that they have revived notions of a necessary link between economic and political forms of liberalization. Whereas the orthodox view of liberal scholars and politicians has been, and for many corporate CEOs still is, that authoritarian regimes are more likely to institute free-market neoliberal reforms and create the political conditions for rapid economic growth, the "new" ideology is that political liberalization (the institution of liberal democracy) either is the necessary precondition for or the inevitable result of the prescribed market-oriented reforms. In this context, the U.S. and international institutions such as the World Bank have turned against the dictatorships and authoritarian regimes they once nurtured or supported. In the name of democracy and as its self-appointed guardians, they now promote the institution of liberal democracy and even require it as a condition of access to aid, loans or investment capital (on this point see the World Bank's 1997 *World Development Report*).

Needless to say, this issue remains unsettled. What is clear is that the democracy now called for by the U.S. involves what Robert Dahl, *inter alia*, has termed "polyarchy," an elite-led form of liberal democracy. Not only is there no effective form of popular participation or substantive democracy in this institution, but under conditions of globalization, effective decision-making on key policy issues, including the regulation of capital, have been shifted towards international institutions, such as the IMF, the World Bank and the G-7 forum, that are notoriously undemocratic in their political processes.

At issue here is the capture of the state by global capital, or its reorientation towards the interests vested in the globalization process. In this context, the role of the new neoliberal state can be defined in terms of three critical functions: (1) to adopt fiscal and monetary policies that ensure macroeconomic stability; (2) to provide the basic infrastructure necessary for global economic activity; and (3) to provide social control, order and stability. The role of the neoliberal state prescribed by these functions has been to facilitate accumulation on a global scale and, it would seem, to regulate labour, which for some reason is less mobile today than it was in an earlier era of globalization from 1870 to the First World War. To assume this role, the state has been generally downsized, decentralized and modernized, and has had its regulatory and policy-making capacities hollowed out.

Another matter of particular concern to global capital is the question of governance, or the capacity to govern. The problem is posed by Ethan Kapstein (1996), Director of the U.S. Council on Foreign Relations, in terms of the growing social inequalities in the global distribution of incomes which, he argues, exceed the level at which the forces of opposition and resistance can be contained. At issue is an emerging and potentially explosive level of social discontent which could all too easily be mobilized into political movements of opposition and resistance. The forces generated and mobilized by these move-ments, Kapstein fears, are likely to undermine and destabilize newly formed democratic regimes committed to market-oriented or friendly economic re-forms. As a result these regimes are unlikely to stay the course, underlining the political will needed to fully implement the prescribed medicine of structural adjustment. The governability of the whole process, he concludes, is at risk, threatened by mounting forces of opposition and resistance.

Labour in the World Economy

The brunt of the capitalist globalization process has been borne by labour, the restructuring of which in effect has been the major mechanism of structural adjustment. This process has two major dimensions *vis-à-vis* labour. On the one hand, the capitalist development process has separated large numbers of direct producers from their means of production, converting them into a proletariat and creating a labour force which at the global level was estimated to encompass 1.9 billion workers and employees in 1980, 2.3 billion in 1990 and close to 3 billion by 1995 (ILO 1996). On the other hand, the demand for labour has grown more slowly than its supply. The process of technological change and economic reconversion endemic to capitalist development has generated an enormous and growing pool of surplus labour, an industrial reserve army that is estimated at one-third of the total global labour force. An estimated 50 percent of the enormous proletariat generated by capitalist development is either unemployed or underemployed, eking out a bare existence in the growing informal sector of the Third World's burgeoning urban centres or on the margins of the capitalist economy.

Our prognosis for the first decade of the 21st century is that the deepening crisis in Asia and the continuing crisis in Latin America will lead to an enormous growth of informal workers with incomes at or below the level of subsistence; large-scale movements of impoverished workers and peasants back and forth between urban and rural economies; the cheapening of industrial production and a decline in well-paid jobs in the advanced capitalist countries; the growth of poorly paid service jobs; and a worldwide crisis of living standards for labour.

Technological innovations, largely related to the processing of information, will lead to the growth of a relatively small elite of well-paid software engineers and executives and a mass of poorly paid "information processors"—the new proletariat. The outsourcing of labour-intensive computer work to low-wage areas is already a growing social phenomenon. Thus, the centrality of wage labour—contrary to the prognosis of the globalization theorists who talk about the "disappearance of wage labour"—will greatly increase even as it is impoverished. Insofar as the new information systems are linked to the vast movement of speculative capital, they can be seen as an integral technical instrument in the assault on productive capital and the living standards of wage workers.

The social and political implications of this change are momentous. For one thing, it will generate a radically different social structure and system of class relations. For another, it highlights the strategic position of labour. Combined with the growth of a huge industrial reserve army (mainly informal and contingent in form) and its depressant effect on the wages of the employed, the change wrought in the labour force and the social structure of society will undermine and weaken the capacity of capital to discipline labour and to stimulate the accumulation process.

Forces of Opposition and Resistance

For the sake of analysis, the economy and society are often portrayed as a system, which is to say, a set of interconnected structures, the conditions of which are objective in their effects and whose operation (on people, classes and nations) can be theorized by reference to "laws of development." The problem with this systems perspective is that it is all too easy to confuse an analytical tool—in this case a theoretical model—with reality. In this confusion structures are reified and their conditions are attributed an objectivity they do not have. As a result the structure of economic and social relations that people enter into is viewed as a mould into which they must pour their behaviour. And the institutionalized practices that make up the structure of the system appear as a prison from which there is no escape, subjecting individuals and entire nations to forces that are beyond their ability to control, let alone understand. Needless to say, this view breeds complacence and resignation—and notions of inevitability. Globalization appears as an immanent and intelligible process to which adjustments must be made.

The reality, however, is otherwise. In fact, the system, if it exists (and for the sake of analysis we too assume that it does), is fraught with contradictions that generate forces of opposition and resistance—of social change. However, as a matter of principle, for the sake of both analysis and political action, we argue that there is nothing inevitable about globalization viewed either as a process or a project. Like the underlying system, it is instituted by an identifiable class of individuals—transnational capitalists—and advanced in their collective or individual interests related to the accumulation of capital.

Chapter 2

Globalization:
A Critical Analysis

The term "globalization" has been used in a multiplicity of senses. Concepts like "the global interdependence of nations," "the growth of a world system," "accumulation on a world scale," "the global village" and many others are rooted in the more general notion that the accumulation of capital, trade and investment is no longer confined to the nation-state. In its most general sense, "globalization" refers to cross-national flows of goods, investment, production and technology. For many advocates of the globalization thesis, the scope and depth of these flows have created a New World Order, with its own institutions and configurations of power that have replaced the previous structures associated with the nation-state.

Globalists have been engaged in a debate with critics over the meaning and significance of the changes in the capitalist political economy. The debate revolves around whether the present stage of capitalism represents a new epoch or is basically a continuation of the past, an amalgam of new developments that can be understood through existing categories of capitalist development. Included in this debate is a discussion of whether the term "globalization" itself is useful in understanding the organization and nature of the flows of capital, goods and technology. Counterposed to the concept of globalization is the notion of "imperialism," which attempts to contextualize the flows, locating them in a setting of unequal power among conflicting states, classes and markets.

This chapter is an effort to rethink the concept of globalization at both the theoretical and practical levels. The fact that capitalism today has spread to practically every geographical region of the world, subsumes all economies under its sway and exploits labour everywhere for private accumulation raises several specific analytical questions that will be addressed.

First, from the perspective of conceptual and historical analysis, what are the origins of the transnational flows of capital, goods, services and technology? Is globalization a phenomenon of early or late capitalism? If the latter, how is it similar or different from the former? What interstate relations have allowed for international flows of capital and trade in commodities? Who were the social agents and what were the objectives of these flows? If what is described as globalization existed earlier, why is it deemed a novelty today? If there is not a linear process leading to globalization, is it more appropriate to examine cyclical tendencies towards outward flows (to the world market) and inward flows (internal to the nation-state) of capital and commodities? If the direction of flow is variable, what are the determining socio-economic and political institutions and classes? At a more general level, if the flows vary over time and place, subject to the influence of different political actors, what does that tell us about the argument of globalist theorists that globalization is inevitable and the counter-argument of critics who say that it is contingent?

In answer to these questions, we proceed to critically analyze several of the basic premises of globalization theorists: the claim of inevitability, the notion that globalization represents a novel development, and its denial of alternatives. We will also analyze the divergence between the grand claims of the globalists' theories and their meagre explanatory power—their claim to be the filet mignon of social theory while their results approximate baloney. (Hence we can introduce the concept of "globaloney" as a way of highlighting the contrast between globalist rhetoric and contemporary realities.) In the following section, we will turn towards an analysis of the political, economic and technological causes of the increasing transnational flows of capital and commodity trade. There we will focus on the macrodynamics of the capital-labour relation and of state power as a basis for rejecting a technological interpretation of these dynamics. We argue that historic changes in political and class power in the context of a severe crisis of accumulation led to the creation of conditions favourable to increased flows in previously closed areas and that technological innovations were at first the consequence and then the cause of these increasing flows.

The political changes that facilitated external flows also had profound distributional consequences. Our argument here is that the growing power of capital over labour with the liberation of capital from state-imposed restrictions also led to a massive re-concentration of wealth. This argument proceeds from the notion that a key to understanding globalist thinking is its use as an ideology to justify growing social inequalities, greater social polarization and the increasing transfer of state resources to capital. Even if globalization theory has little intellectual merit, we argue, it does serve an essential political purpose as an ideological rationalization for growing class inequalities.

The last section of this chapter focuses on resistance, opposition and alternatives to the New World Order. If we are correct in pointing to class and state relations as the decisive nexus, then it follows that changes in class relations and power can create the basis for an alternative to "globalization." The final section examines a key element in globalist ideology: privatization. The chapter concludes with a positing of alternatives that call globalist dogma into question.

Conceptual and Historical Analysis

Historically the international flows of capital and commodity trade have taken place via three routes: through (1) imperialist and colonial conquest, (2) trade and investment among advanced capitalist countries and (3) exchanges among Third World countries. Each route embodies different relations and has had different consequences. The imperial-colonial flows of capital led to unequal accumulation and a division of labour in which economic diversification and industrialization in the imperial centre was accompanied by specialization and vulnerability to raw material fluctuations in the colonized regions. The second route of international flows, among advanced imperial centres, was "mutually compatible" in that foreign capital was regulated to complement internal capitalist development. The third route towards globalization, through exchanges among Third World countries, was limited by the intrusion of imperial powers and the relationships of Third World economies with their imperial centres. The main periods of intra–Third World exchanges occurred before these geographical entities were colonized and during the post-colonial industrializing phase.

The theoretical point here relates to the long history, diversity of sources, and differential relations and consequences that accompany the expansion of international flows of capital and commodity trade. The historical fact is that the U.S., Africa, Asia and Latin America have a history of several centuries of ties to overseas markets, exchanges and investments. Moreover, in the cases of North and Latin America, capitalism was born "globalized," in the sense that most of their early growth was based on overseas exchanges and investments. From the 15th to the 19th century Latin America's external trade and investment had greater significance than during the 20th century. Similarly, as shown by Blackburn (1998), one-third of English capital formation in the 17th century was based on the international slave trade. It is only in the middle of the 19th century that the internal market began to gain in importance, thanks to the growth of wage labour, local manufactures and, most significantly, a state which altered the balance of class forces between the domestic and overseas-oriented investors and producers.

The significance of the historical shift from a globalized to a domestic path towards development was based on the emergence of middle classes determined to play a central role in the political economy *vis-à-vis* financiers and staple and grain-producing agro-exporters. The transition was not smooth: in the U.S., the Civil War, in which globalizing plantation owners were subordinated to the interests of western farmers and eastern industrialists, cost two million lives. In Latin America, civil wars and overseas intervention raged throughout the 19th century as globalizers and domestic producers battled over the direction of the economy. Major wars (the Opium War, Perry's expedition to Japan, etc.) were waged to globalize Asia, while emerging domestic producers resisted under the leadership of traditional elites. The point is that globalization in its old imperial form based on European traders, manufacturers and local agricultural and mining elites was seen as a major obstacle to development by the modern emerging producers. The fact that the immediate opponents of globalization were decrepit emperors (China) or corrupt dictators (Latin America) should not obscure the fact that globalization as it had emerged from the 15th to the 19th century had become a serious obstacle to the development of a modern economy.

Sociologically speaking, the objects and subjects of globalization up to the 20th century were distinct groups. While capital and goods expanded across national boundaries, they were centred in specific nation-states. The results of expansion provided unequal benefits among classes in both the capital exporting and receiving countries. Today this tendency is even more marked, even as countries which previously were objects of capital flows and commodity trade have themselves become exporters. The crucial difference today is the presence of transnational capitalists from the former colonial countries who are engaged in capital export and establishing regional dominance.

The cases of China, Hong Kong, Taiwan, South Korea, Chile, Mexico and Saudi Arabia are only a few instances. The point, however, is that the multiplication of new centres of accumulation and the addition of new billionaires from the ex-colonial countries does not change the qualitative class and national relations: much of Latin America, Africa and Asia continues to specialize in primary goods exports, labour power with high rates of exploitation, and substantial imbalances in payments for rents (royalties) and services (insurance and interest). In effect, the expansion of capital flows and commodity trade via unequal relations in the contemporary period is a continuation of the imperialist relations of the past. The subjects of globalization—the principal traders, investors and renters of services—have interests antagonistic to those of the objects of their policies—the workers, peasants and national producers in the targeted countries. What is described as globalization is thus essentially a perpetuation of the past based on a deepening and extension of exploitative class relations into areas previously outside of capitalist production. The globalist claims of novelty and the assertion that we are entering a new stage of the world economy are largely based on the assertion that accretions and expansions of capitalist relations are sufficient to define the new period. Globalist ideologues forget that past economic activities were also rooted in international exchanges and production and that the current expansion based on international flows is not the predominant engine of capitalist reproduction. Moreover, the shifts in the axes of capitalist expansion from domestic production and exchange (enlarging the home market) to the world market has always been contingent on the political and socio-economic composition of the state, which orients economic policy.

It is useful to compare and contrast the concepts of globalization and imperialism to highlight the analytical weaknesses of the former and the strengths of the latter. The relative explanatory power of the two concepts is revealed by their measures of power; specifications of agency; understandings of regional, national and class inequalities; and explanations of the directional flows of income, investment, and payments (royalties, interest, profits, rents).

The concept of globalization argues for the interdependence of nations, the shared nature of their economies, the mutuality of their interests and the shared benefits of their exchanges. Imperialism, in contrast, emphasizes the domination and exploitation by imperial states and multinational corporations and banks of less-developed states and labouring classes. In today's world it is clear that the imperial countries are less and less dependent on the Third World countries they trade with: the composition of traded commodities is increasingly rich in information and low in the raw materials that characterize Third World exports; imperial countries have diverse suppliers; the major economic units are owned and operated in large part by stockholders in the imperial countries; and profits, royalties, rents and interest payments flow upward and outward in an asymmetrical fashion. In addition, within the international financial agencies and other world bodies, the imperial countries wield disproportionate or decisive influence. In comparison, the dominated countries are low-wage areas, interest and profit exporters (not importers), virtual captives of the international financial institutions and highly dependent on limited overseas markets and export products. Hence the concept of imperialism fits the realities much better than globalization.

With regard to specification of the social agency involved—the mainspring of transnational flows of capital and commodity trade—the concept of globalization relies heavily on diffuse notions of technological change and information flows and the abstract notion of "market forces." In contrast, the concept of imperialism sees the multinational corporations and banks and the imperial states, as the driving force of the international flows of capital and commodity trade. A survey of major events, world trade treaties and regional integration themes is enough to dispel any explanation based on technological determinism: it is the policy-makers of the imperial states who establish the framework for global exchanges. Within that shell, the major transactions and organizational forms of capital movements are found in the transnational corporations, supported by international financial institutions, whose personnel are appointed by the imperial states. Technological innovations operate within parameters that further this configuration of power. The concept of imperialism thus gives us a more precise idea of the social agencies of worldwide movements of capital and trade in commodities than the notion of globalization.

Data covering long- and short-term flows of incomes at world, national and class levels consistently show an increase of inequalities between imperial states and dominated states, investors and workers, agro-exporters and peasants. The assumptions of the theory of imperialism are compatible with this outcome; the assumptions of globalization theory are not. Moreover, there is a robust relation between the growth of international flows of capital and the increase of inequalities between states and between CEOs and workers. The best face that globalists can put on the matter is to shift from an argument for greater general prosperity to justifying inequalities in terms of unequal rewards for differential contributions. In a rather self-serving and tautological fashion, this argument depends on emphasizing the contribution of capital and devaluating the role of labour. Even here the concept of imperialism, with its focus on the value creation of labour and the value appropriation by capital, is more to the point:

it sheds light on the different loci of exploitation (labour, dominated countries) and accumulation (capital, imperial firms and states).

The structure of the international flows of income, investments and royalty payments does not correspond to any notion of an interdependent world. In contrast, singular concentration and unidirectional flows towards imperial-based corporations makes sense and is easily explained by the theory of imperialism.

The same is true regarding military policy and intelligence operations. The flow of intervention is unidirectional, from the imperial centres to the dominated countries. There is no mutual penetration of military commands, but only the extension of military missions from the imperial centre to the dominated countries. In legal terms, only the imperial countries raise claims of extraterritoriality (the supremacy of their laws over the laws of other sovereign nations); the dominated countries invariably are the targets.

These empirical measures allow us to argue for the greater scientific utility of the concept of imperialism over globalization. Both as an explanation and as an organizing principle of the major structural relations in the world political economy, the notion of imperialism has become more, not less, relevant.

The struggle in the world today is not only between different conceptual, historical or analytical frameworks. It involves living forces. As important as the issue of theoretical clarification is, it is crucial to look at the political actors engaged in the struggles. To this we turn.

Advocates, Adversaries and Ambivalents

Although a variety of international exchanges are not embedded directly in imperial relations (exchanges between imperial states, exchanges between dominated countries, exchanges regulated by regimes of popular accumulation), we will focus on the imperialist component of global flows of capital and commodity trade.

There are essentially three "classes" or "actors" in the world political economy: the advocates and beneficiaries of globalization; the adversaries and exploited classes and states; and those who experience both exploitation and benefits and waver in their response. The proponents of globalization, both now and in the past, are always from the ascending countries within the world economy. In this logic the principal supporter is the hegemonic state. Obviously its superior competitive position gives it little to fear and much to gain from opening the economy. Nevertheless, two caveats are in order: not all classes in ascending nation-states are beneficiaries—mainly the large dominant enterprises prosper. Secondly, while proclaiming the universality of global principles (free trade, free markets and free remittances), the ascending powers frequently restrict entry to protect political allies of their regimes (in backward sectors of their economies) and establish privileged trading zones to exclude competitors.

While ascending states and their dominant economic enterprises are the main proponents of globalization, their political and economic counterparts in the dominated countries are also staunch advocates. Here the internal divisions are crucial, as are the structural effects. Agro-business and financial groups, importers, mineral exporters, and big manufacturers for export markets or subcontracted sweatshop owners are all strong advocates of globalization.

Hence globalization is both an imperialist and a class phenomenon. The asymmetrical income flows affect the growth of the internal market as a whole but favour the rapid growth of export enclaves and the enrichment of local classes in the global circuit.

A third group supportive of globalization, and subordinate to the first two, includes high-level state functionaries (self-styled technocrats), academics and publicists linked to the international circuits. For the imperial countries, they manufacture the theories and concepts that can be used to justify and prescribe globalist programs, strategies and tactics. Academic mentors in prestigious universities of the imperial countries have trained a long list of globalist advocates from dominated countries. Frequently, academics shape the economic programs of dominated countries to maximize the interests of global capital and receive lucrative consultation fees. Their former students shape government policies, engage in corrupt business practices and accumulate private fortunes through privatization policies.

The fourth group promoting globalization includes key elements of the dominant capitalist class—bankers, financiers, and importers and exporters of goods and services. They are advocates of free trade as well as beneficiaries, up to a point. The point of differentiation comes when large foreign-owned commercial traders displace local commercial groups. Otherwise, individuals in this sector, particularly where they do not have ties to local producers, tend to be staunch advocates of globalist principles of free trade. Together this bloc is a formidable configuration as long as it retains state power. Its principal power base is its position at the node of trade, finance and investment transactions, and the amount of money at its disposal to finance political campaigns and social organizations. Yet money, though singularly important, is not the only resource: social power and mass organization are also potentially crucial sources of political power.

Adversaries of globalization make up in numbers what they lack in financial power. The major adversaries of globalization in the dominated countries have been the peasant movements, particularly in Latin America and parts of Asia, and to a lesser degree in Africa. Free trade policies have led to the devastation of local producers, unable to compete with cheap grain imports, for example. Subsidies to agro-export producers have stimulated the concentration of land ownership, credits and technical assistance at the expense of small producers. The introduction of technology by corporate agro-producers on extensive holdings has replaced the labour of local peasants and created a mass of displaced producers. The imperial state's eradication of non-traditional crops (coca, poppies, etc.) has undermined world market niches for small farmers. As a result we witness a growing mass of radicalized peasants and landless rural workers in key countries such as Brazil and Mexico, India, the Philippines, Ecuador, Paraguay, Bolivia and elsewhere.

The second major adversary group or class confronting globalization are the workers in both the imperial and dominated countries. Workers in France, Germany, South Korea, Brazil, Argentina, South Africa, and many other countries have engaged in general strikes against globalization policies. In the imperial countries strikes have been mounted against threats of plant relocations; cuts in pensions, health plans and vacations; and, most important, the massive growth of job insecurity. In the dominated countries workers have mobilized against low wages, despotic working conditions, autocratic managerial rule, long workdays and declining social benefits.

The third class of adversaries is the bulk of the public employees affected by budget cuts, privatization and massive loss of purchasing power. Once again the opposition of this class is found in both the imperial and dominated countries.

The fourth class is small business, particularly provincial classes affected by cutbacks of public subsidies, deindustrialization, and privatization of minerals and transport, which have impoverished the interior of the country and concentrated wealth in a few enclaves in the major cities. Floods of cheap imports have bankrupted many local producers and provoked widespread protests based on multi-sectoral alliances against the central government. Protests of this sort have occurred widely in Argentina, Bolivia, Colombia, Ecuador, South Korea, India and Peru, at least prior to the Fujimori dictatorship.

In the past one would have included non-competitive or newly industrializing nations as part of the adversarial alliance against globalization. However, that is a difficult position to maintain since the governing and ruling classes of these countries have become beneficiaries of the global circuits and define policy in accordance with imperial imperatives of free trade, free markets and free flows of capital.

A third category of classes is ambivalent towards globalization—for example, industries that have difficulty competing in the global market and yet benefit from the reduction of social payments and declining wages; manufacturers who are bankrupted by overseas competition and "convert" to importing and other commercial activity; low-paid wage workers who consume of cheap imported goods; and peasant families who lose migrant family members, see the prices of their produce decimated by imports but depend on overseas remittances freely reconverted. What are decisive in the swing of these sectors are political intervention, organization and struggle. When the globalist classes are in command, the ambivalent classes adapt to rather than resist globalist encroachments. When the subordinate classes are in ascendancy, the "ambivalents" join in civic strikes, increase demands for state protection and favour state regulation of sweatshops and assembly plants.

The division among advocates, adversaries and ambivalents cuts across classes, even as the major beneficiaries are found in the imperial classes and the exploited are found in the dominated countries. The point is that the international networks that link competing advocates and exploited adversaries are unevenly developed. The advocates have their own international forums and organizations and act in common, but the exploited adversaries remain fragmented. There is a gap between the structural affinities of the adversaries and their subjective dispersion. A key point is *the control of the nation-state by the advocates and beneficiaries and their capacity to wield it as a formidable weapon in creating conditions for global expansion*. The weakness of the adversaries is in part organizational—opposition is built around sectoral demands without strong international ties and ideological commitments. Adversaries have been sidetracked from the struggle for state power by the rhetoric of "civil society" and the notion that "the nation-state is an anachronism."

The configuration of advocates, adversaries and ambivalents is intimately tied to the distributive outcomes of globalist politics. There has been a geographical reconfiguration of wealth. The TNCs and transnational banks (TNBs) in the imperial countries (of North America, Western Europe and Japan) and Hong Kong, Saudi Arabia, Taiwan and South Korea concentrate the vast majority of the world's assets and wealth, along with enclaves of wealth in the dominated countries among the billionaire directors of new conglomerates emerging from privatization programs.

In the imperial countries, former industrial and agricultural regions have been battered, particularly areas of militant unionism. The key regions of impoverishment in the dominated countries are the city suburbs, rural and provincial towns, and older mining and seaport regions. Within the working classes, children, women and ethnic minorities have been paid below general wage rates and have virtually no protective coverage. Their main defence is employment turnover, as in the case of Mainland Chinese working in coastal factories owned by diaspora millionaires. Migrant workers, the unregulated (so-called informal) sector and young people in temporary employment are tyrannized at the workplace by global capital's absolute power of hiring and firing and its threat to relocate. Downwardly mobile public employees, teachers and health workers have been at the centre of social struggles throughout Latin America and parts of Europe and Asia as wage and salary levels decline.

While the mass of old and new workers experience relative or absolute declines in living standards, new classes of billionaires emerge in finance, sweatshop manufacturing, mass entertainment and drug, pornography and contraband activities. The latter is particularly strong in the former USSR and Eastern Europe.

Attitudes towards globalization are clearly defined by structural position and distributive consequences: globalization ideology and its universal appeals are grounded in mystifying its profound class roots and class inequalities. Globalization's continuing powerful ties to the nation-state and the ruling classes within those states contradict its appeal to universalism and abstract internationalism.

The Cyclical Nature of Globalization

The development of capitalism has been accompanied by shifts in its nature and in the particular sectors of capitalists who have directed the state. The capitalist state in turn has been at times influenced by the demands of the labour movement and left -wing parties, and by economic processes (crises, depressions, inflation, crashes, etc.) and technological breakthroughs. These changes have had a powerful effect on shaping the direction and proportions of capitalist investment inwardly and outwardly.

Over the past five centuries capitalist expansion has alternated between dependence on global flows and the deepening of the internal market. The early colonial conquest led by mercantile capitalists, trading companies and slave merchants was the driving force of early globalization (15th to the 18th century), and the growth of protectionism and national industry (from the late 18th to the mid-19th century) stimulated the growth of domestic industries and the relative decline of global flows as centrepieces of accumulation. In Asia, Africa and Latin America, pre-colonial productive systems (some, like East Indian textiles, with marked capitalist features) had been oriented towards domestic markets and/or long-distance non-European trade (within Africa and Asia). Colonization set the stage for the emergence of settler colonists who displaced indigenous ruling economic elites and reoriented the economies towards the world (European and later North American) market. In the 19th century, national independence movements in Latin America led by the indigenous export elites (mine owners, landowners and merchants) deepened the process of globalization. Latin America's integration into the world market become more pronounced, except for cases such as Paraguay which attempted to initiate industrial-protectionist policies similar to the Euro-American approach.

Beginning in the late 19th century the last great push (prior to the present) towards externally generated growth began, with the notable exception of Germany and the U.S. The latter countries combined heavy protection of emerging industries with selective imperial expansion. "Globalization" involved *laissez-faire* economic policies far in advance of what is practised today: travel without passports, absence of labour and environmental legislation, no currency controls, limited powers to central banks (if they even existed), etc. This period ended with or—some might argue—led to the First World War. There was a brief revival during the 1920s, and then it definitively closed (or so it seemed for over a half century) with the World Depression of 1929. The re-emergence of globalization or international flows of capital and commodity trade between 1945 and 1997 was gradual, only accelerating after the end of the 1980s. Even today global trade does not account for the major part of the goods and services that go into the GNP, even as it has been growing rapidly in recent years.

In the Third World the *laissez-faire* policies accompanying global integration were weakened by the First World War, as new manufacturers and middle-class producers emerged, demanding greater protection and development of the internal market.

As the internal market gained relative importance, a process of class differentiation took place between national producers and the allied popular classes (labourers, peons, peasants, etc.) on the one hand and the export globalist classes (merchants, traders, large landowners, mine owners) on the other. The crash of 1929 sealed the fate of the globalist strategies, even as it did not definitively displace the export classes. From the early 1930s to the 1970s, Latin America's GNP was increasingly based on production for domestic markets, even as local producers continued to depend on export elites to generate foreign exchange to finance capital imports. The reversion of this pattern and the return to globalist dependence on external flows of capital and commodity trade began in the 1970s, but it has been a prolonged, highly unsuccessful effort to create a new source of dynamic growth. The Latin American country with the highest resource endowment (metals and minerals, timber, fisheries, fruit) that fits in with world market conditions, Chile, has been the most successful in making the transition. It is also the country that has the highest rate of exploitation of its non-renewable resources and thus has the least sustainable development. Most other countries, which depend relatively less on resource exploitation, have had only limited capacity to sustain reasonable rates of growth across economic sectors and classes and over time.

In Asia, North America and Europe the push towards dependence on external flows of capital and commodity trade has been uneven: while growing across the board, it has also been selective (combined with protectionism), integrative (exchanges between advanced capitalist countries predominate) and still based on the nation-state for substance, support and promotion.

Globalist claims of an economy tied to international exchange is thus a slowly emerging, cyclical process which is still deeply implicated in national economies and highly dependent on the nation-state for its projections abroad. The principal actors, the TNCs in their majority, still receive the bulk of their profits from the domestic market, even as the percentage from overseas earnings increases. Subsidies for technological innovations, plant construction, export promotion, labour control and tax write-offs, which are essential components of multinational corporate growth strategies, are still formulated within and by the nation-state.

What accounts for past and present outward cycles of capitalist expansion? Essentially we can identify three general, interrelated sources: changes in the world political economy such as wars, crises and the opening of new markets; the ascendance of export classes to political and economic power; and the changing composition of the state and the reallocation of resources to further an outwardly expansive economic strategy.

Far from being a linear process, international flows of capital and commodity trade historically have been interrupted and ruptured for extended periods of time. At least over the 20th century, this was the exception rather than the rule as capitalist rivalries incited nationalist protectionist measures, wars stratified the economy, and social opposition channelled resources internally.

The current wave of globalization is meeting stiff resistance in Latin America, Europe and Asia and has a problematical basis of social support, even as its legitimacy as an economic program is increasingly being called into question. What is unquestionable is that the tendency towards greater dependence on external flows is increasing and the power and willingness of states to proceed and deepen the process is growing. Under current circumstances the economic linkages between markets and multinational corporations has had a wrenching effect on workers, employees, farmers and peasants. A break with globalist state strategies will involve a period of socio-economic dislocation and a particularly high cost for financial corporations, multinational executives and their supporting classes. The point, however, is that the breakdown of Communism, the defeats of the revolutionary Left and the subsequent decline of labour and social movements provided optimal terrain for the imposition of globalist policies.

The political nature of the high profits is evident in the stagnant economic growth pattern that accompanies globalization. Japan, Germany and the U.S. overall have shown meagre growth results despite a resurgence in recent years. The so-called technological revolution has been of little or no significance in stimulating overall growth. In fact, the more technologically backward countries—China, India, Chile and Turkey—have shown the most growth, based largely on intensive and extensive labour exploitation, extraction of raw materials and production of cheap manufacturing goods. The process of internationalization of capital is thus based on exploiting new frontiers and locating sites for high profits—not on developing and deepening the forces of production. The international movement of capital and commodity trade is thus creating more capitalism, more wage workers and more exports and imports but overall has failed to overcome the tendencies towards stagnation.

If external opportunities do not lead to dynamic growth, what accounts for the ascendancy of the export classes? The answer can be found in the shifts in political and social power within the nation-states and their extensions outward from the imperial centre to the rest of the world. The basic fact of the matter is that the capitalist class in the West has to a greater or lesser degree inflicted severe defeats on the working class in every sphere of life: in state control, social policy and ideology; at the factory level in work rules, wages, bargaining power and employment; and at the personal level in vulnerability, consciousness and fear.

Since the early 1970s the capitalist class has taken advantage of a highly bureaucratized trade-union movement divorced from the rank and file and highly dependent on state favours to roll back labour's bargaining power. While capitalists have developed close ties to the political parties of the state and thus wield effective power over their politicians, labour bureaucrats have continued to depend on essentially the same capitalist parties to further their interests.

While capitalists have developed a forthright and coherent strategy that bars concessions on welfare issues, labour bureaucrats have remained tied to an earlier concept of social contracts and the welfare state and have been unable and unwilling to develop an anti-capitalist strategy or consider a socialist alternative. While capitalists have taken hold of the state, labour remains a pressure group, an outsider, linked to sectoral struggles and narrow wage issues. While capitalists dominate the mass media, labour lacks any alternative media; while capitalists launch wave after wave of anti-labour legislation, intensifying the class struggle from above, labour turns towards service activities as its members decrease.

The centrality of class struggle in defining globalist policy is evident if we compare where it has gone the furthest: In the United Kingdom and the U.S., where strikes are few and often lost, and France and Germany where trade unions wield the strike weapon and workers still retain a large state sector, social programs and national industries. In the Third World the transition towards the globalist model has proceeded furthest under conditions where labour was most severely repressed by the state—in Mexico, Chile and Argentina.

The *reverse* pattern was also evident in the past. From the early 1930s to the mid-1970s, the advance of the middle and working classes undermined the power of the export classes and made the growth of the domestic market the centre of economic policy. The creation of a welfare state and the proliferation of public enterprises were products of the collapse of the export model and the crisis and displacement of the classes which supported it. The growth of non-capitalist countries in Europe, Asia, Eastern Europe and Latin America and the growth of nationalist regimes in Africa forced the Western European and U.S. capitalist classes to compete for the allegiance of the working class by offering wage and welfare concessions. Export capitalists were harnessed to internal demand. Globalization was tempered by worker and peasant militancy, and the spectre of Communism made social welfare a necessity for capitalist survival.

Working-class defeats in Brazil in 1964, Indonesia in 1966, and throughout Latin America in the 1970s, China's counter-revolution from within in the late 1970s, the collapse of the USSR and the conversion of European social democrats to neoliberals and U.S. liberals to free-market conservatives were political events that transformed state policy from a force mediating between globalization and welfare into a straight-out instrument for supporting international flows of capital and commodity trade.

The change of class power and the recomposition of the state are the basic conditions underpinning the growth of international flows and the emergence of globalization as an ideology to legitimate power.

Globalization, Past and Present

Is "globalization" in the contemporary context different from that of the past? The answer depends on what we are looking at. In the past, during periods when export classes predominated, globalization was much more significant than in contemporary times in its impact on growth. This was particularly true for the imperialist centres and the newly colonized countries between the 16th and 19th centuries. Nevertheless, in entire regions and countries the capitalist mode of production was incipient or non-existent, particularly in rural areas of the Third World and even in parts of Europe. Today there is nary a country or region that has not been incorporated into the capitalist mode of production. Unlike those in many parts of the world in previous centuries, today's market exchanges take place within the capitalist system.

Secondly, for a greater part of the 20th century substantial regions of the world were organized in a non-capitalist system, a form of collectivism, which did not operate within the capitalist mode of production. In the last decade these areas have been incorporated and subordinated to the logic of capitalist accumulation. In the case of most of the USSR, the would-be capitalists resemble 16th-century English pirates, plunderers and slave runners engaged in accumulating wealth through non-economic means ("primitive" or initial accumulation).

The significant continuities are found in the point of origin of globalization, in the advanced imperial countries (though the particular countries have changed) and in the unequal effects it has on the classes and nation-states in the imperial relation. Today, as in the past, major trade takes place via the giant European, Asian and North American firms. Today, as in the past, the greater part of the profits is appropriated by the ruling classes linked through investments, trade, rents and interest payments. As in the past, the nation-state is the principle political instrument for organizing global expansion: trade treaties, subsidies, labour controls, military intervention and ideological promotion of free trade doctrines are all essential functions performed by the governing elite of the nation-state. Then, as now, the nation-state is unable to control speculative booms and busts, the tendencies towards overproduction and stagnation crises inherent in the capitalist mode of production.

The apparent "novelty" of the contemporary drive towards globalization is found in the fact that it comes out of a prolonged period of inward-oriented growth under a coalition of class forces that elaborated an ideology (Keynesianism, Communism, corporatism) and policies in which external exchanges and investments were subordinated to the growth of protected industries and the enlargement of the domestic market. If one took a longer view of economic history, predating the ascendancy of inward directed development, one would find substantial structural similarities to the current pattern of globalization.

The difference today is that the earlier period of outward development ended with a deep crisis and a near collapse under conditions of war and depression. The current drive towards globalization has yet to enter its "final phase," although there are clear indications of a continuing propensity towards crisis. For example, both in the present and past, speculative activity tends to out-run productive investments; collapse is proceeded by a period of prolonged stagnation, a pattern also evident in the post-war period in the U.S., Japan and Western Europe. With inequalities heightening and social discontent deepening, it is probable that globalization is, in the words of one investment banker, "coming to the limits of political acceptance of these approaches" (*New York Times*, June 20, 1997, A-10).

As mentioned earlier, the major difference today is that capitalism has spread everywhere and is the only economic system at the moment. This means that the direct adversaries of capitalism are not other states or regions resisting capitalist encroachment, but classes (the working class, peasants, etc.) located within the system. The opposition is not from pre- or post-capitalist elites or excluded classes, but from those incorporated and exploited—those who create value.

The second "new feature" of globalization is the greater volume of capital movements. Transfers of wealth across national boundaries, particularly financial transfers, far exceed past movements. This is made possible by large organizational networks and new electronic technologies. These movements, however large, operate through many of the older networks that predate the current boom in globalist expansion. The various ethnic diaspora networks (Chinese, Indian, Middle Eastern, Jewish, etc.) and the extended family conglomerates (particularly effective are the Asian Chinese) influence the modern channels of banking and investment. In Western Europe and North America pre-existing family and class networks have deepened their influence through electronic innovations. Hence while volume of flows increases, the decisive decision-making units are embedded in earlier, pre-globalist social formations.

The transmission and accumulation of information is more rapid and immense under contemporary globalization, but it does not seem to have made much of a difference in breaking open a new period of robust growth. Even Japan and South Korea, the foremost leaders in the new technology-induced development during the 1970s and 1980s, are bogged in slow growth. Despite the self-laudatory posture adopted by Clinton, the U.S. wallows at a level of GNP growth that barely keeps up with population increase. The technologies are different than those of the past but in themselves have not led to a new class structure, economic dynamic or state structure. The new technologies are embedded in pre-existing classes and nation-states and in the larger constraints and imperatives of the capitalist system. The notion of information as "the new capital" is, of course, nonsense, as is the idea that the mass of new information and the glorified clerks feeding and processing information are the new captains of the economy.

The crucial point of information accumulation and communication is its analysis and use, as well as the conceptual framework used to formulate the questions that orient information analysts. These are not autonomous actors, but rather individuals and classes embedded in structures of power—configurations that turn information at times into capital gains or losses. While information is an important element in earning profits, it is so because capitalists employ information collectors to do the menial work of punching in charts, tables and graphs, summarizing data and putting it online in succinct and usable forms.

Swift movement of capital allows for shifts in capital location and rapid accumulation but also exaggerates existing volatility without adding anything to capital stock. Velocity is not directly related to the growth of productive forces. It largely operates in a parallel sphere. The paper economy is only tenuously related to how the real economy functions. This does not mean that it could not have a major impact on the real economy, for example, if there was a major crash in the financial markets or the stock exchange. This type of globalization, while novel in its volume and speed, has not significantly changed the structure and operation of the real global economy in a qualitative way. At most, it has increased the autonomy of capital movements by giving individual agents greater access to more locations for money transfers. But even that is a relative autonomy because governments have chosen not to regulate this area, not because of the greater volume (trillions of dollars per day) or ease of movement (a touch of the computer), but because the nation-states that most benefit (the U.S., Western Europe, Japan) have "deregulated." Precisely because high-speed computers can process billions of items a second and precisely because of the greater economic integration of capital and states, it is potentially possible to set forth new sets of regulations.

Finally, contemporary globalization has deepened and extended the international division of labour. Cars, for example, are made of parts from factories located in distant nation-states. Information collection, processing and analysis are outsourced to workers in different regions. The process of exporting labour-intensive industrial work to the Third World and retaining a mass of low-paid service workers and an elite of high-paid executives in the imperial centres has advanced. But this is a continuation of the past international division of labour, between mining and agricultural workers in the Third World and manufacturing and service workers in the imperial countries. What has changed is the inclusion of manufacturing activities in the former Third World. This means greater proletarianization (larger numbers of wage workers) in some settings. The key problem for the theory of a new international division of labour is the fact that most industrial output, both in the Third World and the imperial countries, is for domestic consumption and is produced by domestic owners. There are, of course, a few countries in which foreign exports and investors predominate, particularly in durable consumer goods, cultural services and financial sectors.

Returning to the initial question, Is contemporary globalization different from that of the past? The answer is "yes" in quantitative terms and "no" in terms of the structures and units of analysis that define the process. Moreover, the main difference between past and present—the fact that the former had an "end point" (crises and collapse) and the latter is still fairly robust—is in itself a problematical issue.

Globalization: Inevitability or Contingency

One of the central tenets of globalization theorists is the idea that globalization is inevitable, that technological, economic and political developments have converged so as to exclude any forms of economic growth other than that based on transnational flows of capital and commodity trade. The claim, more normative than scientific, is that globalization is the highest and last stage in history in which all countries and economies are linked together through the capitalist market. One early spokesman for this idea, Francis Fukuyama (1991), wrote about "the end of history" in which markets, democracy and prosperity had put an end to conflicts, authoritarian regimes and the reign of necessity.

The notion of the inevitability of particular political-economic processes has a long and ignoble history of inevitable refutation. What looks to observers absorbed by conjunctural successes as a predetermined outcome for all future generations is usually based on a tunnel vision of history in which all events are prefigured in thought and predestined. In this tautological view of history, what happened had to happen, what is happening is a product of a singular set of events, and that which exists today has a singular difference with all past history in that it lacks the points of conflict or contradictory processes of the past. This view of history as a linear process of determined events is, of course, false: divergent outcomes from generally similar circumstances have been the norm.

For example, "similar economic processes and colonial experiences" (structural similarities) have had widely divergent outcomes. China in the 1940s was similarly underdeveloped as in the 1920s, yet in the 1920s the counter-revolution succeeded, while in the later period the revolution was victorious. Similarly, post-World War II post-colonial outcomes varied because of contingent factors: political intervention, consciousness, organizational capacities, leadership, strategies, etc.

The emergence of globalization in the past was determined by a plethora of structural and historical circumstances, and emerging antagonistic class and state relations engendered by earlier cycles of globalization led to political ruptures and the relative demise of globalization and indeed, in some cases, of the capitalist system. In each period of global expansion, globalist theorists emerge to glorify, legitimize and gratify the leading classes of the global project, using the language of "Pax Britannica" or the "American Century."

More reflective globalist theorists at least recognize the demise of globalist expansion in the past and try to develop a different line of inquiry, conceding the imperfections of the past but marking out the singularity of the present "global world order."

By ignoring past contradictions and how they play themselves out in the present, globalist ideologues fall back on a kind of technological determinism. By making blanket claims about the magical qualities of the new computer and electronic systems, they hope to convince or delude the populace into believing that the new global system is the product of and guided by science, technology and reason, which have erased or undermined class and anti-imperialist conflicts. The emergence of contrary phenomena—that is, major class conflicts and anti-imperialist struggles—is relegated to a residual category of "anachronistic phenomena" or seen as the last gasps of outmoded groups and ideologists.

But labelling is not explanation; nor is residual categorizing an adequate way to deal with burgeoning movements that are centred in the vortex of the globalist imperative. The linkages of the new rural and provincial social movements in Latin America and Africa (the Democratic Republic of the Congo/the former Zaire) with urban struggles and the growing explosiveness among the new generation of the working classes in France, South Korea and Germany, speak to the profound cleavages inherent in domestic exploitation to maximize global market shares.

To deal with the notion of inevitability on a less philosophical and more analytical level it is important to examine the origins, dynamics and future perspectives of the current version of globalization.

In the first instance, the technologies that are cited as determinant existed prior to the current big push towards globalization. The addition or application of technologies has not had a major impact on global growth, which, as we mentioned earlier, has been largely stagnant. Technological innovation has been incorporated into global processes that are shaped by decisions in the political and socio-economic sphere. The origins of the most recent wave of globalization can be found in the political process associated with the ascendancy of capitalism in its neoliberal or "free market" form.

The early starters on the neoliberal road towards free market capitalism were found in Chile. Exclusively a product of the military *coup d'état*, the neoliberal program of free market reforms were subsequently implemented by the Reagan and Thatcher regimes. This is not to say that TNCs and financial capital were not operating in the world market prior to these political regimes. It is to say that the globalizers had to share power and resources with local capital, trade unions and popular political forces. Henceforth the compromise between internal market development via the welfare state and the international flow of capital and commodity trade was ruptured either by political force, military dictatorship or executive decree within a minority electoral regime.

The origins of globalization as an economic strategy were thus the consequence of an ideological project backed by state power and not the "natural unfolding" of the market. The fact that in the period preceding globalization the major technological breakthrough took place in a variety of non-globalist settings pokes holes in the ideological veil that techno-globalists throw over the process of capitalist development.

Contingency, not inevitability, marks the origins and unfoldings of the globalist project. Otherwise it is difficult to explain the constant, frequently irrational and frantic efforts of the G-7 to prop up failing regimes such as Mexico, and to make capitalism irreversible by accelerating economic reforms that destroy production and impoverish millions in the former USSR and to extend NATO affiliation to Eastern Europe and the Ukraine. Surely the practitioners of globalization, if not the ideologues, are aware of the conditionalities and contingencies of their project. Since globalization theory has a strong ideological component, it is important to confront it in those terms.

Globalization as Globaloney: Rhetoric and Reality

One of the major characteristics of vulnerable social systems is the exaggerated claims made on their behalf. Behind these claims is the belief that sheer assertion of invincibility or inevitability will compensate for structural weaknesses. The whole ideological edifice constructed around the globalist perspective of export capitalists and financiers is a cogent example of this. However, the notion that ideological hegemony and normative prescriptions of a desirable outcome can sustain an otherwise fragile political economic enterprise provides a poor substitute for substantive programmatic analysis and politics.

The term "globaloney," coined by Bob Fitch (1996), captures the tendentious and tautological arguments put forth by globalist theorists. In the first instance, globalists posit a general progression towards globalization which draws all nations and peoples into a common set of market relations. It is hard to know what to make of such a view in the context of widespread and wholesale rejection of the globalist project by electorates and civil societies all over the world. Here we need but refer to the North American Free Trade Agreement (NAFTA), the Maastricht treaty, and the free trade doctrines proposed in North America, Europe and Asia. It seems that the absence of general support becomes a catalyst for even more exaggerated claims—from the best to the "only" policy, from an advance in the economy to "the end of human history." However, it is precisely such unfounded claims, particularly as to the inevitability of globalization, that in the face of fragile social support can be put under the category of "globaloney."

The notion of inevitability as framed by globalists has the same kind of messianic message that patent medicine makers attributed to their products and itinerant preachers vowed would affect non-believers: if it is not here, it is coming; if it is not visible, it is just over the horizon; if you are experiencing pain, prosperity and well-being are "around the corner." There is a bit of charlatanism in all this, designed to beguile the innocent or attack those who have lost faith in other inevitabilities and have a need to recur to the new faith.

Beyond the globaloney is the hard fact that the great majority of nations and the immense majority of humanity are opposed to globalization in practice, if not in thought. That is why globalist politicians so often disguise their beliefs and present themselves as critics of globalization—all the better to practise it after they take power. Clinton (in the U.S.), Menem (Argentina), Cardoso (Brazil), Fujimori (Peru), Chirac (France), Prodi (Italy) and Caldera (Venezuela) all ran for office as critics of free marketeering, an essential element of globalism. Today in Europe, Asia and Latin America massive opposition to globalist policies is plainly visible. As a *New York Times* heading (June 16, 1998) put it, "U.S., Lauding its economy, finds no summit followers." If there are no sheep at the summit, it is because there are no donkeys in the streets. The article said one of the key economic advisors to the South Korean president tersely remarked about Clinton's advocacy of globaloney for the rest of the world: "South Koreans would not stand for that kind of economic instability."

The second feature of globaloney is the assertion that it is the "wave of the future." Here the ideologues paint a futuristic world of high-powered technology that operates through global markets to produce quality goods and deliver advanced services that are consumed by growing multitudes. The reality, however, is very different: social conditions on the eve of the 21st century are in fact reverting to those of the 19th century. For one thing, health care all over the world is becoming more precarious and more dependent on income levels. In the U.S. more than sixty million people have no or inadequate health care and over ten million children are not covered. Job insecurity is on the increase as managers assume the power to hire and fire and subcontract part-time and temporary work in a fashion reminiscent of the times of Charles Dickens. Impoverished families are forced to work at below-subsistence, minimum-wage jobs or go hungry. More workers work longer hours today than they did in the 1970s. Retirement age is reaching nearly seventy years old. Employers no longer provide pension plans. Private employers for private gain employ prison labour on a large scale. The number of children in orphanages is growing, as is the number of children living in poverty. Inequalities approach or surpass 19th-century levels. A more appropriate ocean metaphor for globalization (than "wave of the future") is an undertow pulling working people back into an ignominious past. The future for most of the young generation looks insecure and fearful both in Europe and North America, and for good reason. It will be the first generation since World War II that will be downwardly mobile. To argue that globalization is the "wave of the future" is to promise upcoming generations a prolonged work life with declining wages and without job security or social assistance. To deny this reality and project a rosy future is the essence of globaloney.

The "wave of the future" ideology is tied to a specific group of capitalists operating at the centre of the globalization project: the investment bankers and brokerage firms that have moved to the forefront of the richest U.S. companies. Goldman Sachs, Wall Street's biggest private partnership, will probably earn close to $3 billion in 1997. In 1975 brokerage and investment banking firms earned $4.8 billion; by 1994 annual profits had grown to $69.5 billion. In comparison, Microsoft, the biggest and most successful high-tech firm, had after-tax profits of only $2.2 billion. Clearly, *globalization is the wave of the future for speculators and financiers*. But it would be the height of deception to confuse this rosy picture with the lot of the rest of humanity. Deliberate obfuscation of class differences in referring to advances of profits for some and the reversal of living conditions for the many is part of the polemical style of practitioners of globaloney.

After all their arguments have been exposed and refuted, the last refuge for scoundrels is to throw up their hands and, like Thatcher, cry "there is no alternative," a self-serving rationalization for the failures of globalization. This argument is simply a confession of failure, a denial of resistance and an attempt to demoralize adversaries. This stratagem is usually based on a simple dichotomy of failed Communism and ongoing globalization, thus compressing complex experience in boxes that exclude the rich mosaic of past experience and current alternatives. The argument here—or assertion, to be more precise—assumes a triumphalist posture. It is based on a superficial survey of the world today, projecting globalist ideology into previously hostile areas. The problem is that this visionary approach deals with epiphenomena over a relative short period of time. The analysis lacks depth because it avoids internal conflicts, the instability and volatility of unregulated speculation, and the lack of a centre of economic dynamic. Profits grow, but they do so based on lower labour costs and a compression of standards of living and conditions of work; while stock markets go up, forces of production stagnate; while new technologies proliferate, their impact on the real economy is overshadowed by the gains of speculators.

Essentially three lines of criticism can be levelled against globalists. First, global expansion is rooted in history and shaped by particular political, social and cultural conditions. Globalists attribute inevitability to a conjunctural correlation of forces that are subject to reversal. Second, the socio-economic interests embedded in the globalist project are minorities, both in the imperial countries and among their collaborators in the dominated countries of the global network. It is a mockery of social analysis to confuse how this minority defines and pursues its interests with the needs, interests and future of the whole of humanity. Moreover, it is the height of obtuseness to overlook the differential effect that globalization has on different classes, races, generations and genders. Third, to attribute behavioural attributes and political commands to abstract entities such as the market is to abdicate one's responsibility as an intellectual to identify the institutions and decision-makers who are the market makers. The attempt to reduce all markets to one market owned and operated by a specific configuration of class forces and under the tutelage of a particular state formation is the ultimate exercise in abstract reductionism. It makes sense to argue that the classes which predominate dictate contemporary forms of market exchanges. But one should also acknowledge there are other real or potential markets, present and future, in which other actors can play a role and condition exchanges to provide outcomes very different from those of today's market.

To approach the market in an authentically analytical way, as opposed to the abstract reductionist way of the globalists, means in the first instance to examine the class relations that shape exchanges; and in the final analysis to examine the class-distributional effects of market exchanges. The debate between globalist adversaries and globalists is in part about method, between those who pursue a systematic analysis of exchanges and those who deduce outcomes from abstract impersonal forces to whom they attribute human qualities (such as "market imperatives").

The ideological confrontation with globalism and its relegation to the status of globaloney is only part of the debate. Equally pertinent is the debate over the dynamics of globalization.

Dynamics of Globalization: Politics, Economy and Technology

The "big push towards globalization" was political and economic. Politically the "big push" was a result of a dramatic change in political power away from leftist, populist and nationalist regimes towards globalist governments. In social terms, the "big push" resulted from the defeat and retreat of trade unions, and the declining influence of the working class, lower middle class and peasantry. The ascendancy of the social classes engaged in international networks of capital and trade, and particularly the financial sector, set the stage for the globalist counter-revolution. What began in certain Third World (Chile, Mexico) and imperial centres (the U.S. and the U.K.) spread throughout the world in an uneven fashion.

Globalists did not merely react to "failures" or "crises" of leftist regimes; they vigorously intervened to bring about the outcome they predicted. This active role was massive in scope and involved direct military intervention, ideological and cultural saturation, arms races, and political alliances with the Vatican and philanthropic foundations. For example, in Latin America, globalist classes emerged out of the violent military regimes that destroyed the opposition, creating hundreds of thousands of victims. In Africa millions were killed in surrogate wars that destroyed the possibility of independent development in Angola, Mozambique and elsewhere. The Reagan regime sponsored an arms race that was deliberately directed towards bankrupting the Soviets, who willingly cooperated. In Eastern Europe, particularly in Poland, the Vatican played a decisive propaganda and material role in pouring millions of U.S. Central Intelligence Agency (CIA) funds into the Solidarity organization. In Eastern Europe, billionaire speculator George Soros poured in millions of dollars to cultivate Czech, Hungarian and Polish intellectuals who later became ardent pro-capitalist, pro-NATO politicos.

The internal crises of these regions played into this proactive globalist campaign by neutralizing potential popular opposition. The net effect of the initial undisputed ascendancy of the new globalist classes was to weaken public control and limitations on capitalist exploitation of resources, markets and labour, and the handing over of important levers of accumulation in the mineral, financial and manufacturing fields to private investors. The powerful role of the nation-state in holding down wages and slashing social programs liberated immense funds for private enrichment of the globalist classes. The nation-state, far from weakening with globalization, became an essential political support in spreading the message. Imperial regimes, influential in the

IMF and World Bank, conditioned loans and credits on so-called "economic reforms," thus imposing a uniform globalist policy. Unpopular structural adjustment policies (SAPs) deepened the power of globalist classes and extended their sway over the national patrimony through privatization and deregulation. The nation-state and its imperial policies were essential elements in the "big push" towards globalization.

Finally, the nation-state's political intervention in "bailing out" troubled overseas investors (Japanese and U.S. banks), speculators (Mexico, 1994) and TNCs (Lockheed, Fiat) suggests the continuing role of politics in sustaining the crisis-prone globalist perspective.

The "big push" from the political side was the counterpoint of a confluence of economic developments that engineered the dynamics of globalization. Essentially, four factors preceded and contributed to the "big push": (1) an overaccumulation crisis, (2) a profit squeeze resulting from labour/capital relations, (3) the intensification of international capitalist competition and (4) the massive growth of financial markets as a result of deregulation.

These "economic processes," of course, cannot be separated from the class relations and political configurations of which they form an integral part. The overaccumulation crisis refers to the massive growth of profits with shrinking space for investment at acceptable rates of return. Put another way, the more capital grew within the bounds of the nation-state, the smaller the rate of profit as more capital pursued smaller market shares. A radical solution would have been to change the class structure to increase demand, but that would also have exacerbated the problem of the declining rate of profit. The reactionary solution, the one pursued, was to break down internal constraints on external movements to overseas markets, in the process forcing down domestic costs over the long term. Globalist classes look at the mass of local producers in part as a cost, not simply a market. Globalization was a solution to the overaccumulation crisis on terms acceptable to the investor class.

The second and related economic determinant of globalization were the constraints imposed by labour/capital relations. The profit squeeze was rooted in the immobility of capital: in face-to-face relations, with the welfare state as a mediator, labour was able, for almost a quarter of a century, to extract economic concessions whose cumulative cost became an unacceptable burden to capital. By reproducing wage/capital relations through overseas investments abroad at sites of production with lower costs, the capitalist class created a global labour market that boosted profit margins and applied downward pressure on the local labour market; hence globalization ruptured the post–World War II capital-labour equilibrium in this class's favour.

The movement of capital abroad was stimulated by the growth of international competition. The powerful export push from Asia and Europe forced the U.S. to invest overseas to open production sites closer to consumers, circumvent protective barriers and learn about local markets. The Europeans and the Japanese who opened production sites to ply the U.S. and Canadian markets followed a similar pattern. Integral to this process of competition was the constant intervention of the nation-state on behalf of their TNCs, demanding equal treatment, taxation, uniform labour laws, etc. The growth of multipolar regional economic blocs was paralleled by intra-bloc alliances between states and their TNCs, giving superficial observers the idea that the nation-state was becoming "anachronistic," "weak" or "peripheral." In fact, as is evident at Maastricht meetings, GATT gatherings, G-7 summits, etc., the nation-states hammer out the rules of the game for global expansion and competition.

Finally, and perhaps most important, the dynamic of globalization is in great part fuelled by the massive growth of financial markets. "Most important" because it is this sector that has shown the greatest volume increase in flows of capital and has had the least effect in stimulating world growth of productive forces. The paradox of massive globalization and puny growth of the major global actors is explained by the dissociation between massive financial flows and the real economy.

The deregulation of financial markets, the massive introduction and subordination of high-technology communications and information systems to financial imperatives, is probably the most salient element of globalization. To emphasize the financial character of a good part of what passes for globalization is not to deny the large-scale movements of goods and investments in minerals and manufactures. It is to say is that the level of widespread financial specula-tion far surpasses the value of the real assets of the companies "bought and sold" in the stock markets of the world. If we add all the other speculative devices (derivatives, currencies, futures, junk bonds) that are traded via financial channels, we get a truer sense of what the real motor of globalization is—hardly dynamic, hardly likely to benefit the masses, hardly likely to produce socially useful productivity gains. It is no wonder that globalists refer to countries (peoples and economies) as emerging markets. They see them through the tunnel vision of the financial investment and brokerage houses, and what they see are short-term windfalls (interest differentials), sell-offs (privatization) and sites for low-cost production (*maquiladores*). The key element in all this was a shift in the social composition of the regulatory regime and a new set of rules governing financial flows. The centrepiece of the new regulatory regime was precisely the undisputed reign of globalist policy-makers divorced from labour and tightly meshed with the leading globalist financial actors.

Where does the much-vaunted technological revolution fit into the picture of the primacy of political and economic determinants of globalization? Contrary to what many globalist ideologues say, it has an important but secondary role. These innovations themselves are based on state-sponsored or -subsidized research, later transferred to the private sector. Pre-existing eco-nomic forces largely determine the application of the technology. Even the most resourceful new high-tech entrepreneurs must sell to the fastest-growing economic sectors, namely those firms already embedded in globalist networks. Increased speed of transmission and access to information do not add significantly to the contours of the global economy. What are most essential are the ruling concepts that govern the basic institutions involved in the exchange of information, capital and trade in commodities. The ruling concepts are capital accumulation, high rates of return, greater market share and lower labour costs. High tech is the handmaiden of globalist "financial engineering," rejigging flows to accommodate short-term decisions based on immediate financial reports. The emphasis on quantity of data and the rapidity of processing reflects the need to make rapid investment decisions based on short-term shifts in the paper or real economy. Hence, high technology is reinforcing the most volatile and unproductive of economic activities, paper exchanges in the financial field.

It would be an exaggeration to deny the other multiple uses of high tech in reordering labour and consumer patterns, personal communication, etc. But the multiplicity of uses is precisely the point: at the institutional level the use of high technology is more adaptive to existing global classes than given to breaking down domination, exploitation and stagnation. The social contradictions engendered by globalization are exacerbated by high tech applied from institutional sites of power. And high tech has no internal corrective measure to ensure any other outcome.

The dynamic of globalization can be analyzed not only in its origins and expansion, but also in its distributive consequences. For what results from globalization can have serious consequences for its future.

Distributive Consequences of Globalization

The distributive consequences of globalization cannot be separated from the patterns of ownership and control of institutions, the class structure and the state. It is not possible to talk of "equity" or "market socialism" by looking at or tinkering with distributive mechanisms or outcomes. This has become clearer than ever today when owners and producers relocate or threaten to relocate their sites of investment and employment if redistributive, environmental or tax policies are not to their liking. There is an indissoluble link between ownership, production and equity on the one hand and equity and sustainability on the other.

The world ascendancy of globalist classes has provoked a serious social crisis affecting wage workers, peasants, employees and the self-employed throughout the world. The growth and penetration of globalist policies have engendered a significant increase in inequality between the minority within the globalist loop and those exploited by it. While the growth of inequality of income between social classes is one consequence of the globalist ascendancy, several other inequalities cut across national and cultural boundaries. Taxes have become increasingly regressive: government tax revenues increasingly come from waged and salaried groups, while the percentage from multinational corporate capital is declining. This is in part because of numerous legal loopholes and the ability of corporate tax lawyers to devise tax shelters and shift the loci of earnings to countries with lower tax rates (what is called "transfer pricing"). Parallel to the regressive tax system are the increasingly regressive state subsidies or spending programs. Corporate entitlements in the form of low-interest loans, export incentives, subsidies for plant construction, land grants, infrastructure development, research and development, etc. have been accompanied by sharp reductions in social transfers to the waged and salaried. State subsidies for multinational corporate capital grows, while the share for wage workers, pensioners, low-wage families, the ill and injured, single-parent families and children declines.

These social inequalities are the result of two structural factors: the growing concentration and centralization of ownership through mergers, buyouts or joint ventures and the tight integration of the state with the globalist corporate elite. The centralization of political decisions is an essential element using state resources to strengthen the profits and growth of concentrated capital. Today the pattern of asset ownership in the advanced imperial centres resembles the pattern of land ownership in what used to be pejoratively called the "banana republics": less than 5 percent of the population owns close to 90 percent of the privately held assets. Moreover, a handful of brokers and banking investors reaps the multibillion-dollar fees that accompany the buying and selling of firms and the stock transactions made by private and public investment funds.

The greatest social crisis is precisely in the countries which have advanced furthest in globalization. The number of workers without medical coverage, non-unionized workers, and temporary or part-time workers with little or no social benefits (vacations, pensions) is greatest in the U.S., followed by the U.K. The much-vaunted low unemployment rate of the U.S. in contrast to Europe is counterbalanced by the highest rate of low-wage, vulnerable workers—conditions unacceptable to European labour movements.

A similar process is occurring in the Third World. Argentina and Brazil have unemployment rates of 18 and 15 percent respectively, rates that have multiplied with the globalization of their economies. Similar processes have occurred in Eastern Europe where living standards have fallen between 30 and 80 percent since the transition to capitalism began in the late 1980s. The model Third World country, Mexico, has seen wage-earning income levels plummet to 30 percent of their levels a decade and a half earlier.

The specific mechanisms by which the globalist classes perform this income and property counter-revolution is through ideology (neoliberal or free market) and legislative packets, so-called structural adjustment policies, including the privatization of lucrative public resources and the development of a new statism which finances and directs the whole process. The neoliberal ideology provides an intellectual gloss to the process of growing inequality through several conceptual devices: it emphasizes the individual as the basic unit of analysis and the notion of individual responsibility is used to obfuscate concentrated economic activities and adverse social consequences. By obscuring the centrality of the concentration of institutional power and the impact that it has on living standards, neoliberal ideology depoliticizes the problem of power and socio-economic inequality, while shifting the burden of dealing with globalist-induced problems to the family, individual or local community. This in turn frees up personnel and funds to promote global expansion and accumulation.

The ideology of neoliberalism argues for free markets when in fact most exchanges of global firms take place within these enterprises. Free market ideology obscures the tight relations between imperial states and overseas investors, the increasing interdependence of the state and global firms, and the interrelations among global firms that shape political agendas.

The structural power of the globalist classes is both a cause and consequence of the so-called "structural adjustment policies" that have been informally or formally implemented. The SAPs are in reality a process of "income reconcentration" through cuts in social spending, corporate tax reductions and increased subsidies. The concentration of power in the hands of employers at the expense of wage workers (dubbed the "flexibilization of labour") leads to rigidities in the hierarchy of the corporate organization. Employers unilaterally fix terms for hiring, firing, outsourcing, subcontracting and other means of increasing the rate of exploitation, lowering labour costs and increasing profits for global ventures.

The advance of SAPs is directly related to the resistance of labour. And the resistance of labour is tied to the internal structure of the unions, the ideology of the union leaders, and the accessibility and rotation of leaders. Where there are democratic structures within the unions, when the leaders confront organized opposition, where the leaders are imbued with anti-capitalist ideology or at least see the union as a movement rather than a business, and where leaders are challenged or replaced by legitimate rank-and-file alternative leaders, the unions have been more successful in blocking the implementation of SAPs and the full globalist agenda. This is the case in France, Italy and Germany. In contrast, in the U.S., where union leaders run oligarchic organizations, in which millionaire union officials run the union as a business through bureaucratic machines that manage pension funds and lucrative real estate holdings and marginalize the members, the unions have been incapable of opposing the globalist agenda. It is no wonder that President Clinton was able to gloat over his success in implementing regressive economic reforms: he does not have democratic, radical trade unionists to contend with.

The U.S. economy is the prototype of globalist ascendancy. Clinton's administration even speaks of it as a model. But it is a model for globalist classes and is firmly rejected by labour everywhere else. Even European leaders frown on its application, fearing that the rigid pursuit of its implementation would provoke a major social upheaval.

The globalist project is reaching its political limits in many parts of the world. Resolution of the contradiction between empire or republic involves breaking the social organizations that sustain the beliefs and interests of millions of wage workers, families and retirees. We are entering a period of prolonged crisis and possible upheaval. The so-called Anglo-Saxon model of globalization may be exportable only if the internal social relations between classes (capital/labour) are drastically transformed. The process of gradual or piecemeal change is underway: cuts in social budgets and plant relocations in Germany; privatization and the ending of wage indexation in Italy; high rates of unemployment and segmented labour conditions in Spain.

The "defensive struggles" of European labour reflect a belief that the choice is between the residue of the previous welfare state or globalist capital. What is clear is that the ascendancy of globalization has not been accompanied by the retention of the welfare state, let alone its expansion. Clearly the social polarization of interests, conditions and structural positions requires a rethinking of the productive system and, more fundamentally, the nature of ownership. To deny the centrality of private profits in its most organized and extended form (multinational corporate enterprise) is to lose sight of the possible solution. To focus on policies and immediate outcomes as the politics of the day and not on the structure and internal composition of the state (the powerful nexus between globalist classes and the executive) is to ignore the essential tool for transforming the ownership and property forms that direct the globalist project.

The irrationality of the privatization effort is undermining the environmental conditions for the reproduction of globalist expansion. New classes, regions and recreation and breathing areas are being voraciously exploited: Antarctica, the Amazon, George's Bank, major cities, the ozone layer. The policy of privatization not only involves a massive transfer of public wealth to billionaire globalists, but it is a license to exploit without constraint. To speak of sustainable growth while the imperial state, the World Bank and globalist investors and politicians promote privatization and pillage is an obscenity, Nowhere has privatization been accompanied by conservation. Rather, it always has been associated with heightened pillage, resource exhaustion and abandonment of people and lands.

Privatization has taken place on a world scale but nowhere has it led to the dynamic development of productive forces. If we discount population growth, per capita growth in the U.S. is less than one percent, and in Europe and Japan close to zero. Privatization is the private skimming or pillage of existing wealth and assets. It is a substitute for creating new firms and products and discovering new markets. The boom in the stock markets parallels the declining growth of the real economy. Speculative growth feeds off of stagnation. The greatest growth is from mergers, firings and reductions of better-paid jobs. Apart from the abnormal case of the U.S. with its hyperbloated oligarchical unions, sociopolitical revolts against globalization are underway.

National Policies and Globalization

Probably the most widespread misconception circulated by globalization ideologues is the notion that the nation-state is anachronistic (or "weak") before the onslaught of globalizing corporations and new international actors.

The reality is otherwise: never has the nation-state played a more decisive role or intervened with more vigour and consequence in shaping economic exchanges and investment at the local, national and international levels. It is impossible to conceive of the expansion and deepening involvement of multinational banks and corporations without the prior political, military and economic intervention of the nation-state. Nor is it possible to understand the expansion of the market in the former USSR, China, Eastern Europe and former radical Third World countries without acknowledging the vital political role of the imperial nation-states, particularly the U.S., in fuelling an arms race and subsidizing cultural and religious propaganda. The most elementary and important trade agreements (GATT, NAFTA, ASEAN) and trading blocs (EU, NAFTA, Mercosur) were formulated, codified and implemented by nation-states. The major policies stimulating vast tax windfalls, massive subsidies and lower domestic labour costs have all been formulated by the nation-state. The scale and scope of nation-state activity has grown to such a point that one needs to refer to it as the "New Statism" rather than the free market. Globalization is in the first instance a product of the New Statism and continues to be accompanied and sustained by direct state intervention.

Too often, glib commentators, business journalists and publicists have argued that the "state" as we knew it has been superseded by a new kind of international order in which TNCs have become autonomous. Other ideologues have argued that the market has replaced state functions and reduced its role to the minimum compatible with law and order. Not surprisingly, many ex-leftists or self-styled "new thinkers" have argued that a "third economy" is coming into being based on NGOs and local community-based organizations rooted in what they dub "civil society." Finally a group of fringe thinkers believe that something called the "world system" has bypassed the nation-state and is in the process of establishing a suprastate entity which has yet to be fully disclosed, perhaps for absence of data.

The pervasiveness of the ideology of the dissolution of the nation-state is matched by the ignorance of its advocates of the major events and forces that shape and continue to propel the international flows of capital and commodity trade.

The centrepiece of globalization is the overarching political framework: the role of the state in eliminating the welfare state, diminishing regulations on overseas flows and demolishing political and economic constraints in overseas markets. These building blocks set in place by the nation-state have been followed by a linear column in the form of nation-state appointees to the IFI who design, implement and enforce the extension of policies throughout the world via the so-called SAP. The cupola of globalization is the short-term, day-to-day, micromanagement of the global economy by the middle-level functionaries who supervise individual investments, sectoral exchanges and monthly commercial balances.

The political-economic role of the state is accompanied by the deep penetration of the police, military and intelligence agencies of dominated nations by the U.S. Former domestic agencies such as the Federal Bureau of Investigation (FBI) and the Drug Enforcement Agency (DEA) now freely circulate at the highest levels of overseas state structures. U.S. drug certification programs extend U.S. power to shape appointments in the ministries, armed forces and police. The legal principle of extraterritoriality is promoted by Washington's assertion of the supremacy of its laws over those of supposedly sovereign nations—as in the case of the Helms-Burton law. All this suggests very forcefully that the imperial nation-states are pushing to the limits their capacity to bolster the role of multinational corporations and, more important, to increase the market share of international flows that accrues to their ruling classes.

If the ideology and rhetoric of globalists regarding the supposedly weak or anachronistic state do not reflect reality, what purpose do they serve? First, they serve to disarm their critics, to discourage oppositional social forces from creating an alternative to globalist-dominated capital. Second, they disorient the political struggle, for if not over the state, which is now supposedly non-existent, what could the struggle be about? Third, they encourage political and social groups to operate in the interstices of the dominant system, but on a small scale.

The purpose is to create dependent links to the macroeconomic system dominated by the globalist classes. The great majority of NGOs, in fact, are neither non-governmental in funding nor in their local collaborative activities. Finally, the purpose is to create an open-ended category such as "civil society" inhabited by harshly exploitative global sweatshop owners and to describe it as a locus for political democracy and private local economic initiative. This discourse ignores the multiplicity of links between the main actors of "civil society" (the ruling classes) and the apex of the state.

Identifying the dynamic and central role of the nation-state in the current phase of "globalization" allows us to identify the tremendous potentialities of the state as a centre for alternative forms of economic organization. These could be public enterprises, self-managed co-operatives and decentralized planning in the reallocation and redistribution of income, credit, land and technical assistance. Investment reallocation by the state presupposes fundamental changes in ownership in which the state plays a powerful role in a juridical, political and economic sense. Nation-state power is the basis for shifting production and consumption from the centrality of the global markets to the local, turning global exchanges into supplemental activities. Nation-state power is the basis for innovation and technological organization rooted in deepened social solidarity and community ties and for tying productivity increases to greater free time.

State power is essential to workers' self-management regimes—to the running of enterprises and returning productivity and competitive gains back to the collectivity of producers.

State power is an essential link to a new internationalism: as a successful example of an alternative to globalism. It is also needed to provide political, educational and cultural activities that strengthen horizontal ties among movements across the world, as a prelude to the emergence of other alternatives.

State power redefines the issue of markets by placing it in a new socio-political context in which social relations give primacy to the producer classes. The market of the popular nation-state is based on exchanges guided by the political criteria of social profits—gains that accrue to the general social wage and not to individual or firm profit-takers. The local and national markets are shaped by the new configuration of popular power, which shapes global exchanges—the inverse of today's globalization process.

The search for alternatives to globalization involves a profound rethinking of the comparative advantages of privatization and socialization in historical perspective. It is clear that the tendency under socialization was for more working people (wage, salaried, self-employed) to have more free time, greater job security, wider health coverage and more access to public higher education. The tendency was towards greater gender concern than is occurring under the privatization juggernaut. Comparative data on living standards in the countries currently experiencing privatization show a sharp decline in the quality of life, in particular for the younger generation. As the age of retirement recedes, exploitation is extended into old age. As managerial prerogatives increase, job-related stress and insecurity intensify and work benefits (health, vacations, etc.) shrink. Objective observers can argue that the obsession with the needs of the CEOs and their profits (disguised by the term "competitiveness") means that the working class becomes degraded. Workers in Europe who retain four-to-six-week vacations are described by the *New York Times* as "coddled." CEOs in Europe who have 40:1 salary ratio to workers are described as "underpaid" or "behind the times" by *Forbes* because they are far below the 240:1 ratio of U.S. CEOs.

The privatization ethos is an ill-disguised effort to create a type of Western despotism rooted in the absolute power of capital to control the state, impose a singular ideology and intimidate the labour force. The advanced model is the U.S.

Socialization provides an alternative democratic model in which capital becomes social capital by its formal subordination to the new organization of state power and the decentralization of authority to the constituent committees of production, consumption and environmental protection. Productivity increases fund health plans for everyone; public education is open to those who are academically qualified, retirement and alternative careers are open at age 50 or 55; work hours are reduced to twenty-five or thirty. Socialization not only redistributes wealth but also reorientates production and the media to serve democratically chosen social values. It provides a qualitative deepening and extension of the social values enunciated by the golden age of the welfare state. It is post-globalist socialism built on democratic and internationalist principles.

Resistance on a World Scale

A review of resistance to globalist politics must take into account the great variety of social forces that have taken the lead in different socio-economic settings, with varying degrees of intensity and a broad gamut of strategies. Nonetheless, certain general tendencies are evident beyond national and regional specificities.

First, while electoral vehicles have been one source of opposition, extra-parliamentary action has been the most widespread and effective approach to blocking or limiting the application of globalist policies. Since most anti-globalist electoral opposition is confined to the legislature, and a minority at that, globalist policies continue to be applied by executive decree and/or through globalist influence over the legislature. Electoral fraud, as in the case of the election of President Salinas in Mexico or the executive's blatant purchase of congressional votes, as in Brazil under Cardoso, debilitate the role of electoral institutions as points of opposition. Second, centre-left electoral opposition, once elected to office, has almost uniformly assimilated the globalist ideology in order to conform to the demands of the leading classes, the IFIs and the pre-existing state institutions. The most recent example is the FMLN (Farabundo Marti para la Liberacíon Nacional) mayor of San Salvador, Hector Silva, who sees the arch-proponents of globalization, the IMF and the World Bank, as allies in the development process. Former revolutionary groups, upon turning to electoral politics and entering political office in the seventies and eighties, have almost always abandoned their opposition to globalization and accepted its postulates.

As a result, all the groups adversely affected by globalization have turned towards extra-parliamentary activities and organization: general strikes in France, Italy, Argentina, Brazil, Bolivia, South Korea, etc.; land occupations in Brazil, Paraguay, El Salvador, Mexico, Colombia, Guatemala, etc.; urban revolts in Venezuela, the Dominican Republic, Argentina, etc.; and guerrilla movements in Mexico, Colombia, Peru, Zaire, etc. Extra-parliamentary movements have become the chosen form of expression in view of the impotence and co-optation of electoral parties.

The second characteristic shared by opposition groups is that they all start as movements to defend rights and interests threatened by the globalist ruling classes. Whether to protest loss of employment, privatization of public enterprise, or cuts in social security programs, living standards, pension plans or public educational facilities, the initial point of confrontation is over the aggressive rollback. Provoked by globalist appropriation of new sources of profits and reduction of costs, the movements respond. Within this common defense of past popular gains, some of the movements have taken the offensive and sought to advance towards structural changes—the peasant movements of Chiapas, Mexico, the Landless Workers Movement (MST) in Brazil, the Revolutionary Armed Forces of Colombia (FARC) peasant movement and the coca farmers of Chapare, Bolivia, have all created co-ops and established community-based economies that are in opposition to globalism and oriented towards developing the domestic market. As yet a minority, there is a growing anti-globalist and even incipient anti-capitalist consciousness among the mass movements currently engaged in defensive struggles.

The third characteristic of all movements in opposition to globalism is the tendency to form coalitions with or incorporate environmental, gender, ethnic or racial groups and struggles. The globalist project has a multiplicity of negative impacts—exploiting and polluting, impoverishing and excluding— that worsen living conditions and deepen interclass and intraclass inequalities. This confluence of groups challenges the efforts of the IFI and local regimes to fragment and depoliticize the different entities into a series of self-serving and isolated cultural organizations divorced from class-based political struggle.

Apart from the common feature of resistance to globalization, several points should be kept in mind. First, opposition is uneven among countries and within countries. Opposition in Europe and, in particular, France is obviously more advanced than in, say, the U.S., and Brazil and Mexico are more advanced than Chile and Peru. What distinguishes the level of struggle are the levels of political awareness, the traditions of struggle, the internal structures of mass organizations, and the insurgent or bureaucratic origins of the opposition.

Within countries certain sectors, regions, classes and ethnic groups demonstrate greater resistance than others. In Argentina the provinces have been in the forefront of opposition, while Buenos Aires lags behind. In Brazil the landless workers are far more combative than the urban slum dwellers or the trade unions. In Venezuela the urban poor of Caracas have been more active than the official trade unions. In general, public sector workers have been more active than those of the private sector (in Chile, Argentina, Brazil, Mexico, etc.). With some notable exceptions, the centre of more radical struggle has been the rural areas and the provinces, while the urban industrial sectors have been basically engaged in a defensive phase. But these are not hard and fast distinctions. In Europe and Asia it has been the workers from the most advanced sectors (transport in France and metal workers in South Korea) who have spearheaded the struggle. The spread of the opposition and its growing depth outside of the electoral arenas has created a firm base for a systemic alternative. Conversely, apart from electoral politics, the social base of globalist politicians and economic elites has become more fragile. The ideological and institutional centre of globalism is the U.S., and it is there that it stands unchallenged because of the long-standing oligarchic nature of the trade unions (which sets them apart from most workers) and the co-opted leadership of the major ethnic, gender and conservationist groups who function as mere pressure groups on the dominant globalist parties. Once one moves away from the U.S. the picture changes dramatically, particularly in Europe, Latin America and Asia. A similar process occurs in examining the internal political dynamic of these countries—a superficial view that looks only at the electoral process gives an impression of the solidity of globalist perspectives. However, moving beyond electioneering to everyday mass struggles and organizations and individual preferences, one finds a broad swathe of opposition to various or all elements of globalist politics.

The basic question that hasn't been resolved or is constantly posed is, if there is such general opposition, why hasn't globalism been overthrown? The answer is two-fold: more groups have been thrown back onto limited resources and thus are largely engaged in defensive struggles; and, while various alternatives are being elaborated, none have achieved general acceptance, or they remain embedded in sectoral or local settings.

Alternatives to Globalization

For years the critics of globalization repeatedly evoked the need to create an alternative. While some intellectuals continue to do so, and many others continue their passive and impotent reflections on the impermeability of the globalist onslaught, a few have begun to examine the real world and the emerging alternatives created by militants and activists.

These new alternatives should be understood not only in terms of what is being created but also in terms of what is being rejected. This can be succinctly summed up as "neither free market nor bureaucratic statism." Within these parameters, the emerging alternatives need to be analyzed further to distinguish them from the small-scale projects that globalist IFIs fund to absorb the discontent generated by their management of the macroeconomy. The alternatives of today are found in the local projects of insurgent groups and/or in the programmatic transformation of movements in struggle. In the first case, there are a variety of alternative forms of socio-economic organization, ranging from the Brazilian rural co-operative network organized by the MST that includes over 150,000 families, to the self-governing Indian communities under Zapatista leadership in Chiapas, to municipal enterprises organized in China, to the emerging, socialist-led regional rural producers in Colombia and Bolivia, to the proposals to democratize the universities in Chile and Argentina, and to the self-management proposals set forth by the radical wing of trade unions in France, South Korea and Italy. What differentiates these sectoral or small-scale activities from the IFI and NGO local projects of alternative development is that they are part of a larger political project of social transformation. They are initiated by insurgent groups in confrontation with the globalist state and classes and they usually are internally democratic. The leaders are elected by and responsible to the local communities (unlike the NGOs which are dependent on and responsible to their foreign donors). Thus these small-sale alternatives are building blocks for large-scale transformation; these alternatives are born of struggles that increase class and national consciousness and point towards the creation of an anti-globalist hegemonic bloc based on democratic collectivist alternatives. What unites these alternatives is their struggle for a social economy, one that combines sustainable growth, entrepreneurship and economic democracy.

Differences among the alternatives abound—labour relations, the scope of private ownership, the reliance on the market, etc. What is clear, however, is that social interests condition market exchanges: the "markets" are essentially local or national, with external exchanges subordinated to the deepening of the internal market. The principal issue is the systematic elaboration of micro-institutional relations to the macro level, the translation of programmatic transformation into specific institutional settings. The principal political problem is the struggle against technocratic intellectuals tied to globalist conceptions who seek to amalgamate popular social programs with liberal economics ("market socialism") and rigid collectivists who fail to understand the variety of forms of popular production (co-operative, public, household, etc.). The image that some intellectuals have that there is a need to create an alternative is, of course, an expression of their ignorance of existing alternatives in the process of creation and/or their unconscious acceptance of the globalist argument that there are no alternatives. Instead of repeating timeworn clichés about the "need for alternatives," it is more appropriate to relate to the alternatives now in the process of elaboration by movements in struggle.

The alternatives are there to be given greater substance, coherence and projection into the nation-state and beyond. Even now, international links are being forged between movements in national struggle against the globalist classes, each with their own local economy and programmatic transformations. If nothing else, they add another affirmative element to the critique of globalist ideology: there is an alternative to be found in the very struggle to overthrow the dominant globalist classes.

Chapter 3

Globalization as Ideology:
Economic and Political Dimensions

One of the fundamental issues facing critical intellectuals today is the corruption of political language, the obfuscation of capitalism as it presently exists through the use of euphemisms and concepts that have little relationship to the social and political realities they purport to discuss. We can observe this kind of mystification simply by glancing through the financial pages of the daily newspapers. A term like "economic reform" has nothing in common with its traditional usage and common-sense meaning—redistribution of income, increase of public welfare. The concept now refers to the reconcentration of income, upward and outward; the transfer of public property to private monopolies; and the reallocation of state expenditures from social welfare for workers and small farmers to export subsidies for giant corporations.

The same problem emerges with the whole repertoire of concepts elaborated over the past two decades by the ideologues of neoliberalism to justify and disguise the growing socio-economic inequalities and authoritarian political practices that accompany capitalist hegemony. A serious discussion of major social and political problems today must begin by clarifying and demystifying concepts such as "globalization."

In this chapter, we argue against the concept of "globalization" and in favour of the concept of "imperialism" as a more precise way of describing and interpreting the context within which political and social issues are framed. We then proceed to discuss the issue of citizenship within the broader framework of a critical view of "democracy" and democratic transitions, introducing the concept of "neo-authoritarianism" to explain how electoral processes have led to perverse and lopsided socio-economic inequalities. With reference to this imperial, neo-authoritarian framework, the chapter will examine "official" and critical views of citizenship, focusing on the distinction between formal and substantive practices of citizenship.

In the second part of this chapter, we discuss the rise and decline of democracy and citizenship in Southern Europe in the context of the new imperial order and the consolidation of its subordinate position within that system. The concluding section discusses prospects for change. It focuses on a series of contextual probabilities which could detonate large and long-term transformations.

Global Myths and Imperial Power

Globalization or U.S. imperialism? That is the question. At the end of one millennium and the beginnings of another a definitive answer can be given: the world economy is increasingly dominated by U.S. economic power. The dominant view in the 1980s and early 1990s was of a world of "global corporations" that transcended national boundaries—what some called a "global village" and others referred to as interdependent states linked by international corporations. But this perspective is no longer tenable. Systematic analysis of the composition of the international economy conclusively demonstrates that U.S. multinational corporations are far and away the dominant force and becoming more so over time. Ideas of a "bipolar" or "tripolar" world, of a more diversified world economy based on the emergence of the Asian miracle economies, are a mirage. The idea of a European counterweight to U.S. power, anchored in a resurgent and united German economy, is not evident, at least not in terms of the giant corporations that shape the world economy.

To the extent that globalization rhetoric persists, it has become an ideological mask disguising the emerging power of U.S. corporations to exploit and enrich themselves and their chief executive officers to an unprecedented degree. Globalization can be seen as a code word for the ascendancy of U.S. imperialism.

U.S. Corporate Dominance

A recent survey reported in the *Financial Times* (January 28, 1999) of the world's biggest companies based on market capitalization showed that among the 500 biggest companies in the world, the U.S. accounts for 244, Japan 46, and Germany 23. Even if we aggregate all of Europe, the total number of dominant companies is 173, still far less than the number owned and controlled by the U.S. Thus it is clear that European and not Japanese capitalism remains the only competitor with the U.S. for dominance of the world market. The acceleration of U.S. economic power and the decline of Japan in 1998 was manifest in the increasing number of U.S. firms among the top 500, up from 222 to 244, and the precipitous decline of Japanese firms from 71 to 46. This tendency was accentuated in the next few years because U.S. multinational corporations were buying out large numbers of Japanese enterprises, as well as Korean, Thai and other firms.

If we look at the largest twenty-five firms, those whose capitalization exceeds $86 billion, the concentration of U.S. economic power is even clearer: over 70 percent are U.S., 26 percent are European and 4 percent are Japanese. If we look at the top one hundred companies, 61 percent are U.S., 33 percent are European and only 2 percent are Japanese. To the degree that the TNCs control the world economy, it is largely the U.S. that has re-emerged as the overwhelmingly dominant power. Insofar as the very largest companies are the leading forces in eliminating smaller companies through mergers and acquisitions, we can expect the U.S.-based TNCs to play a major role in the process of concentration and centralization of capital.

The Myth of "Emerging Markets"

Beginning in the mid-1970s, corporate journalists, investment bankers and academics began to refer to the end of Third World dependency and the rise of Asia as a new centre of world capitalism. Today those pronouncements ring hollow. All of the emerging countries together (in Latin America, Asia, the Middle East and Africa) account for 26 of the 500 leading companies—only 5 percent. What is even more significant is that because of economic crises and privatization policies, many of these companies have been taken over by U.S. or European capital and they are in effect subsidiaries of the giants of the Euro-American empire. For example, in Latin America most of the telecommunications and electrical power companies—among the biggest companies in Latin America's business world—are owned by European TNCs. Privatization in Brazil, especially of Telebras, Latin America's biggest company, has extended the Euro-American empire.

The leading economic sectors among the top 500 companies are banking, communications, pharmaceuticals, office equipment, computer software and insurance. The U.S. predominates in both finance capital and high technology. The biggest company in the world today is Microsoft, followed by General Electric. U.S. imperial power is based on the four-legged stool of finance, high tech, pharmaceuticals and energy resources.

The dynamic shift in economic power can also be illustrated by looking at the number of big national companies with significant increases in value between 1997 and 1998: among the top twenty-three companies, thirteen were U.S. and ten were European—no companies from Asia or Latin America made the list. In contrast, among the companies whose capitalization has decreased significantly, twelve were from Japan, five were from other Asian countries and only five were from the U.S. and Western Europe. The increasing value of U.S. and European companies gives them more capital to extend their empires while the decreasing value of Japanese, Southeast Asian and Latin American companies makes them vulnerable to buyouts.

The precipitous decline of Asia as a world economic power coincides with the end of the Communist challenge to Euro-American power. The "rules of capitalist cooperation" between the imperial centres and "emerging markets" have changed dramatically. In the previous epoch of systemic confrontation, emerging Asian capital was seen by Washington as a strategic ally to be pampered with easy access to markets, loans and investment money, and its state regulations and protectionist policies were conveniently overlooked. In the contemporary, post-Communist period of intercapitalist competition, all the rules have changed. Asia is perceived as a competitor, a target to conquer. Washington and Wall Street apply strong pressures to liberalize, privatize and deregulate its financial markets. The resulting economic crises in Asia provide a tremendous opportunity for U.S. and European companies to conquer lucrative Asian enterprises and eliminate competitors.

Comparative Advantages of U.S. Corporations

Even in the darkest days of their relative decline in global power, during the mid- 1970s to mid-1980s, U.S. companies possessed several strategic advantages that they were later able to fully exploit to regain world supremacy.

First, U.S. corporations have undisputed control over the U.S. political system to a degree that is not imaginable in Europe. Both the Democratic and Republican parties are committed to expanding corporate power abroad even at the cost of sacrificing social programs at home. Whatever minor differences exist over marginal issues, Congress, the Presidency and the Federal Reserve (the U.S. central bank) are oriented towards promoting overseas expansion.

Second, U.S. trade unions represent only about 10 percent of the private-sector labour force and, more significantly, are totally dependent on and linked with the two major parties. There is no social democratic or left political threat to the two-party consensus on big business overseas expansion. U.S. trade union officials cooperate with companies firing workers, reducing social benefits, and implementing work rules that maximize corporate power. They force workers to accept technological changes and job reclassifications to a far greater degree than European or Asian trade union officials. As a result, big U.S. companies have been able to accumulate capital and expand overseas without confronting any of the political resistance found in Europe or Asia.

Third, the U.S. has the lowest corporate tax rates of any industrialized country. Corporate taxes account for 10 percent of federal revenues, but income taxes on wages account for 47 percent. The U.S. has the highest percentage of workers without health coverage of any of the industrial and semi-industrial countries. Combined, these factors provide U.S. companies with greater profits to buy out competitors and finance mergers leading to more dominant positions in the world market.

Fourth, the U.S. Treasury Department can finance the nation's huge current account deficits by issuing dollars—the major currency of exchange in world markets. No capitalist competitor has this privileged ability to finance its negative balances.

Fifth, U.S. Treasury Department officials are the most influential members of the IMF and the World Bank and are thus in a position to enforce economic policies that increase the vulnerability of rival countries and facilitate U.S. corporate takeover by lowering barriers to U.S. financial investment invasions.

Finally, the U.S. imperial state, via a multiplicity of agencies (Commerce, CIA, Pentagon, Treasury), has concentrated its efforts on undermining the Japanese economy, retaining influence in Europe (via NATO) and seizing assets in Asia and Latin America through a combination of political and military interventions that shape the development agenda in the direction of free markets. These internal and external political and economic advantages have provided U.S. companies with the internal resources and international framework for large-scale mergers and overseas expansion, leading to the re-emergence of the American economic empire.

And it is *empire*, not globalization, that explains why the U.S. economy continues to grow while Asia experiences massive bankruptcies and the Brazilian economy collapses. The contrast between big U.S. companies' increasing capitalization and the decreasing capitalization of firms in Asia and Latin America cannot be explained by an "interdependent" global economy. Rather, the growth of profits, interest payments to banks and buyouts by TNCs that precede and accompany Asian and Latin American collapse are best understood as the successful operation of the U.S. imperial order. The crises of its competitors are an opportunity for U.S. business and facilitate low-cost purchases of enterprises and banks in Korean, Japan and Brazil. Devaluations lower wages in countries where U.S. companies operate, and cheap consumer goods stoke U.S. consumer spending.

A good illustration of how "crises" have benefited the U.S. and European empire is found in the takeovers of profitable enterprises. In 1998, U.S. and European TNCs invested $47 billion in purchasing Brazilian firms. In 1999, with the debt, devaluation and depression in Brazil, more lucrative purchases by Euro-American companies there were forthcoming. In Korea over 53 percent of U.S. foreign investments were directed at taking over existing operations from Korean nationals. In 1998, as Japanese industry declined 6.9 percent, U.S. banking and financial corporations were making deep inroads into the Japanese financial and real estate market.

The growing economic empire was matched by the growing willingness of the Clinton administration to use force in Iraq, Central Europe, Asia and Africa, to increase the U.S. military budget and to appoint hard-line presidential intelligence and security advisors to direct covert and overt military interventions. Washington is prepared to defend its newly regained economic ascendancy by all means necessary: by free trade if possible, by military force if necessary.

According to most advocates of the "globalization" theory, we are entering a new epoch of interdependency in which stateless corporations transcend national frontiers, spurred by a third technological revolution and facilitated by new information systems. According to this view the nation-state is an anachronism, movements of capital are unstoppable and inevitable, and the world market is the determinant of the macro and micro political economy. Neoliberalism is an ideological derivative, with its emphasis on free markets, free flows of capital, and privatization.

The result, according to globalization theorists, will be a progressive, dynamic, modernizing world of prosperous nations. The contrast between the promises of globalization theorists and contemporary realities could not be starker. Instead of interdependent nations, we have dramatic contrasts between creditor and debtor nations; multibillion-dollar corporations appropriating enterprises, interests, royalties and trade surpluses; and billions of workers and peasants reaping poverty and miserable existences. Structurally, we find that over 80 percent of the major multinational corporations control their invest-ment, research and technology decisions out of their home offices in the U.S., Germany and Japan. Multinational corporations are based on worldwide operations, but their control is centralized.

The most striking refutation of globalization theory is found in the contrast between the relative prosperity of capitalism in the U.S. and Europe and the collapse or depression of economies in the rest of the world. The crises in Asia, Latin America, the former USSR, etc. were fuelled by pressures from the Euro-American powers, who encouraged liberalization, deregulation and indebted-ness. Today U.S. and European TNCs benefit via cheap buyouts of banks and corporations, exploit low-wage labour and exercise greater control over trade and macroeconomic policies. It is a strange concept of "globalization" that describes pillage and profit in the same breath as interdependence and stateless corporations. The great concentrations of profits and interest accrue to the accounts of TNCs and banks headquartered in the U.S. and Europe.

The concept of imperialism is much more precise in defining the current concentration of wealth and power, the centralization of capital and the distribution of benefits and losses from economic crises. And the historic focus of imperialism today is in the U.S.

The return of U.S. ascendancy has contradicted theories about the immi-nent decline of the U.S. U.S. banks and investment houses are increasingly dominant in Asia and Europe. U.S. cultural commodity exports have expanded geometrically and U.S.-appointed officials in international financial institu-tions are seen to act as direct spokespeople for U.S. multinational corporations and banks.

Equally important, through NATO and its expansion in Eastern Europe, the U.S. now has a greater presence and influence in Europe than at any time during the Cold War. U.S. influence is seen in its military presence in, for example, Bosnia, Iraq, Yugoslavia (Kosovo) and Macedonia. U.S. influence in the United Nations, and particularly its control over the U.N. inspectors in Iraq, is now public knowledge. Washington's violation of U.N. mandates in its bombing of Iraq and its challenge to the World Trade Organization via unilateral sanctions against Europe on the bananas issue are symbolic of the arrogance of imperial power.

It is difficult to argue against the imperial nature of international relations, and even more difficult to deny the ascendancy of the U.S. within the imperial system. To continue to deny economic and military realities with continued reference to the "global nature" of the economy is essentially to obfuscate information about the principal actors and beneficiaries within that system.

The Internationalization of Capital and the Pursuit of Profits

The internationalization of capital has become the subject of considerable debate. At issue has been what we would argue to be a misplaced concern about international competitiveness. The search for competitiveness provides a potent rationale for policies of structural adjustment: competitiveness is said to be necessary to adapt to the changing requirements of the new world economic order. The issue in this non-debate is how to identify the driving force of overseas expansion. However, we argue that the search for profits rather than "competitiveness" underlies the "internationalization" of capital.

Overseas profits are today the principal source of profit for a growing number of firms. The profile of the corporations that derive the bulk of their profits from overseas activities varies and thus "internationalization" is not a uniform phenomenon. Internationalization of capital has gradually evolved over time among certain types of TNCs. The internationalization of capitalism—the movement of multinational capital—in fact has little to do with abstract notions of "competitiveness." It is more directly related to rates of profit. The main driving force for the growth of investment abroad ("capital flight") and the relative decline of a domestic economy is the higher rate of overseas returns.

When the percentage of foreign assets equals a corporation's percentage of overseas profits there is no comparable advantage between foreign and domestic investment. But when overseas profits are proportionally higher than overseas assets, then there is a comparative advantage in this kind of investment. We analyze the profit-making of U.S.-based TNCs in relation to earnings from their domestic market and overseas. We then turn to examine profitability in relation to assets in both domestic and overseas markets to determine where and to what degree profits to assets ratios are higher. In both instances we analyze profitability and rates of profit over a thirteen-year period.

Although internationalization of capital is a growing reality, it is important to put it in perspective. In 1993, 22 percent of the one hundred largest TNCs earned more than 50 percent of their revenues from foreign sources. The U.S. market is still the primary source of revenue for three-quarters of the TNCs even as U.S. corporations expand overseas. Nonetheless there are clear indications of an historic shift. Between 1980 and 1993, among the top one hundred TNCs, those earning more than 50 percent of their profits overseas increased from 27 percent to 33 percent of the total (see Table 1). In other words, one-third of the largest corporations earned the bulk of their profits from overseas investments.

Table 1. Largest 100 firms earning over 50 percent of profits overseas

	50–74 percent	75 percent and over	Total
1980	22%	5%	27%
1993	20%	13%	33%

Source: *Forbes*, July 18, 1994: 276–79; July 18/19: 102–4.

The dependence of TNCs on overseas profits is growing and has become for many a strategic need. In 1980 only 5 percent of the largest TNCs earned over 75 percent of their profits overseas. By 1993 that figure had increased two and a half times to 13 percent. For this minority, U.S. state policy promoting NAFTA, GATT and other international free trade agreements is crucial to growth and continuing operation.

The issue of U.S. firms becoming "competitive" to oppose being squeezed out by foreign competitors does not square with the data. In 1980, 44 percent of U.S.-based TNCs had lower than average rates of profits or losses, but by 1993 that figure had declined to 35 percent (see Table 2). By the early 1990s a growing number of firms were earning high to super profits. High profits were based on profit to asset ratios of 1.50–1.99, and super profits on ratios of 2.0 and over.

Table 2. Rates of profit of largest 100 U.S.-based TNCs, 1980 and 1993

	Losses	Below Average	Above Average	High Profits	Super Profits
1980	1 percent	43 percent	35 percent	12 percent	7 percent
1993	9 percent	26 percent	25 percent	14 percent	14 percent

Note: Rates of profit are calculated by ratio of profits earned overseas to foreign assets. Hence, a corporation whose percentage of foreign earnings exceeds its percentage of foreign assets by a factor of two would be classified as earning super profits; a firm earning between 1.5 and 1.99 would be classified as high-profit; 1.00–1.49 as above average; and below 0.99 as below average.

In 1980 the high and super profit earning TNCs amounted to 19 percent of the firms, but by 1993, 28 percent of the U.S.-based TNCs were in the high-profit bracket. However, there was an increase in the percentage of TNCs that had overseas losses between 1980 and 1993. In 1980 only one firm showed a loss compared to nine firms in 1993. The "competitiveness" argument about a profit squeeze applied to a very limited number of firms, though a number that is growing alongside a large number of firms who have consolidated robust profit margins. Along with the growing number of U.S. TNCs earning the bulk of their profits overseas, we must take note of the increasing number of firms earning exceptional rates of profit. Internationalization of capital appears to be based on penetration and consolidation of favourable positions in overseas markets, as manifested in high rates of return for a growing number of U.S. firms. However, this is not a risk-free venture, as along with the growing number of big winners there has been an increase in "losers."

Going international has been the road to super profits. The 1980s was a transitional decade in the breakdown of nationalist, socialist and welfare barriers to worldwide capitalist expansion. The decline of wage and welfare payments and the increase in favourable state regulations and tax policies facilitated domestic accumulation for global expansion. And the converse is also true: global expansion has led to a reduction in wages and fringe benefits in the U.S. The importance of international investment in TNC profits is one reason why the U.S. government is so actively promoting global and regional "free trade agreements." By opening up overseas investment opportunities, the U.S. government promotes higher rates of profits while reducing domestic living standards. The TNCs have succeeded at least temporarily in selling the idea that the global market or the capitalist world system is responsible for reductions in U.S. living standards, instead of the TNCs own drive for higher profits. As Louis Uchitelle of the *New York Times* writes, "Instead business is seen [by workers] as also a victim caught in a global competition that forces cost-cutting and lay-offs." (*New York Times*, November 20, 1994, 4-1).

The New Imperial Order
The new imperial order and the promotion of the interests of the dominant economic institutions through neoliberal policies have profound consequences for democracy and society. At the structural level, external and non-elected officials play a major role in shaping macroeconomic and macrosocial decisions that affect the basic structures of the economy and the living standards of nations.

Today, in many parts of the world, officials designated by the U.S. Treasury in the World Bank and IMF decide on government spending levels, property relations (private versus public ownership), development strategies (export or domestic markets) and many other decisive aspects of social existence, bypassing the electoral system. These external political actors respond to the imperatives of their home governments and national TNCs. In most cases, local political elites implement regressive macroeconomic policies without consulting their electorate or even the elected legislature. The presumption of political decision-making by these external representatives of corporate power fundamentally alters the nature of electoral political systems.

If authoritarianism is defined as a system where decisions are made without public consultation or accountability, the growing influence and power of the non-elected officials of international financial institutions is one important pillar of that system.

However, the influence of non-elected financial actors from the outside forms only one aspect of the growth of authoritarianism, albeit a very important one. The growth of NATO with its central command structure dominated by

U.S. military officials and its increasing role in defining national boundaries, extending its reach into Central Europe, for example, is another dimension of the new authoritarianism. The re-satellitization of Eastern Europe via NATO command is a vivid reminder that yesterday's defenders of national independence are today's eager clients of U.S. hegemonic aspirations.

The style of the new authoritarianism is different from that of the old repressive regimes. In the past, authoritarianism had a military face and denied individual freedoms and electoral competition. The new authoritarianism is a hybrid, combining electoral processes and individual freedoms with highly elitist decision-making structures. Elections occur, but there is no correspondence between the populist and social democratic rhetoric during the electoral campaign and post-electoral governance, when harsh neoliberal austerity measures and structural adjustment policies are applied. The deliberate use of political deception calls into question the function of "competitive elections" in providing real voter choice and a true means for the electorate to influence the political process. The increasing use of executive decrees to implement the neoliberal agenda (of privatization, structural adjustment policies, etc.) is much more akin to the style of the old authoritarian regimes than to democratic practices.

Equally important, the routine threats of capital flight by TNCs to undercut social reforms, and the amplifications of those threats by political executives, are a form of blackmail that denies voters and legislatures the ability to discuss and pass laws. The use of such threats are antithetical to a civic culture, where all the socio-economic actors accept the rules of the democratic game and are free to discuss policies without coercion. The case of the resignation of former German Finance Minister Osker La Fontaine is instructive. His attempt to redress certain fiscal inequities was countered by the threat of German corporations to move out of Germany. Prime Minister Schroeder proceeded to force the issue, resulting in the resignation of La Fontaine and the scuttling of the social reform agenda. The electorate, which had voted for social reform, was marginalized and corporate capital had its way. The democratic process in Germany was sacrificed to meet the demands of centralized corporate power.

Neo-authoritarianism is a hybrid system that combines elite decision-making and electoral processes, elected legislators and non-elected corporate decision-makers and electoral campaigns and decrees, undermining the notion of a civic culture. In this context it is important to critically examine the meaning of citizenship from two angles: "formal" and "substantive." *Formal citizenship* refers to the legal attributes attached to a citizen according to a written or unwritten constitution. *Substantive citizenship* refers to the capacity of individuals to exercise those powers in actual debate and in the resolution of political issues. Today, citizens are systematically denied the right to address and vote on the most profound and substantive issues that affect their lives, including state spending, taxation, privatization, austerity programs, and subsidies for TNCs. To cover up this denial of citizenship, elitist defenders of the liberal state refer to amorphous notions of "civil society" and "globalization."

We live in class societies where socio-economic inequalities are now sharper than they were over the last three decades of the 20th century. "Civil society" includes billionaire investors and bankers who accumulate fortunes buying and selling enterprises, closing enterprises and firing thousands of workers, as well as low-paid, contingent workers lacking elementary labour rights. The socio-economic inequalities and the exploitative relations within "civil society" define very distinctive conceptions of citizenship and political action. For wealthy, elite corporate managers, citizenship consists of influencing macroeconomic decisions; for workers, citizenship consists of adapting to those decisions or engaging in class politics to resist them.

The point is that the concept of "civil society" is too general and inclusive to explain the divisive economic policies generated by one class in society against another. The exercise of substantive citizenship is closely associated with a class politics that recognizes the distinctive and unequal relations within civil society and the interlocking relations between dominant classes in civil society and the state.

Substantive citizenship is in profound conflict with the coercive practices of TNCs. The overt and covert threats of TNCs to move capital, close factories and fire workers significantly undermines free debate and the democratic legislative process. The corporate gun pointed at the heads of workers and legislators precludes democratic politics.

Citizenship can only function when citizens can elect decision-makers while not under the thumb of external actors responsive to U.S. or European political and economic elites. Citizens cannot engage in meaningful debates within a civic culture where threats and blackmail are the weapons of one set of interests. Citizenship requires that preferences expressed and chosen during electoral campaigns have some direct correspondence to government policies. Social Democrats who talk to the people before elections and capitulate to the TNCs after elections not only put their reformist credentials into question but also undermine the legitimacy of the electoral process.

Conclusions

The re-emergence of imperial relations—mistakenly described as "globalization"—has wrecked havoc on democratic practice. As democracy has been redefined as centralized elite decision-making with elections, the role of citizens as protagonists of public policy debates has declined. The result is greater voter apathy, increased abstention, rejection of political incumbents, "anti-voting" and increased resort to extra-parliamentary action.

The prospects for a new realignment of socio-political forces and the possibility of a new, more participatory politico-economic order (deep democracy or socialism) are contingent on several factors:

1. The spread of capitalist crises from Southeast Asia, South Korea, Japan, Latin America, Russia and the ex-USSR to the U.S. and Europe. There are plausible reasons to believe this is possible, given the constraints that the collapse of these markets has on the profit realization of the biggest corporations in Europe and the U.S.
2. Large-scale socio-political changes are looming on the horizon in key regions affected by the crises. In China, political unrest is growing throughout the interior of the country as massive layoffs occur and safety nets are non-existent. In Brazil, depression has provoked increasing confrontations at many levels—from state governors to landless workers. Similar social challenges are emerging in Indonesia, Russia, etc., devastated by economic collapse.
3. The military-political confrontation provoked by Washington and NATO's military partition of Yugoslavia could become a prolonged military conflict, destabilizing the Balkans and leading to more general warfare, creating uncertainty among investors and precipitating financial crises.
4. The boom in the U.S. is fuelled in part by an exaggerated speculative bubble that is unsustainable. Stocks are vastly overvalued, savings are negative and the performance of the productive economy has no relation to the paper economy.

If any or all of these events become reality we are likely to see the growth of extra-parliamentary politics in the West and the radicalization of the political process in the South and East. Established parties, even or especially the Socialists, deeply convinced of their own mission as guardians of the status quo and believers in their own myths of belonging to the Centre-Left or "third way," are structurally incapable of extricating themselves from a political economic order in crisis. New socio-political movements will probably initially take the form of the unemployed councils in France, peasant-farmer confrontations with the state, the general strikes of the Danish workers, etc.

The ravages of neoliberalism are already provoking a profound rethinking of the mindless "liberalization" which has condemned hundreds of millions to poverty in Asia, Latin America and Russia. There is a strong likelihood of a turn towards inward development against imperialist "globalization"; a revival of a Socialist project—the resocialization of bankrupt private enterprises as an alternative to foreign takeovers; higher levels of public planning and a return to popular assembly–style democratization of public and private space.

In Southern Europe, the crises and rethinking of the post-1970s trajectory might lead to a revival of the "spirit of 1974"; crisis brings out the best and worst in people. For declining ruling classes there is always the option of repression to retain power and subsidize their losses; for the popular classes, councils and assemblies, there is solidarity—the re-emergence of citizenship in place of patron-client relations.

One-quarter of the capitalist world cannot prosper when three-quarters are in deep crisis: the laws of capitalist accumulation cannot operate in such restricted circumstances. What is clear is that the current success of capitalism in Europe and the U.S. is largely based on dismantling the social welfare state and refusing to comply with any meaningful social pact. As we have seen, even the minimal fiscal reforms proposed by former German Finance Minister La Fontaine were rejected and he was ousted. This raises a fundamental question: If social welfare as it has historically been understood in Europe is no longer feasible under existing capitalism, what are the alternatives? We are reminded here of one President Kennedy's rhetorical flourishes, which contained a profound truth: "Those who make reform impossible make revolution inevitable."

Chapter 4

Capitalism at the Beginning of a New Millennium:
Latin America and Euro-American Imperialism

A good place to begin a review of Latin American capitalism is Harry Magdoff's *Age of Imperialism*. The last two decades of 20th-century capitalist development in Latin America have witnessed an unparalleled period of prosperity for U.S. multinational banks and corporations as well as nearly unchallenged political power exercised from Washington. Notwithstanding the current intellectual consensus that has formed around the concept of globalization, the dynamics of these developments in Latin America can best be understood in terms of the workings of Euro-American imperialism. Although it has long and deep roots in the region, it was not until the 1980s and 1990s that imperialism, arguably the highest and final stage of capitalism, effectively came of age in Latin America, creating the conditions for its consolidation.

Several issues are central to our discussion of the current configuration of capitalist power in Latin America at the beginnings of the 21st century. First is the growing evidence of a hegemony of the U.S. over the global capital-accumulation process. Throughout the 1990s, U.S. capital and its imperial state increased their positions and weight in the global economy, engaging in a veritable frenzy of mergers and acquisitions of leading corporations in strategic sectors: in 1998, 244 of the top 500 were American (up from 222 just the year before) and so were 61 of the top 100. In Latin America, ten of the top twenty corporations were U.S.-owned. This emerging hegemony and growing economic power, and the corresponding decline in the position of European and particularly Japanese capital, is paralleled by a series of strategic moves to establish control over the levers and institutions of global finance and "governance," as well as military power.

Second, this unparalleled wealth and power of Wall Street and Washington in Latin America is a relatively recent phenomenon, coming after several decades of nationalist and populist policies that limited the depth and scope of U.S. imperialism and blocked its hegemony.

Third, despite diverse efforts to reactivate the national economies in the region, these economies have been beset by a propensity towards ever-deepening crisis. Conditions of this crisis include a pillaging of resources of staggering proportions and ever-larger bailouts of U.S. investors organized by the U.S. imperial state and its adjuncts in the "international financial community."

Fourth, while the conditions of poverty and social inequality in the distribution of productive resources and income are embedded in deeply entrenched economic and social structures, the current ascendancy of U.S. imperialism in the region has led to a reversal of the limited gains made by the working and middle class and to a serious regression in living standards.

Fifth, the capitalist transition from a rural, agricultural economy to an urban-centred industrial economy has led to a new and fundamental social division in Latin American society. On one side of this divide is the bourgeoisie, dominated by a handful of super-rich billionaires linked to the circuits of global capital and a small cluster of export-oriented multinational corporations. On the other side is the growing mass of impoverished, exploited and marginalized workers found in the burgeoning informal sector of the region's urban economies, stripped of social rights and protective labour legislation.

Sixth, a new political language and theoretical discourse has been constructed to obfuscate the workings of U.S. imperialism in the region and elsewhere. The multinational banks and corporations—which are taking over productive enterprises, appropriating assets, dominating markets and extracting profits on the basis of cheap labour—are no longer understood to be agents of the imperialist system; they are now viewed as facilitators of globalization, the growing integration and interdependence of the world economy. The transfer of income from labour to capital and its reconcentration are viewed as mechanisms of internal adjustment to the requirements of the global economy. The purchase and takeover of public and state assets is dubbed "privatization." The removal of restrictions on foreign investment, the liberalization of markets and the deregulation of private enterprise—all policies designed to increase the rate of profit on invested capital—are viewed as forms of "structural adjustment." The imperial prescription of macroeconomic policies is described as "stabilization." The imposition of economic structures designed to attract foreign capital, the bailout of investors and the increased level of control over military and police under the pretext of anti-narcotic campaigns are dubbed "free market" or "market-friendly" policies. The accommodation of "third sector" popular organizations to the interests and policies of the imperial state is described as "good governance" or the "strengthening of civil society," a critical factor in "the economic development process." And the profit-seeking actions of the dominant class are viewed as the socially oriented and subjectively meaningful behaviour of new economic agents, or, in "postmodern" terms, as the actions of diverse individuals searching for their social identity. With the dissolution in thought of the operating structures and material conditions of the capitalist system, classes also disappear. Even the economically and politically dominant capitalist class, the social base of the imperialist system, is replaced by a multiplicity of social actors and individuals, each struggling to define and position themselves in the context of the new global economic order and its heterogeneous conditions, which are viewed and treated as subjective rather than objective.

To enter into a discussion of capitalism and imperialism in Latin America, one must first discard the euphemistic, imprecise and obfuscating terms and discourse that have come into fashion and return to the more precise and rigorous categories of Marxist analysis.

Historical Origins of Imperial Hegemony in Latin America

From the 1930s to the mid-1970s, U.S. imperialism in Latin America was constantly challenged by nationalist, populist and democratic socialist regimes and movements. Generally these challenges were reformist rather than revolutionary, in that they called into question elements of the imperialist project but not the whole system.

In the 1930s and 1940s, President Cardenas of Mexico nationalized U.S. petroleum interests, while Vargas in Brazil, Peron in Argentina and the Popular Front in Chile promoted national industry under protective trade barriers, initiating a widespread movement towards the nationalization of strategic industries in the region. In the 1950s, Guatemala's president Arbenz expropriated United Fruit land and redistributed it among the peasants, provoking a CIA-led coup against his administration. A radical-nationalist revolution of sorts took place in Bolivia in 1952, followed by a social revolution in Cuba that challenged imperial hegemony in the region. The 1960s and early 1970s saw the emergence of populist, nationalist and democratic regimes and movements throughout the continent. This "long half century" of social and political advance led to significant social and economic legislation that legalized trade unions, provided basic social benefits and extended public education and health care to substantial sectors of the industrial working class, public employees, and in a few cases (Chile, 1970–73) the peasantry.

This period was not a "golden age" of development or a paradise for workers, because they were still exploited. Peasants were excluded from social legislation, and the economies still depended heavily on primary-goods exports to the industrially advanced countries. Nonetheless, constraints on capital were still in place, and under various populist regimes the income distribution between capital and labour improved significantly. In the case of Chile under Allende's socialist regime, labour received close to 60 percent of the income derived from social production, an advance which was soon reversed by the subsequent Pinochet regime, which created conditions that by 1989, after seventeen years of neoliberal policies, had reduced the share of labour in the national income to 19 percent, one of the lowest in the world.

The two-class system of peasants and landlords that had prevailed in the pre-depression period was replaced by a more complex structure that included workers, a petite bourgeoisie and an industrial bourgeoisie. A wave of nationalization in the 1960s and early 1970s led to state control of the strategic sectors of the economy. In some cases imperial firms were generously compensated and many found lucrative new investments. Tariff barriers fostered national industrialization but did not prevent multinational corporations (TNCs) from setting up branch plants. However, these TNCs generally had to abide with legislation relating to content, employment of nationals, and foreign exchange requirements. The TNCs' direct investments and their repatriation of profits were also restricted, forcing them to resort to subterfuges such as transfer pricing so as to have profits surface in less restrictive economies.

Latin America's national-populist regimes did allow the TNCs to make substantial profits on invested foreign capital and operations. However, in the wake of the Cuban revolution, new and more radical measures were on the agenda of many governments, creating conditions for political reaction. A new class of wealthy business operators and bankers chafed at the labour legislation and the controls placed on their capital, as well as at measures designed to redistribute productive resources such as land. This class turned towards both the armed forces and the TNCs for support in breaking the populist alliance and to secure greater overseas market shares, financing for ventures and access to new technology. Thus was formed the social base for the counter-reform politics and the ascendancy of U.S. imperialism that characterized Latin American capitalism over the next two decades.

The Political and Ideological Basis of Imperial Ascendancy

According to the ideologues of neoliberalism, the "free market" has become the dominant model because of the failures of "statism." But the historical record suggests otherwise. The "free market" emerged in Latin America precisely in reaction against the success of social reform and was imposed on the basis of violent political intervention.

Washington, acting in concert with the Latin American military. overthrew democratically elected governments in Chile, Argentina, Brazil and Uruguay. Newly installed dictators, supported by the international financial institutions, then proceeded to dismantle social and protectionist barriers, denationalize the industrial and banking sectors, and privatize public assets. Free market policies were enforced by draconian regimes that killed thousands, jailed and tortured tens of thousands and forced millions into exile. Political linkages between TNCs, Latin American transnational capitalists and the state were strengthened, while U.S. hegemonic aspirations became a reality.

The centrality of state violence and imperial state intervention in the construction of the new neoliberal configuration gives the lie to those who argue that the institution of the "new economic model" was due to the greater efficiency and rationality of the market. The expansion of U.S. imperialism was not the result of impersonal, amorphous and inevitable global forces; much less was it an inevitable "imperative" of "globalization" or of the "world capitalist system." Rather, the new configuration of power is the result of a class war conducted at national, regional and international levels. The agenda behind this war is not only to spark a renewed cycle of capital accumulation but to create conditions that will allow the forces of U.S. imperialism to advance and expand into other parts of the world. In effect, Latin America has been set up by U.S. capital not only to be pillaged of its resources but as a staging ground for an impending battle for the world market among the leading centres of capitalist power.

The New Imperial Order in Latin America

There is abundant evidence that the elite members of Latin America's transnational capitalist class and imperial "enterprises" benefited enormously from U.S. hegemony in the last quarter of the 20th century. The nature of the New Imperial Order in Latin America can be grasped in terms of the deep structural ties that have served as means of surplus extraction and by an examination of the class/state relations which have sustained these ties.

The New Imperial Order is built on five pillars: large, long-term interest payments on external debt; massive transfers of profits derived from direct and portfolio investments; buyouts and takeovers of lucrative public enterprises and financially troubled national enterprises, as well as direct investments in sweatshops, energy resources, and low-wage manufacturing and service industries; collection of rents from royalty payments on a wide range of products, patents and cultural commodities; and favourable current account balances based on the dominance of U.S. corporations and banks in the region through traditional market "familiarity" and historical ties.

Interest Payments on Debt
The statistics concerning interest payments on external debts, are staggering. Most of the original capital (in the form of syndicated bank loans) was extended in the 1970s, when U.S. commercial banks rapidly expanded their international operations so as both to use their surplus capital and capture anticipated higher rates of return. By 1982, up to $257 billion of loans were extended to governments and the private sector in Latin America, particularly Argentina, Brazil and Mexico, which accounted for over 50 percent of the accumulated Third World debt. With the onset of the "debt crisis" in 1982, bank loans to the region were drastically reduced, although over the course of the decade, the accumulated external debt held in the region grew from $257 billion to $452 billion, despite total annual interest payments of $170 billion, resulting in a net drain so large that the then president of the World Bank was prompted to note that "a transfer of resources of such proportions is ... premature" (*Financial Times*, January 27, 1986).

By the 1990s, when the flow of capital to the region had significantly changed in composition (to equity rather than debt), the IFIs trumpeted the end of the debt crisis, notwithstanding the fact that the majority of countries still had to service their external debts at a level—50 percent of export earnings—that the World Bank defined as "critical." However, as Table 3 suggests, the problem of external debt, although now regarded as "manageable," is by no means over. By 1998 the total external debt in Latin America climbed to $698 billion, an increase of 64 percent from 1987, the peak year of the debt crisis. However, what is significant about this debt is not so much its magnitude (about

45 percent of regional GNP) but the sheer volume of annual interest payments made to U.S. banks, causing a huge drain of potential capital. In just one year (1995) the banks received $67.5 billion of income from this source, and over the course of the decade well over $600 billion, a figure equivalent to around 30 percent of total export earnings generated over the same period, at enormous economic and social cost.

Table 3. Debt and debt payment, Latin America, 1982–98
(billion U.S.$, annual averages, current prices)

	'80	'87	'90	'91	'92	'93	'94	'95	'96	'97	'98
Debt Stock	$257	474	476	491	450	526	547	607	627	650	698
Percent of GNP	36	66	45	45	42	37	35	30	35	33	36
Debt Payments	$30	47	41	39	37	38	35	36	35	33	35
Percent of Exports	36	37	32	26	26	28	29	29	-	-	-

Source: World Bank, *World Debt Tables, 1994/95; World Development Report*, various years; CEPAL, 1998b: 25.

Portfolio Investments
Enticed by a program of neoliberal reforms, private capital has flowed into Latin America at an accelerated rate from 1991 (Table 4). Portfolio investments in stocks and bonds accounted for the lion's share of total capital flows over the decade and, like FDI, were highly concentrated in the most industrially advanced countries of the region—Brazil and Mexico. In the years that had led up to the 1980s debt crisis there had been a net outflow of portfolio investment, which reflected not only the volatility of this form of capital but was a symptom of capital flight. This outflow also reflected the conditions that had led to a persistent increase in current account deficits throughout the region and a highjacking of reserves of hard currency held by central banks. The early 1990s saw a boom in portfolio investments attracted by high interest rates and opportunities in emerging markets, but subsequent years saw considerable ups and downs and in and out movements in the flow of portfolio investment as investors responded to government adjustments and manipulations of exchange and interest rates and to changing conditions. In general, countries in Latin America have tended to rely more on foreign portfolio investment than on FDI. Since 1992, inward portfolio investment flows (bonds and notes issued by governments in the region) have far exceeded inward FDI flows.

Table 4. Equity capital flows into Latin America
(accumulated billion U.S.$)

	1981-89	1990	1991	1992	1993	1994	1995	1996	1997
FDI	83.0	8.7	11.6	17.6	17.2	28.7	31.9	43.8	56.1
Portfolio		-0.9	16.6	28.1	74.4	63.1	5.4	50.9	32.5

Source: For portfolio, IMF, *International Financial Statistics*, various years; for FDI 1990–97: UNCTAD (1998: 256, 362), based on data provided by the U.N. Economic Commission for Latin America and the Caribbean (ECLAC), Unit on Investment and Corporate Strategies. According to Securities Data (*Excelsior*, January 16, 1999), $54.4 billion of FDI was used to purchase existing corporate assets in 1998.

Foreign Direct Investments
Throughout the 1980s, global capital was used to create equity in developed countries while bank loans were directed primarily towards the developing countries. But in the 1990s the direction and composition of capital flows changed significantly, and there was a relative shift towards equity investments in both portfolio and direct forms. From 1978 to 1981 syndicated bank loans accounted for 82 percent of capital flows to Latin America, but from 1990 to 1993 they accounted for only 32 percent. But by the end of the millennium, equity investment accounted for over three-fifths of such flows—a third in portfolio form and around 45 percent as FDI. Capital showed increased preference for Latin America's "emerging markets" and assets because of the highly favourable conditions presented by the region's extensive privatization programs, macroeconomic stability, liberal government policies and stock of natural resources, markets, labour and "created assets." Over the course of the 1990s, the flow of direct investment increased by 223 percent worldwide, but in Latin America the rate of increase has been close to 600 percent. Brazil, Mexico and Argentina accounted for 62 percent of this FDI, and Chile, Colombia, Peru and Venezuela accounted for another 26 percent. The inflow of FDI to the region (as shown in Table 4) was reflected in the rapid growth of its accumulated stock and the increase in its share of gross fixed capital formation—from an annual average of 4.2 percent from 1984 to 1989, to 6.5 percent in 1990 to 1993, 8.6 in 1993 and up to 11 percent in subsequent years, a level that reflects the disproportionate weight of the TNCs in the region's economy.

Most of this FDI has been used to purchase the assets of privatized public enterprises and financially troubled "private" enterprises in the region, with little capital formation involved. Together, such acquisitions account for 68–75 percent of all FDI in the region. The unproductive nature of this FDI is reflected in statistics on the explosion of mergers and cross-border acquisitions, which has led key industrial sectors and top corporations to fall into the hands of U.S. corporations, the major agents of U.S. imperialism. By 1999 over thirty-three of the top one hundred Latin American corporations had fallen victim to foreign investors, mostly American. And the economic power and effective control exercised by these corporations over the Latin American economy is much greater than the size of its stake (about 3.5–5 percent of the regional GDP). This is because the actual assets held and controlled by the affiliates of the imperial firms is about 3.5 times greater than their stock of inward FDI. In addition, corporate control is strategically concentrated and exercised.

The influx of FDI into the region has revived concern about its negative impact on balance of payments. In Brazil, for instance, the current accounts deficit increased from $1.2 billion in 1994 to $33 billion in 1997, as inflows rose from $3 billion to $17 billion. A study by Varman-Schneider (1991) suggests that this problem is regionwide and connected to the issue of capital flight, which appears as a residual in balance of payments data. Varman-Schneider shows that large inflows of debt and equity capital, the growing deficits in current accounts and the depletion of hard currency reserves are all connected to the phenomenon of capital flight, which in many cases reaches and even exceeds the proportions of the external debt. And these problems are connected to the enormous profits made by Wall Street money managers and investment banks in their speculative, short-term investments. A recent report, for example, points to the enormous profits made by a number of investment houses and banks like Chase Manhattan, which doubled and even quadrupled their "normal" rate of profit during the financial crisis in Brazil (Chossudovsky 1999).

The income generated by inflows of FDI is a major source of profit, of which over 50 percent is regularly reinvested, thus accounting for the bulk of FDI (the real inflow of capital is only 6 percent of the total listed flow). Table 5 tabulates different forms of this income. The reported income represents an annual average profit rate of 12 percent on U.S. FDI as calculated by the U.S. Department of Commerce, but a range of 22–34 percent profit as calculated by the U.N. Economic Commission for Latin America and the Caribbean (ECLAC 1998c). Of course, the real rate of return and profit is much higher, because so much of it is unreported or disguised through transfer-pricing but also because it does not include reinvested profits and is calculated after deductions for taxes, liabilities held by parent corporations, insurance and license fees and royalty payments to the same, and "adjustments" related to currency valuations. Nevertheless, even as officially reported, the rate and magnitude of profit repatriation is significant—on the basis of calculations by ECLAC, $157 billion from 1996 to 1998 alone. It provides a crucial source of fuel for global accumulation and the expansion of U.S. imperialism.

Table 5. Payments of income on equity investments and rates of profit
(billion U.S.$, annual averages)

	1993	1994	1995	1996	1997
Income from Assets	27.5	34.7	41.6	40.0	59.0
FDI	14.5	16.6	16.2	17.8	28.9
Other	12.9	18.1	25.4	22.2	30.1

Sources: IMF, various years; UNCTAD, 1998: 267–68; U.S. Dept. of Commerce, BEA, March 4, 1999.

Royalties and License Fees
The U.S. battle to include "intellectual property" clauses in the Uruguay Round of the GATT is related to the fact that royalties and license fee payments have become increasingly important to the U.S. balance of payments (see Table 6). Between 1982 and 1992 these payments totalled over $1.3 billion, but throughout the 1990s they exceeded a billion dollars a year, representing a growing charge made annually by parent corporations in the U.S. against the operations of their affiliates in Latin America. Not only do these payments constitute a form of rent, which can be collected without adding value to production, but they allow parent companies to lower their rate of declared profits in the host country. In recent years, payments of royalties and license fees are also on the increase, growing by 14 percent in 1996 and another 20 percent in 1997.

Table 6. Royalty and license fees payments to the U.S. from
Latin America (billion U.S.$, average annual payment)

Years	1985–90	1991–93	1994–95	1996	1997
Average payment	$0.9	$1.1	$1.6	$1.4	$1.7

Source: UNCTAD 1998: 268; U.S. Dept. of Commerce, BEA, "U.S. Direct Investment Abroad: Capital Flows," 1994, 1999.

Commodity Trade
Cumulative returns for U.S. direct investment in a broad range of economic sectors and high profit margins for its biggest corporations are of vital importance to the U.S. economy. But of equal importance is the role of trade between the U.S. and Latin America. Close to a fourth of U.S. exports are directed towards Latin America, and this is the only region in the world that provides the U.S. with a significant current account surplus. Without this surplus, the U.S. foreign accounts deficit would be significantly greater, the dollar would be weaker and the role of the U.S. as the world's premium banker would be much more problematic. Losing its role as world banker would devastate the capacity of the U.S. to finance its huge deficits. Latin America thus represents a strategic reserve, compensating for U.S. trade

weaknesses elsewhere and providing an important inflow of profits to sustain imperial expansion.

The specialization of Latin American economies imposed by the "international financial community" has led to windfall profits for the U.S. and other imperial powers. The doctrine of "comparative advantages," in which specific Latin countries are led to specialize in certain lines of production that reflect their factor endowments, has undercut the process of economic diversification initiated in the national industrial phase. The result has been an overdependence on a limited line of export products that have experienced a sharp decline in price over the years, with a relative deterioration in the terms of trade that is estimated to have cost the region over 25 percent of its potential export earnings. In March 1999 a precipitous decline in the world price of copper, oil and coffee was wreaking havoc in the region, resulting in widespread anticipation of an overall negative rate of growth for the last year of the millennium and a downward adjustment of an earlier and repeated prognosis of sustained growth.

The economies of Mexico and Venezuela have also increased their dependence on oil exports to the U.S., with a disastrous decline in revenues, which in turn has led to savage cuts in social programs and public investments, a substantial decline in living standards and a massive increase in poverty and unemployment. On the one hand, declining revenues have led to the selling-off of lucrative public assets to meet overseas debt payments. On the other, the U.S. economy has benefited enormously from cheap energy sources to fuel its own growth and maximize profits for corporations.

Not only has the structure of U.S.–Latin America trade provided the U.S. with a substantial surplus on its trade account with the region, but it also facilitates the hidden transfer of a large pool of surplus value and profit. For one thing, the affiliates of U.S. corporations dominate this trade and a full 58 percent of this trade takes the form of intra-firm transfers and thus is not subject to the "forces of the market." Further, there is evidence of considerable under-invoicing or falsification of trade transaction documents as a means of gaining foreign exchange outside the control or regulation of the region's central banks. When added to the income lost via the terms of trade mechanism and the income generated on exports and imports, as well as the enormous outflow of income in the form of rents, interest payments and profits on long- and short-term investments, the result is a hemorrhage of the region's lifeblood, enriching local and foreign capitalists but crippling the economy and impoverishing the people.

Stagnation, Regression and the New Dualism in Latin America

The other side of corporate prosperity within the U.S. empire is deepening stagnation and systemic crises in Latin America. As Magdoff and Sweezy have persuasively argued, capitalism in its monopoly phase has an inherent tendency towards stagnation and crisis. Nowhere is this more evident than in Latin America today (see Table 7). Despite the World Bank's and IMF's periodic announcements that Latin America has recovered and is on its way to dynamic growth, such optimistic projections tend to be short-lived as new and more serious crises emerge.

Table 7. Macroeconomic indicators of Latin American development

	1981–9	'90	'91	'92	'93	'94	'95	'96	'97	'98
GNP per capita	-0.9	-2.2	2.0	1.3	2.3	3.8	-1.2	1.8	3.6	0.7
Current account		-5	-22	-38	-41	-46	-52.	-37	-64	-84

Source: CEPAL (1998a: 1, 1998b: 26).

Between 1980 and 1999, Latin America experienced stagnation punctuated by systemic crises and costly bailouts that further weakened the basic productive structures of the economy. The 1980s were dubbed "the lost decade" as the international banks drained the regional economy through massive transfers of debt payments and the first wave of takeovers and privatizations. Renegotiated debts and new loans were conditioned on economic policies which weakened the productive system and undercut employment and public investment in infrastructure that might have forestalled a recurrence of crisis. The "conditionalities" imposed by the IFIs opened up economies in the region further to a flood of cheap imports and loosened controls over capital flows. The result has been a short-term boom in speculative portfolio investments, a weakening of state leverage over strategic sectors of the economy and a greater dependence on and vulnerability with respect to the imperial centres of overseas capital.

Short-term injections of capital from time to time give the impression of a "recovery" and the arrival of the "Promised Land" promoted by neoliberal ideologues. However, shortly after "recovery" would be announced, a trigger event would lead to an assault on the national currency and the central bank's reserves; capital flight estimated to reach magnitudes well in excess of new capital inflows; and the onset of crisis, deepening stagnation and growing un- and underemployment, which expose the fragility of the financial and productive system and the region's utter dependence on imperialist agencies and institutions. Each offered "solution" deepens imperialist penetration, increases profitable opportunities and weakens the "fundamentals" of the economy.

To attract new capital to a deteriorating economy, neoliberal regimes offer higher interest rates to speculators, which leads to a wave of portfolio investment, the sale of lucrative enterprises and an open door to greater flows of imports, thus deepening stagnation as local enterprises go bankrupt. In this connection, it is estimated that 38,000 medium-sized enterprises in Argentina operated by the petite bourgeoisie over the 1990s either went bankrupt or were saddled by crippling debt. In Mexico this development has resulted in the formation of an organization of bank-indebted producers (El Barzon) that has amassed in excess of 750,000 members.

In the same context, local industrialists seek to maintain profits by pushing down wages even more and/or shifting to speculative and illicit activity (drugs, contraband and large-scale corruption involving cost overruns on state contracts). Actions taken to ensure "macroeconomic stability" (to attract portfolio investment) results in an overvalued currency, which leads to declining exports and increased trade deficits, which in turn result in speculative bets and runs on the currency, necessitating new bailouts. The result is a vicious circle of stagnation, crisis, bailout and stagnation that benefits the imperial system and its key corporate and financial agents but subjects the region's policy-makers to considerable problems of economic management and governability.

From Stagnation to Class Crisis

To sustain profits under conditions of chronic stagnation, the Latin American capitalist class has periodically engaged in a direct assault on the working class, attacking its organizational and negotiating capacity. It has also engaged in an indirect assault (via the state) on state-legislated social benefits, reversing the social legislation of the previous period to undermine the capacity of labour to participate in productivity gains. Very little of the capital attracted to the region has been invested productively. Over the course of the 1980s and 1990s the rate of participation of capital in productivity gains has been negative or marginal. Labour has participated substantially in productivity growth, but it has done so without a corresponding increase in its level of participation. In fact, the share of labour in the value added to production and national income (see Table 8) has been drastically reduced by labour restructuring. Thus the working class has undoubtedly borne the brunt of the "adjustment process" generated by efforts to insert the Latin American economy into the "globalization" process.

Table 8. Wages as a percentage of national income

	1970	1980	1985	1989	1992
Argentina	40.9	31.5	31.9	24.9	-
Chile	47.7	43.4	37.8	-	-
Ecuador	34.4	34.8	23.6	16.0	15.8
Mexico	37.5	39.0	31.6	28.4	27.3
Peru	40.0	32.8	30.5	25.5	16.8

Source: CEPAL, several years.

The basis of this "adjustment" is the restructuring of labour in its forms of employment (creating more precariousness), its conditions of work (causing more irregularity and informality) and in its relation to capital. The process can be seen at two levels. It is reflected first of all in conditions that have resulted in a significant reduction of the share of labour in national incomes (and value added). For example, under the Allende regime, Chilean labour received well over 50 percent of the national income. By 1980, however, after five years of crisis and draconian anti-labour measures, this share was reduced to 43 percent and by 1989, after seventeen years of military dictatorship and free market reforms, to 19 percent. In other countries can be found variations on the same theme. On average, the share of labour (wages) in national income has been reduced from around 40 percent at the beginning of the adjustment process to below 20 percent, and this development has been paralleled by an even greater reduction in the share of labour in the value added to the social product. Other structural changes can be seen in the reduction of jobs in the formal sector of production and in an associated decline and disappearance of the industrial proletariat.

Structural change *vis-à-vis* the working class has also been evident in the fall in the value of wages and the worsening of wide disparities in the distribution of earned incomes among households. In many cases, wage levels in the early 1990s were still well below levels reached by 1980 and, in the case of Argentina and Venezuela, by 1970. The Bank of Mexico estimates that at the end of 1994, that is, before the later outbreak of crisis, wages had maintained barely 40 percent of their 1980 value. In Venezuela and Argentina workers have not yet recovered wage levels achieved in 1970.

As for the pattern of developments that relate to the distribution of income and the compression of wages, Argentina provides the exemplar: in 1975 the ratio of income received by the top and bottom quintiles of income earners was eight to one, but by 1991 this gap had doubled and by 1997 it was a staggering twenty-five to one. In the extreme but not atypical case of Brazil, the top 10 percent of income earners receive forty-four times more income than the bottom. And in other countries we witness the same growing social inequalities in the distribution of wealth and income—at one extreme, the sprouting of a handful of huge fortunes and an associated process of capital accumulation, and, at the other, the spread and deepening of grinding poverty. ECLAC estimates that over the course of the structural reforms implemented in the 1980s the rate of poverty in the region increased from 35 percent to 41 percent of the population, but that in the first half of the 1990s the incidence and rate of poverty was somewhat reduced in eight of the twelve countries it examined. However, a closer look at the statistics suggests either sleight of hand or outright obfuscation and lies—poverty was reduced by redefining the poverty line according to the World Bank's base measure of $1 a day. By other, more reasonable measures related to the capacity of the population to meet its basic needs, the rate of poverty has continued to climb to up to 60 percent of all households by some estimates. In any case, the minimal progress identified in the first half of the 1990s disappeared in the second half.

On the political level, the adjustment of workers to the demands of imperialism is reflected in the destruction of their class organizations and in a generalized weakening of their capacity to negotiate collective agreements with capital. These developments, as well as the notable failure or incapacity everywhere of the working class to resist the imposition of the New Economic Model (NEM) or SAP, reflect a new correlation of class forces in the region. In the 1970s, workers confronted a concentration of armed force and repression, as well as a direct assault by capital on their organizational capacities and conditions of social existence. In the 1980s the major mechanism of adjustment was the restructuring of the capital-labour relation based on forces released during the change in economic policy.

In the 1990s, within the same institutional and policy framework, the working class also confronted a major campaign by organizations such as the World Bank for labour market reform. The aim of this campaign was to create political conditions for a new and more flexible regime of capital accumulation and mode of labour regulation: to give capital, in its management function, more freedom to hire, fire and use labour as needed; and to render labour more flexible, that is, disposed to accept wages offered under free market conditions and to submit to the new management model of its relation to capital and the organization of production. As the World Bank constructs it, widespread government interference in the labour market and workplace (minimum wage legislation), as well as excessive (monopoly) union power, have distorted the workings of the market, leading capital to withdraw from the production process, and thereby generating the problems of unemployment, poverty and informality that plague the region.

To solve these "problems," labour legislation protecting employment have been replaced by laws that enhance the arbitrary power of employers to fire workers, reduce compensation for firings and hire temporary and casual labour. Such deregulation of the labour and other markets has led to new rules that facilitate new investments and the transfer of profits, but also result in massive decimation of stable jobs for workers, increased marginality for and within many communities, and sharply polarized national economies.

Disparities in income distribution and access to productive resources are reflected, at one extreme, in a concentration of income within the capitalist class and the spawning of a number of huge fortunes—*Fortune*'s billionaires. Worse, much of the income available to this class is undeclared. For example, revenues from narco-trafficking by capitalists in Mexico, the proceeds of which are distributed among crony politicians, bankers and others and exceed revenues from Mexico's principal export (oil), are grossly under-reported.

The poorest households dispose of a reduced share of income that, in any case, is growing little or not at all in real terms. One result is the generation of new forms and conditions of poverty which have even reached into the middle classes. In fact, a striking characteristic of imperial-induced inequality is the growth of the urban poor and the changing class composition of the poor: the new poverty is urban rather than rural and extends well beyond the working and producing classes into the once proud but now decimated middle class. While rural poverty continues to be the rule, the fastest growing number of poor today are found in the cities. The new urban poor are not simply "rural migrants" but include downwardly mobile workers and members of the lower middle class who have been fired from their jobs and found employment in the burgeoning informal sector. The growing army of urban poor in Latin America now constitutes a second and third generation of workers who increasingly live in shantytowns, unable to follow the earlier generations' occupational ladder towards incremental improvement. One consequence of this development has been the skyrocketing growth of crime directly linked to family disintegration and concentrated among young people who earlier would have channelled their grievances through trade unions or the factory system.

The New Dualism: First World, Fourth World

Presidents Carlos Menem, Fernando Cardoso, Ernesto Zedillo and Eduardo Frei at one time or another all announced the entrance of their respective countries (Argentina, Brazil, Mexico, Chile) into the First World. They showcased modern shopping malls, the boom in cellular phones, supermarkets loaded with imported foods, streets choked with cars, and stock markets that attract big overseas speculators.

Today, 15–20 percent of Latin Americans share a "First World" lifestyle: they send their kids to private schools; belong to private country clubs where they swim, play tennis and do aerobic exercises; get facelifts at private clinics; travel in luxury cars on private toll roads; and communicate via computer, fax and private courier service. They live in gated communities protected by private police. They frequently vacation and shop in New York, Miami, London or Paris. Their children attend overseas universities. They enjoy easy access to influential politicians, media moguls, celebrities and business consultants. They are usually fluent in English and have most of their savings in overseas accounts or in dollar-denominated local paper. They form part of the international circuit of the new imperial system. They are the audience to which presidents address their grandiloquent First World discourse of a new wave of global prosperity based on an adjustment to the requirements of the new world economic order. Despite the ups and downs of the economy they benefit from the imperial system.

The rest of the population lives in a totally different world. Cuts in social spending and the elimination of basic food subsidies have pushed peasants towards malnutrition and hunger. Large-scale redundancy of factory workers and their entry into the "informed sector" means a subsistence existence and dependence on the "extended family," community-based charities and "solidarity [soup kitchens] for survival." Slashed public health and education budgets result in increasing payments and deteriorating services. Cuts in funds for maintenance of water, sewage and other public services have resulted in a resurgence of infectious diseases. Declining living standards measured in income and living conditions is the reality for two-thirds or more of the population. There has been a decline from Third World welfarism to Fourth World immiseration.

As the crisis of the system as a whole deepens, the elite classes intensify the exploitation of wage labour. As the costs of associating with First World powers increases, the elite diverts a greater percentage of state revenues towards subsidizing their partnerships at the expense of social programs for working families.

As debt payments accumulate, and interest, royalty and profits move outward, declining incomes shrink the domestic market. Bankruptcies multiply and competition for declining overseas markets intensifies. The crises become systemic and economies totter on the verge of collapse. Stagnation turns into depression, and major banks and financial institutions go bankrupt, fuse or are bought by overseas financial groups. Overseas speculators threaten a fast exit. International bailouts put in place to prevent imminent collapse become larger and more frequent.

Responses to Crisis: Reform or Revolution?

In the past several years, voices within the imperial consensus have begun to question the workings of the "new economic model" based on the operations of the "free market." International functionaries, intellectuals, politicians and business leaders have spoken of the need to "bring the state back in." While accepting the basic premises of the free market, they have called for limited state intervention to soften the blows of the market by financing job training, poverty alleviation (or reduction), and self-help programs. Some have argued for capital controls to encourage productive investments of capital rather than "speculative investment." While supporting privatization, they question the "transparency" of sell offs to cronies at non-competitive prices. They criticize high unemployment but avoid tackling structural causes, preferring to call for greater "flexibility" and job training. In effect, they promote the free trade model but argue for, *inter alia*, an agrarian bank to finance small and medium producers on the verge of bankruptcy as a result of the influx of cheap imports, and for the need to expand the social base of production. Some of these proposals have been implemented but have failed to stem the deepening crises; others have been shelved once the critics enter the government.

However, a more consequential and extra-parliamentary opposition is growing which questions the "globaloney" of the dominant classes. New socio-political movements like the Zapatista Army of National Liberation (EZLN) in Mexico, MST in Brazil, FARC in Colombia, and peasant-Indian movements in Ecuador, Bolivia and Paraguay are openly challenging neoliberal regimes and their imperialist backers. Although their tactics vary from large-scale land occupations to guerrilla armies and a wide gamut of other mass actions in between, all these movements have called for the socialization of strategic sectors of the economy, far-reaching land redistribution and the reduction of overseas debt and other transfers.

The size and scope of extra-parliamentary struggle is significant. The MST has organized hundreds of occupations covering twenty-four states and has settled 500,000 families. Organized as a national-political movement, the MST has successfully unified urban and rural workers in a common struggle against neoliberalism. In Colombia, FARC controls half of all rural municipalities with an army of fifteen thousand militants and support from close to a million people. In Argentina, Brazil and Mexico, rank-and-file industrial workers are organizing class-based trade unions to challenge state-run unions. While full-blown, alternative programs are still being elaborated, these movements are struggling to form anti-imperialist regimes that can begin the reconstruction of the domestic market, regain control over the essential levers of the economy, redistribute wealth and create a participatory form of democracy to replace the elite-driven, foreign-based electoral systems that describe themselves as democracies.

Conclusions

The neoliberal parabola has run its course. Since the 1970s, when neoliberalism burst on the scene under the guns of the military and the tutelage of the CIA and the Pentagon, a new course has been inaugurated that has savaged the working class and peasantry, demolished the welfare state and cleared the way for unrestrained capitalist expansion. Fuelled by massive loans from the IFIs, an influx of multinational corporate capital and large-scale, long-term private lending, the regimes consolidated their rule. They secured support among the petite bourgeoisie and better-paid workers with easy credit and cheap imports. The boom, however, ended quickly with the world stagflation crises of the early 1980s, which led to a virtual economic collapse and almost a decade of regression. Popular discontent, elite malaise and intervention by Washington led to political transitions from military to electoral politics largely within the "shell" of neoliberal economies and authoritarian state institutions. The electoral elite deepened and extended the free-market policies and institutions inaugurated by the previous regimes. Vast sectors of the economy were privatized by executive decree, debt payments were met at the cost of social programs and austerity programs were imposed on the populace. Electoral campaigning bore no resemblance to subsequent government policy: promises of social reform preceded harsh reductions in social spending; full employment promises were followed by mass redundancies; and rhetoric defending the national patrimony was followed by the privatization of strategic and profitable enterprises.

Capital returned to the region in the 1990–93 period, most of it in the form of speculative portfolio investments or buyouts of enterprises. And an underlying stagnation of productive forces is still a reality, as is the propensity towards crisis. The Mexican crash of 1994–95 signalled the decline of neoliberalism, resulting as it did in a massive wipe-out of productive employment and a collapse of the financial system. The "rescue package" of $20 billion saved U.S. speculators but subjected Mexico to overt colonial control, its future oil revenues mortgaged to the U.S. Treasury Department.

By the end of the millennium, the conditions of long-term stagnation and crises were becoming more and more visible. Foreign reserves were being depleted, bailouts multiplied as currencies threaten to collapse, and negative growth rates and double digit unemployment (Brazil, 18 percent; Argentina, 14 percent) were matched by a permanent reserve army of underemployed (the informal sector) reaching 50–70 percent of the population. Export earnings were crashing; imports were being reduced; debts, domestic and overseas, were reducing state resources that could have been used to stimulate the economy. The neoliberal cycle was crashing even as the regimes continued to apply empty formulas to enrich a narrowing circle of class cronies, the upper 10 percent of the population.

The Old Left of the 1970s and 1980s, mired in electoral contests and social-liberal accommodations to the status quo, shows little imagination and less audacity in organizing radical ruptures with the system. Populist military figures like Hugo Chavez emerge as "radical outsiders" who quickly come to terms with overseas bankers and investors while rhetorical flourishes frustrate mass expectations. The gap between the objective conditions of crisis and the subjective revolutionary response is widening, as the crisis becomes more systematic. The NGOs founder in the interstices of the system, their local projects and self-help micro-enterprises an ineffectual sop in view of collapsing living standards. But the new radical socio-political movements in their rural settings have deep popular roots "outside" the system and are engaged in the construction of a new revolutionary subjectivity.

The fundamental problem is to turn sectoral movements into national political formations capable of turning regional struggles into social revolutions. The end of the millennium brought intense hardships, heightened social polarities and new forms of state repression. The new millennium can be a prelude for the rebirth of socialism, but the path is likely to be long and tortuous.

Chapter 5

The Labyrinth of Privatization

Privatization of public enterprises and resources has reached massive proportions throughout Latin America. Every sector of the economy has been affected—highways, natural resources, zoos, parks, steel plants, utilities, telecommunications networks. This chapter is directed towards analyzing the deeper meaning of privatization by placing it in a broader structural and historical framework. This will involve a critical analysis of assumptions about the origins and growth of public enterprises and the internal and external sources of crises in the public sector. An analysis of the nature of privatization and its socio-political and economic consequences will follow. The final section will discuss alternatives to both past public-ownership patterns and contemporary privatization.

We wish to present several theses. First, privatization in Latin America is not an isolated economic decision. It is related to larger political forces acting through local coercive apparatuses rather than a product of "market rationality."

Second, the growth of public enterprises was a response to the failures and crises of earlier free market regimes. Public enterprise development was largely a pragmatic reaction to crises and necessity rather than a product of ideological decrees.

Third, the crises of public enterprises are in large part a product of the failures and demands of private sector corporations and the political style of capitalist politicians.

Fourth, privatization is based on changes in both ideological and class structures, which in turn have had a major role in undermining local representative government and fostering authoritarianism.

Fifth, privatization, rather than "correcting" the evils of state intervention, public monopolies and high-cost services, has deepened them by producing an economic structure unresponsive to domestic users and the lower echelons of "civil society."

The chapter concludes by pointing to a number of alternatives to privatization in which public-private relations are made compatible with the needs of the national majority.

Origins of Privatization

Privatization is not an isolated phenomenon resulting from local circumstances in limited time frames, as was the case in the 1960s or 1970s. Today privatization must be understood as part of a global strategy which has its roots in an attack on civil society and democratic politics, in violent military interventions and in the use of arbitrary executive decrees. Today privatization is carried out under the orders of imperial-controlled "international" banks, by imperial-funded consultants and governmental agencies that devise programs, decide on prices and identify potential buyers. The time frame and scope of privatization is dictated by the economic superpowers, whose priority is to ram through transfers of property that will make the transition to neoliberal capitalism irreversible. Privatization is essentially a political act, having little or no "intrinsic value" as a national economic strategy and certainly not adding anything to the creation of new jobs, higher rates of savings and investment, or new productive forces. The privatization strategy of the imperial centre is in the first instance to homogenize every region of the world economy subject to its penetration, while differentiating access to the world market according to the productive capacities of each region. The process of privatization is thus not principally a means of taking over enterprises and penetrating markets so much as it is a means of eliminating alternative structures of production which could compete or challenge an imperially dominated world. That is why the miserable performance of the privatizing economies does not bother imperial policymakers as much as does the tempo and scope of privatization. Once an economy has been privatized, the fruit of that policy can be harvested by lucrative enterprises or captured markets, without fear of "nationalist" or "socialist" backlash.

The agencies of imperial-induced privatization work through the financial, ideological and political support of military coups (Latin America) or electoral processes (Eastern Europe, Western ex-USSR countries). The process of privatization under either a civilian or military regime usually follows the same procedure: executive decrees with or without the rubber stamp of parliament. The privatization process relegates social organizations, movements and citizens to marginal roles. Massive firings, closure of industries and conversion of manufacturers into importers lead to the decline of well-paid unionized factory workers, the growth of irregular work in the informal sector and greater numbers of low-paid employees. To contain the social effects, imperial regimes and financial institutions foster non-governmental organizations to reabsorb the populace in local activities in the interstices of an economy dominated by TNCs, banks and the export sectors. NGOs contribute to the weakening of civic and social movements that confront the neoliberal model imposed by imperial centres.

The irony is that the convergence of the "market" rhetoric of the imperial banks at the top and the "civil society" ideology of the NGOs at the bottom undermines collective struggles for social change and a positive role for the national state.

The advance of privatization is thus located within a global strategy of empire-building during a period of counter-revolution in the Third World and collapse of Communism in the East.

Privatization and Denationalization

Privatization is almost always associated with the denationalization of an economy. Both policies are strategic means used by the economic superpowers to conquer economies and hegemonize "civil society." The whole post–World War II period was dominated by the efforts of the more powerful Western countries to impose a free market policy against nationalist and socialist regimes restricting access to foreign capital. Privatization was part of a general process of reversing social welfare and reconcentrating income. Instead of transferring income from private corporations through public welfare programs to wage and salary workers, privatization involved the transfer of publicly owned and taxpayer-financed enterprises to private corporations. A "matrix" involving international actors and overseas consultants, advisors and financiers inevitably led to the inclusion of foreign capital as a necessary agency of "privatization." The large size of the enterprises, the efforts to internationalize markets, increased access to overseas financial resources, and the political clout of TNCs resulted in privatization becoming synonymous with denationalization.

The Social Matrix of Privatization

Privatization is part of a general pattern of undermining social organization and popular power and reversing social welfare. In the West and South, public ownership originated more often than not as a result of popular struggles against the liberal export models of the 19th and early 20th centuries. The absence of drinkable water, adequate and inexpensive transportation and investment in strategic electrical and energy sectors led to public demands for state intervention to prevent health epidemics and provide infrastructure to facilitate trade and manufacturing. Only in Eastern Europe was public ownership "imposed from above and outside" and thus was an anomaly in the historic pattern.

Privatization is thus a counter-reform movement against historical trends and part of a general effort to subvert the welfare state, mixed economies and class-based social movements. The irony is that while the free marketers defend the traditional family, their policies encourage the creation of single-parent families and the forced labour of women for low wages. "Left" critics, who supposedly defend wage workers and women's choice, glorify the forced labour of women ("independence") and the "non-traditional family" imposed by the Right. The result is that the reversal of public property undermines the stable social foundation of class and family necessary to sustain concerted political opposition. And the "private choice" ethos of the Left plays into the micropolitics of the neoliberal macro-privatization project.

The origins of privatization are political in several senses. Privatization is part of a global strategy directed towards eliminating political-economic alternatives, part of a domestic strategy to reconcentrate wealth and power, and finally a mechanism for lining up economic resources for imperial accumulation.

Purely economic arguments about market rationality and rational choice have little historical or sociological explanatory power to identify the political framework within which macroeconomic decisions are formulated and implemented. Thus the rationale for privatization is more closely related to doctrinal exegesis than to contemporary realities. Paradoxically the same doctrinairism of the free market ideologues is found in their efforts to explain the growth of public enterprises. They impute the origins of public enterprise to "ideology," forgetting the historical experiences and circumstances out of which the public sector rose.

Public Enterprises: Pragmatism and Ideology

In Latin America the growth of public enterprises coincided with industrialization, increases in public demand for social services, the growth of a technical-engineering middle class and a larger internal market. The political context was the crisis of the export-elite model of a "free market" and the incapacity of the liberal state to meet the development needs of manufacturers, the occupational demands of the middle class, or the health and education needs of the working class.

Public enterprises were essential elements for the growth of private industry. The private sector was unable or unwilling to finance and invest on a scale (or produce at a cost level) sufficient to meet the burgeoning needs of the new productive classes. A coalition of nationalist industrialist forces including the working, middle and sectors of the bourgeois class emerged and supported long-term and large-scale public investments to provide low-cost energy and transportation networks essential to production and distribution. Public sector enterprises produced steel that was sold to private manufacturers at subsidized prices, enabling them to compete and accumulate profits. Public construction of highways, dams, ports, etc. was subcontracted to the private sector, stimulating the growth of private construction firms and manufacturing industries. Amassment of private fortunes via state-promoted activities was the basis for the "export-oriented" activities and joint ventures of many of today's neoliberal big business people. Without the huge push from the public sector to establish basic infrastructure and industry, state financing and contracts, it is hard to imagine where today's free marketers would be.

Fundamentals of Economic Development: The Public Sector

The rise of public ownership in the post–World War II period was largely due to pragmatic considerations. First, public enterprises emerged in economic sectors vital to growth because private national entrepreneurs were unable to mobilize large amounts of capital for long-term returns. Private business people were not willing to take risks or lacked the know-how to enter many of the activities eventually undertaken by the public sector. Foreign private capital was opposed to investing in sectors of the economy that competed with their exports. Only after protective barriers were established did foreign corporations become "multinational" and establish subsidiaries within countries to exploit domestic markets and "jump over" tariff walls.

Second, in some cases, public enterprises resulted from the nationalization of private—mostly foreign—firms. This was usually based on the failure of investors to maintain or modernize their plants or the shift of investment priorities to other regions or economic sectors, which had allowed vital services to deteriorate. In some cases, foreign investors threatened to close down operations, which would have led to massive firings and major social dislocation, thus forcing the government to intervene and incorporate the enterprise into the public sector. Frequently the enterprise was left with debts, deteriorated machinery and high compensation payments, severely undermining the capacity of the state to turn the enterprise into a profitable and efficient firm. This was referred to as "lemon socialism," where the private sector unloaded run-down enterprises at a high cost to the state, while retaining other lucrative enterprises.

Third, privately owned firms in public utilities (water, gas, transport) refused or were unable to provide adequate service or extend services to a burgeoning population, forcing the state to intervene to reach otherwise "unprofitable" regions, provide low-cost services to potential producers and improve health conditions for potential consumers.

Fourth, public enterprises emerged in industries important for national security or conservation, or essential for providing export earnings to finance a broad array of development programs or purchase imports for production and consumption. For example, petroleum, minerals and hydroelectric power provided earnings to finance or subsidize extensive private domestic investment in local industries.

Finally, public enterprises were established during the 1930s depression and World War II to produce domestically what could not be imported, because of a collapse of exports or the liberal economic model or because the major exporter countries were at war and had redirected their production to bellicose activity.

In summary, public ownership emerged and sometimes replaced private activity for pragmatic rather than ideological reasons. It was simply a more efficient manner of diversifying the economy, stimulating economic recovery and mobilizing capacity unused under the previous free market, export model. Public enterprises took the initiative in providing employment and increased the capacity of national decision-makers to shape the development agenda. The shift to public ownership and national development allowed economies to avoid some of the extreme fluctuations experienced during the previous export-based liberal economy based on raw materials and foreign enclaves. Nevertheless, some of the conditions that led to public ownership, the subordinate role it played in fostering private sector growth and the political matrix in which it functioned eventually led to a crisis.

The Crisis of Public Ownership

Both "external" and "internal factors contributed to the crisis in public ownership. "External" factors were those outside the formal organization of the public enterprises, and "internal" factors concerned their structure and functioning.

The public sector was supported by a political coalition that provided votes, technical expertise, economic resources, political leadership and occasional social mobilizations. The coalition included urban labour, public employees, the middle class and capitalists—particularly industrialists, construction contractors and intellectuals. This disparate coalition came under severe pressure as labour and capital developed divergent interests. The trade unions moved beyond securing industrial employment and minimal recognition from the state to demanding wider social legislation, greater employment security and higher wages through social organization and mobilization. Employers, on the other hand, after securing state protection, subsidies and monopoly prices, sought lower labour costs and greater freedom from state and labour obligations to increase profits and diversify their investments. The problem was not simply a profit squeeze (which was not always and everywhere the case) employers wanted to dispose of profits, capital and investment whenever and wherever they wished. The squeeze was not coming from "labour" but from the national-industrial framework, which inhibited imports and transfers of capital. The "profit squeeze" argument was essentially a conservative one (later taken up uncritically by the Left and later intellectually disarmed), because the Right moved far beyond increasing profits to changing the whole framework for capital accumulation, stimulating the advent of what was later dubbed "neoliberalism."

The crisis among the coalition sustaining public ownership resulted from a growing internationalization of "national capital." The pressure was based on large-scale accumulation from high profits accrued under the protectionist regime. "Surplus capital" was channelled overseas in the form of portfolio investments, and overseas partnerships were sought to increase access to technology, markets and financial resources. The alternative of widening and deepening the domestic market was not seriously considered, because it would have involved major changes in land tenure, agrarian reform, vast investments in urban infrastructure and large investments in technology and plant, all of which would defer profits over the long run. Basically the choice was either to support peasants against landlords, who in many cases included industrialists and their immediate families and financial associates, or to seek to appropriate public enterprises and a greater percentage of the state budget and go "overseas." The limits of the internal market had two solutions: the revolutionary choice of deepening the national-industrial project or the counter-revolutionary choice of dismantling it in favour of a reconcentration of wealth strategy and a link-up with overseas capital.

From this historical perspective, public ownership was for the capitalist class a "transitional phase" to liberalism based on political concerns rather than simply a "failure" or "exhaustion" of the so-called import-substitution model. The crisis of public ownership was thus in part based on the weak social foundations on which it was constructed.

The second "external" factor leading the crisis in public ownership was the macroeconomic matrix. In subsidizing and protecting the private sector and in the absence of capitalist concerns about the social wage of labour, the state in general and the public sector in particular began to run budget and trade deficits. The public enterprises paid monopoly prices for products from the private sector and sold services at subsidized prices. The state subsidized imports for private industrialists without demanding commensurate export earnings to pay for them. The state also paid for social benefits for workers, thus lowering the cost of labour for capital.

The imbalances in the macroeconomic indicators reflected the efforts by the national-industrial state to balance the returns to capital and the social welfare of labour. The liberal solution ("managing the macroeconomic indicators") was essentially to transfer the "indebted" public enterprises to the private sector, eliminate social welfare for labour, subsidize the international segments of capital to increase exports and provide high interest rates and high profits in the hope that large flows of capital would enter and balance external accounts.

The problems of high deficits and budget imbalances were serious and related to the functioning of the public sector, but the sources of these problems were as much the matrix in which they functioned as they were their internal organization.

In some contexts, class conflict between labour and capital caused the capitalist class to "dis-invest" and withdraw from the production process, exacerbating problems of unemployment, social insecurity and dislocation. Conflict was occasionally accompanied by factory occupations or demands by workers for state takeovers. When this occurred, production temporarily declined. This led to increases in state subsidies and declines in exports, provoking greater trade imbalances. Not infrequently economic enterprises did lend themselves to public ownership, either because of their size or relation to the economy. Thus, the alleged inefficiency of public enterprises resulted in good part from the public sector demands of social actors engaged in class warfare.

Although "external" conditions were essential elements of the crisis of public enterprises, they were not the only reasons for privatization. Internal factors relating to structure and functioning as well as the attitudes of public sector supporters also contributed to the crisis.

Overemployment was a perennial problem in many of the public enterprises. In many cases the state became an employer of last resort, absorbing surplus labour the private sector failed to employ. The result was high administrative costs, a bloated payroll and unnecessary paperwork, all of which contributed to the image of an "inefficient state sector."

Related to this was the tendency among political parties to use the state as a mechanism for political clientelism. The less ideological parties (but not exclusively) depended on attracting followers and vote-getters through offers of state jobs, resulting in public sector overload, lower productivity and an increased number of incompetent but politically loyal functionaries available to organize the electoral machinery.

Related to, but not identical with, clientelism was the tendency to politicize public employees, focusing on short-term political loyalties instead of ability to deliver results. Thus tactical advantages frequently led to strategic weaknesses, and stagnation and lack of innovation accompanied consolidations of public sector activities.

The rigidity of public sector enterprises resulted in part from the corporatist attitude of the trade unions, which were linked to nationalist or socialist parties that defended and, in some cases, encouraged inefficiencies among public employees. Attempts to increase or improve services to working-class consumers were countered by the pseudo-workerist rhetoric of protecting "working class" interests.

The hierarchical structures of public enterprises in many cases closely resembled those of private firms. As a result, employees and management frequently looked upward and inward, thus avoiding public accountability and external competition that might encourage innovation and efficiency. Finally, the prices of public sector products and services were set by private corporate interests, leading to private subsidies and public losses. The state frequently provided energy to industry below cost, absorbing the losses. The earnings of public enterprises were sometimes not invested internally but transferred to public funds, and thus the public sector failed to modernize and become competitive. In summary, both external and internal political, economic and social forces worked in tandem to generate crisis in the public sector. Implicit in the crisis were the possibilities of reforming the public sector by making it more responsive to the larger populace or dismantling it and handing its resources over to the minority private sector.

Privatization: Means and Consequences

Privatization strategies emerged from a variety of sources. Sometimes they were derived from ideological convictions, as in the case of the dictatorships in the Southern Cone in the mid-1970s. Sometimes they resulted from a desire to curry favour and demonstrate pliancy to international lending agencies, as was the case in many of the electoral regimes in Latin America in the 1980s and later in Eastern Europe and the "republics" of the ex-USSR.

In still other cases, privatization was the decided preference of a new class of export-oriented capitalists who sought to expand their empires while attracting overseas investment partners.

Equally important was pressure from the capitalist superpowers acting directly or indirectly through the World Bank and IMF. The dismantling of alternative development models, particularly approaches that limited the access of multinational banks and enterprises, was always a cherished goal of Western policy-makers. Together with civilian and military elites and emerging transnational investors, they were able to impose the model of "openness," export supremacy and a "market-based" political economy. Once in place, this configuration of power imposed its concepts and constraints on future political and intellectual debates. Henceforward, "serious discussion" revolved around supply-side economics and the timing and manner of transferring public resources to private monopolies (the so-called "market economy"). The whole issue of public enterprise-based national development was banished to Hades.

The important point is that the whole privatization process had its roots in an authoritarian setting and was the result of a shift in political forces at the state level. Privatization was never based on public consultation and, on the rare occasions when consultations occurred, the privatizers lost the vote, as in Uruguay. Nor was privatization based on the demonstrated economic efficiency of the private sector; rather it was founded on policies deduced from doctrine by economists and by generals convinced of their economic truths. Finally, the decisions to privatize were not part of national debates; instead international actors were involved in the design, promotion and financing of the process.

In sum, privatization was an elite, international and highly politicized process, in contrast with the popular, national and pragmatic process of constructing public enterprises. The implementation of privatization mirrored its intellectual origins. It was largely implemented or, more precisely, *decreed* by non-elected officials or elected executives who frequently had hid their true intentions during the electoral campaign. The executives involved in privatization by decree frequently consulted with non-elected overseas bankers or their academic consultants when designing and implementing specific measures. The entire process of privatization thus severely undermined the representative bodies of civil society and marginalized public opinion, effectively mobilizing elites while demobilizing the public.

While the pivatization rhetoric was decidedly anti-statist, in practice the privatizing regimes merely shifted state intervention from financing public welfare to funding private elites. Large-scale state intervention was required to "socialize" the private debts of landlords and bankers, and direct and indirect state subsidies to exporters became the order of the day. State limitations on salaries and the social benefits of labour led to massive increases of wealth at the top. The low prices fixed by the state for the sale of public enterprises allowed big business purchasers to amass windfall profits.

In summary, the ideology of anti-statism became the banner for a new kind of statism in which privatization was financed and organized by the state for the benefit of the private sector.

The Impact of Privatization

Privatization policies not only impacted on the economy but on all of society: on the political system, class structure, domestic market, and transportation and communication systems.

Privatization has deeply polarized the class structure. On the one hand, the buyers of public enterprises have in many cases reaped vast profits, catapulting some from millionaire to billionaire status. On the other hand, the firing of "excess" public employees has pushed many workers into a new class of urban poor and into low-paid, "informal" employment. Workers with job security and social benefits have experienced serious erosion of living standards and downward mobility. Declining social benefits have increased earnings and profits for the new private owners.

The increased prices of services, electricity, transport, etc. accompanying privatization has decreased living standards for wage and salary workers, while increasing profits for the private monopolies that have taken over the public ones.

The privatized sector thus benefits from state subsidies while enjoying the lower wage scales and "flexible" schedules the liberal state has imposed on labour. The "good fortune" of a few dozen billionaires plugged into the privatization process has its counterpart in the marginalization of tens of millions of poverty-stricken workers.

The second major impact of privatization has been on the political system. The strong ties between the private monopolies that benefit from privatization and the executive branch of government has been a central reason why the legislative and judicial branches have been the big losers in the shift to a free market economy. Representative institutions have been bypassed in the process of transferring public property into private hands. The big decisions are decided elsewhere (in the boardrooms of overseas banks), while the parliaments or congresses at best react to decisions already taken.

The end result of privatization is the weakening of democracy and the loss of legislative supervision of essential economic sectors. The primary responsibility of privatized firms is to their board of directors, who in most cases are not even in the country. Congressional committees overseeing public enterprise activities have been deactivated. The private sector is now not responsive or responsible to any public authority, only to private interests.

Privatization brings two basic changes—both negative—to the development of a national economy. First, privatization deprives a national economy of a lucrative source of accumulation, particularly when the new investors send their earnings abroad. Second, the state loses a strategic lever for shifting earnings to new sectors of the economy that may not be immediately profitable but can have positive impacts on employment and the opening of new areas to investment, e.g., infrastructure, education and regional diversification. Privatization in many cases further disarticulates the economy by focusing on production and imports out of enclaves. Thus the provinces are cut off from investment funds, regional railways and airlines are eliminated or cut back, and factories for regional markets are undermined by cheap imports promoted by the privatizing elites. As privatization deepens international integration, it disarticulates the domestic economy, emptying the provinces of economic activity and reducing them to utter dependency on purely administrative activities.

In summary, the political drive to make privatization irreversible has had major negative effects on democracy, social mobility and economic development. Beyond these basic problems are a host of other negative impacts.

The Pitfalls of Privatization

Serious political, economic and ethical issues have arisen regarding the rationales and process of "privatizing" public enterprises. One of the basic rationales for privatization was to put an end to public "monopolies" in order to stimulate competition and promote lower prices and greater efficiency. The fact of the matter is, however, vastly different. The buyers of public monopolies have been private monopolies, large-scale investors who add to their burgeoning economic empires. With the deregulation which accompanies privatization, the new private monopolies have increased prices and cut back services for those unable to pay, thus creating "inefficiencies" in meeting real demand. Competition has not usually resulted from privatization; it has merely reconcentrated ownership in private hands.

The price at which public enterprises are sold is usually a "political price," not its true potential market value. In consultation with advisors drawn from among potential buyers, the political regime sets a price. Frequently, investors linked to the political regime, business associates of the president or senior members of the executive branch benefit from privatization. Corruption on an unprecedented scale has accompanied the process of privatization. In the transfer of public companies to private ownership, hundreds of millions of dollars have greased the hands of politicians, degrading the electoral regime.

Prior to the sell-off of public enterprises, the state engages in systematic disinvestment, provoking a deterioration of services, to arouse public discontent with the public sector and build support for privatization. The state assumes the costs for the retirement of workers and employees, lowers costs of inputs, and provides subsidies, providing buyers with an enterprise with low labour and production costs. Once privatization takes place, the immediate "pickup" in activity appears to be due to the new private owners rather than what it is—the manipulated outcome of deliberate state policy working in concert with privatizing elites.

When selling public enterprises, the regime and the buyers make a big public display of the new agreement signed by both parties. The private sector promises to invest hundreds of millions of dollars, create thousands of new jobs, increase export earnings by some geometrical figure, transfer new technologies, provide low-cost services, etc. In fact, the contract obligations are largely a publicity stunt. Hardly ever are any parts of the agreement lived up to, even in part. Most new investment is at best funds borrowed from local banks, reconverted debt or reinvested profit. In many cases, little new investment occurs. Frequently the original agreement is renegotiated, or "extraordinary" circumstances and economic problems are cited by the firm and usually accepted by the accommodating regime to explain non-compliance. Once in place, firms usually import more than they export, and thus external accounts become more negative. Privatized industries displace local producers and downsize their labour force, thus exacerbating the unemployment situation instead of improving it. Technology is transferred and a rent is paid, but few of the facilities for research and development of new technologies are transferred to the host country.

Privatization absorbs investment capital in existing enterprises instead of directing it to new areas or sectors. In many cases, it displaces national capital instead of complementing it. Many firms that are privatized do not fulfill their expectations with regard to exports, new capital investment or technology, whereas state policy could previously channel capital towards new export activities or to sectors with high capital costs and areas of technological innovation.

Privatization has frequently increased the vulnerability of the economy, particularly when the buyer is a multinational corporation. Decisions regarding plant location, levels of investment and employment are subject to the global strategies of the board of directors of the multinational corporation. Privatization deprives the country of a "school" for entrepreneurial and management training. Public enterprises previously provided local engineers with an opportunity to learn by doing and to apply concepts to strategic planning.

In place of engineers linked to production, a new breed of business graduates with skills in facilitating sell-offs, procuring buyers and opening markets emerges as the dominant type. These specialists, heavily imbued with free market doctrines, are essentially intermediaries tied to overseas operations controlled by foreign investors and bankers and have little contact with local markets and productive forces. The result is frequently perverse pronouncements such as, "The economy is doing great. Only the people are doing badly."

Alternatives to Privatization

One of the most absurd and ill-informed pronouncements of the many that free market enthusiasts are prone to make is that there are "no alternatives to privatization." In fact, there have been and, as we will argue, there are plenty of alternatives to privatization. Certainly, the almost uniformly negative consequences of privatization warrant deep reflection on whether to continue on this self-destructive path.

Previously we summarized the real historical origins and positive roles played by public enterprises. A similar line of inquiry is appropriate in a discussion of alternatives. Measures successfully implemented in the past are relevant to contemporary policy-makers seeking to promote national development.

While free market ideologues argue that foreign investment and free trade are the only alternatives to economic development, we would argue that there is another approach which secures long-term, large-scale growth and the advantages of capitalist development, while minimizing the social, political and economic costs. We argue at two levels: (1) that public-centred development is far superior to private (national or foreign) and (2) that social ownership within the public sector is superior to state.

There are at least three measures associated with public sector development that secure the best of capitalist growth while retaining strategic national control and maximizing social equity.

Fade-out Formulas
From the 1930s to the early 1980s, a number of countries contracted foreign corporations to invest (with a guaranteed profit) in particular lines of activity. In was explicitly understood that this was a time-bound agreement at the end of which public ownership would be phased in and private ownership would fade out. The foreign firm would earn a profit, and the recipient country would gain experience and ultimate control.

Turnkey Operations
During the 1960s, developing nations contracted foreign firms to construct enterprises and organize production for a set price and then "hand over the keys" to the host country. Payment in some cases included a certain percentage of the production on line.

Disaggregating Technical "Know-how" from Ownership
Instead of paying the high price of having foreign capital control strategic economic sectors and thus being at the mercy of its global shifts and priorities, in order to secure technical advance, some countries have disaggregated technical know-how from investment and ownership, buying or renting the former and excluding the latter. Thus they are able to incorporate technical advances into their own social and national priorities.

In economic sectors with high returns and low expertise it may be necessary to form joint ventures, but majority public control can be retained. Profits are shared, but control is public, ensuring that future growth and investment priorities will be integrated into national goals. Thus foreign participation does not displace but complements national involvement, filling a niche within the overall national project.

Within public enterprise, management styles other than vertical management are essential to ensure public accountability. Social control by consumers and producers is an essential antidote to bureaucratic sloth and inefficiency. Private skills need to be incorporated into public enterprise—risk taking, personal initiative, product development, etc. In a word, public enterprises should be far more *entrepreneurial* than in the past. Public enterprise should combine a consultative style in formulating general policy with executive leadership in implementation. Decision-making should look inward and downward before looking upward and outward, linking regions through patterns of transportation and communication, meeting basic social needs and articulating these with export activities.

Public enterprise should consult and be articulated with social movements in the formation of social policy and allocation of social budgets and investments. The reversal of privatization and "globalization" is absolutely essential to any effort to reverse the growing social polarization, regional disintegration and political authoritarianism emerging under free market capitalism. Public ownership, co-operatives, consumer and worker collectives, import substitution in specific lines of economic activity, and selective openings to the world market are all complementary. As diverse and rich development strategies emerge from public debate uninhibited by the fiats and decrees of free market ideologues, the notion of the free market as being the culmination of history will end up in the dustbin of history.

Chapter 6

Democracy and Capitalism:
An Uneasy Relationship

The debate about the relationship between democracy and capitalism has been continuous from the early 19th century to the present. For some scholars capitalism and democracy are in "contradiction" (Shapiro 1990; Meiksins Wood 1995; Overloop 1993). They argue that the "democratic content" of capitalist democracy is a product of popular movements and class struggle rather than an integral element of the expansion of market relations. The resulting merger of capitalism and democracy is seen as a contradictory development sustained by a political equilibrium in which the forces of democracy must constantly be vigilant against a tendency towards authoritarianism inherent in capitalist power.

On the other side are those who argue that the growth of capitalism and democracy are interrelated. Here free markets and free elections are seen as mutually enforcing processes (Schumpeter 1941; Friedman and Friedman 1980), or one is viewed as creating the preconditions for the other: economic liberalization freeing the forces of eonomic development to create conditions for democracy or, conversely, political liberalization and democracy creating conditions for economic development (Diamond 1992; Inkeles 1990; Landes 19669; Lindblom 1977; Rostow 1960). According to this line of reasoning, free markets increase choices, foster individualism and promote social pluralism, all essential ingredients of a democracy. Alternatively, a democratic political system is seen as an indispensable means of securing the optimal or necessary conditions of capitalism, which is viewed as the most effective and efficient form of economic development.

Most of the political and economic debates on the issue of capitalism and democracy since the 1960s have been conducted within the framework of these two schools of thought. However, a third school of thought on the relationship between democracy and capitalism has emerged. Proponents of this school argue that the grand theoretical discourses of both of the other schools overlook the centrality of "the rules of the [political] game" that define democracy independent of popular movements or capitalist markets (Bobbio 1990; Friedman 1990; Offe 1983; Przeworski 1986 and 1991). These scholars argue that social agreement on the rules of political competition (political consensus) guarantees that competing forces will accept the outcomes of electoral and other democratic processes on the assumption that the same rules will enable incumbents to retain power and the opposition to eventually attain power. In this context, Przeworski (1986) is able to explain why or howcapitalism has managed to survive the advent of political democracy. And in the same context,

Offe (1983) argues that the contradiction between democracy and capitalism apparent to many 19th-century liberals and Marxists was resolved in the 20th century with the emergence of mass political parties, inter-party competition and the Keynesian welfare state.

Each of these three conceptions of the relationship between capitalism and democracy focuses on a different sphere of the social system. The critics of capitalism focus on struggles and movements in society; the celebrants of capitalism focus on the genius or magic of the marketplace; and proceduralists, proponents of political "realism," focus on the institutionalized "rules of the game" accepted by the political class. However, while each of these perspectives captures a part of reality, none is able to fit into their theories a number of incongruous, albeit significant and fairly widespread, historical experiences. In fact, we argue that each of these theoretical perspectives is deficient and needs to be supplanted by a perspective that is able to explain the structural, if not contingent, conditions of the capitalism-democracy relation in its diverse historical manifestations.

Prevailing Views on Capitalism and Democracy
One of the problems of the view that capitalism and democracy are incompatible and in contradiction is to explain the introduction and support of democratic regimes by capitalist-oriented politicians in Western Europe in the aftermath of World War II. Also, while it is true that capitalist politicians in the U.S. had resisted the inclusion of Blacks—and, earlier, of women—in the electoral process, their eventual incorporation took place under the aegis of capitalism. And there has been no attempt to reverse their inclusion in the political process despite the warnings given by Huntington (1984) and other political conservatives about the potentially destabilizing effects of such inclusion. More recently, capitalist politicians in Europe and the U.S. have promoted democracy in Latin America, Asia and Africa, even conditioning economic loans and investments on the introduction of free elections and the trappings of liberal democracy and good governance (Leftwich 1993; Robinson 1993; World Bank 1993). While the critics of capitalism argue that this turn towards democracy—or, in the context of Latin America and other parts of the so-called Third World, redemocratization—is incomplete, opportunistic or merely procedural, it calls into question the idea of an inherent contradiction between capitalism and democracy. Indeed, the process of more markets and more elections seems to resonate with Lenin's idea that the bourgeois democratic republic is the ideal institutional shell for capitalist relations to reach their fullest expression within.

On the other hand, the free market theorists of democracy have a serious problem in accounting for the broad swath of historical experiences. As Anderson (1979) has demonstrated, the origins of capitalism in the European absolutist states had little if anything to do with democracy. Nor did the conquest and enslavement of millions of Third World peoples within the

historical context of which, according to Blackburn (1997) and other proponents of a "dependency theory" of capitalist development, the industrial
revolution and early capitalist development was financed.

More recently, from the 1960s to the mid-1980s, the introduction of
market reforms in Asia (Indonesia) and Latin America (Brazil, Chile, Argentina and other countries) was preceded and sustained by harsh military
dictatorships. In the Southern Cone of South America the association of
economic liberalization and the neoliberal model of capitalist development
with what O'Donnell and his associates (1986) termed "bureaucratic authoritarianism," but which most observers regard as military dictatorship, was very
clear in the 1970s. The Argentine political economist Atilio Borón (1981)
would argue that, in the context of U.S. imperialism, capitalist development in
peripheral social formations requires a dismantling of the institutions of
bourgeois democracy, and that economic liberalism both requires and generates
political despotism. In this context, advocates of free markets and democracy
might argue—and in the 1970s many of them did—that there is a "lag" between
democracy and free markets, whereby the latter requires a period of authoritarianism to consolidate in order to setup the basis for the emergence of democracy.

This stage theory fails to account for cases of advanced market economies
reverting to dictatorial or authoritarian rule, such as Italy in the 1920s,
Germany in the 1930s, France in the late 1950s, Greece in the 1960s and Turkey
in the 1980s. Recently "redemocratized" countries such as Argentina, Brazil,
Chile and Uruguay had a long history of democratic politics prior to the
introduction of free market reforms but succumbed to a combination of
dictatorships and free markets before moving towards the current formula of
democracy and free markets (Leiva and Petras with Veltmeyer 1994; Veltmeyer
and Petras 1997). In Brazil, within a few hours of the 1964 *coup d'état* against
Goulart's constitutional and democratically elected nationalist regime and the
installation of a military dictatorship, the colonels received a telegram from
U.S. President Lyndon Johnson congratulating them for "restoring democracy."
The sweeping claims made by the ideologues of free markets and free elections
cannot account for these and other such incongruous experiences. Whatever
their propagandistic merits, propositions about a necessary connection between free markets and democracy have little explanatory power or analytical
value.

On this score, proceduralist theorists have perhaps presented a more useful
analysis of the set of prerequisites for democracy, independent of apparent
ideological considerations. As these scholars see it, the "rules of the game"
specify procedures for electoral competition, alternation and succession, and,
as such, they are based on a political consensus that precludes disruption of the
democratic process as long as the political actors abide by the rules. However,
the problem with this notion of "democratic rules of the game" is that it is
tautological. It assumes what needs to be proven: that the rules in themselves
provide an adequate opportunity for alternative interests and movements to

gain access to the seats of power. In other words, the assumptions made by proceduralists about the parameters of political power preclude analysis of the historical antecedents that shape and give rise to the institutional forces that determine the "rules of the game." For example, institution of "democratic rules of the game" in Latin America took place in the context of a continuation of authoritarian state institutions, which were able to define and condition the fundamental issues of power, social structure and international relations. Likewise, "democratic rules" were instituted in Western Europe under the U.S. military occupation and reconfiguration of fascist states.

The general statement about the importance of procedural rules in sustaining democracy overlooks the manner in which these same procedures have been applied, revised and redefined in different historical contexts to sustain incumbents and their class cohorts in power. What appear as "adjustments" in procedures may serve the same role as a *coup d'état* by denying an opposition the chance to exercise power (e.g., the case of Whitlam in Australia). Latin American cases of incumbent presidents revising constitutional clauses to allow for their own re-elections is but one instance of authoritarian practice within institutionalized electoral procedures. Since these changes are seen as "merely" procedural, they are seen as part of the competitive democratic political system. Ironically, theorists of the centrality of procedures frequently overlook or fail to analyze how subtle shifts in procedure can alter the fundamental content of the democratic process. Equally important, the proceduralists fail to examine the larger political power struggle, the way it impinges on the formation of consensus on the rules of the game and how "procedures" themselves are redefined to perpetuate the authoritarian exercise of power. What appears to be a neutral definition of democracy based on a commonly acceptable set of procedures actually obscures the interrelationship between the political economy and the changing uses and abuses of electoral rules.

Capitalist Democracy: An Instrumental Perspective

Liberal ideologues often speak of democracy, not as a means but as an "end in itself." However, there is little historical or empirical basis for making that claim on behalf of the principal political actors in capitalist democracies, who, regardless of their origin or location in the social structure, clearly represent the general or specific interests of the capitalist class. During periods of more or less stable capitalist rule, this proposition seems to reflect reality. Opposition parties are tolerated, a critical press operates, competitive elections take place and alternation is the norm among parties that share the dominant economic ideology. At these times the argument that democracy and capitalism are at least compatible if not mutually reinforcing appears to have validity.

The crucial issue, however, is to view the onset of democracy, whatever its "popular" or "market" origins, as an unfinished process, as contingent on the perpetuation of a regime of property, power and privilege. If democracy is the culmination of the working of market forces, what about circumstances in which market relations are challenged by social forces within the institutions of a democratic system? If global markets everywhere encourage political democracy, how do we explain external political forces intervening to undermine democratically elected regimes which challenge the dictates of the market and "hegemonic power"? How do we explain the actions of the hegemonic powers, which alternately bolster democratic regimes and military dictatorships supportive of free markets? How do we explain the subversion of democratic regimes that oppose free markets by regimes that are also considered democracies? Clearly more profound forces are at work than the simple affinity of democratic regimes for their counterparts.

At the national level, why do political actors who play by the democratic rules suddenly kick over the table when they lose elections and become or embrace dictatorial regimes? Why do individuals and business associations with longstanding ties to democratic parties and procedures embrace totalitarian solutions and reject democratic outcomes unfavourable to their interests? And why do they return to democratic processes further down the line?

It is clear that democracy is not a universal ideal operating according to larger historical forces or economic laws. Nor is it contingent on the embrace of political modernization and the values and procedural norms associated with it; as we have argued, *these vary over time and place*, in many cases alternating with other sets of political interests, commitments and realities. Nor, as argued by Przeworski (1986) and Offe (1983), among others, is democracy simply a product of popular struggle which modifies the operation of the capitalist system to make it more responsive to majoritarian interests. We have seen how even the most socially advanced capitalist democracies can be transformed into dictatorial states.

The key to understanding the evolution of democracy within the capitalist system, we argue, is to understand its fundamentally contingent nature, always, or at least everywhere we have historical and empirical data. Contingency means that their very existence and non-existence depends on the degree to which democratic rules are compatible with the perpetuation of capitalist property relations, the class structure and state institutions that support the former and hegemonic relations among states.

Capitalists themselves tend to have an instrumental view of democracy in which its virtues or defects are defined in terms of property interests. This understanding allows us to account for the shifting relationships between democracy and capitalism over time and place. When a democratic state is governed by the capitalist class or, more likely, operated in its interests, democracy is viewed as a "good in itself." However, when it provides a platform for transforming social relations and property rights, the tendency is to view it as a "luxury," as expendable and properly replaced by an authoritarian system better able to protect the relations and perquisites of property.

Proceduralists have incorporated this conditionality into their theory of democracy without cognizance of the profound theoretical consequences: that the capitalist threat of reversion to dictatorship if property rights and relations are threatened is a key procedural factor that undermines any pretext to a level playing field or open-ended democratic rule-making. The primacy of capitalist property relations and hegemonic interests over democracy is thus the real meaning of the term "capitalist democracy." Thus there are limits on democracy even within the most "advanced" state committed to democracy as an end in itself. This unwritten "law" can be illustrated by reference to numerous historical experiences in Europe, North America and the Third World. To illustrate this point, we will briefly review some of these experiences with particular reference to the cases of Finland (1918), Guyana (1953, 1961–64), Chile (1970–73), Guatemala (1950–54), Haiti (1991 and 1994), Nicaragua (1984 and 1989), Iran (1954), Germany (1933), Italy (1920s), Spain (1936) and the United States (1877).

In all these cases, popular regimes were democratically elected and then overthrown by military forces backed by the capitalist class and a hegemonic power, in response to an attempt to transform or even simply reform the current system of property relations. There are no cases on record in which the capitalist class has acquiesced to legislation which made deep inroads on the power and prerogatives of property ownership.

Finland (1918)

Shortly after the Russian Revolution of 1917, elections took place in which worker-based socialists sympathetic to the Russian Revolution were democratically empowered to govern. Backed by workers' councils, trade unions and factory committees, the new government adopted a series of measures designed to advance the position of the working class in society. The capitalist class resorted to a series of extra-parliamentary manoeuvres designed to undermine the regime. Where these manoeuvres failed, they supported a military uprising backed by an invasion of German troops who proceeded to massacre, imprison or force into exile about one out of every four workers in the course of overthrowing the democratically-elected regime and installing the authoritarian, pro-capitalist Mannerheim regime. Under this regime, capitalist dominance in the factories and the state was re-established.

Guyana (1953, 1961–64)

In 1953 the majority of Guyanese citizens democratically elected a democratic socialist, Cheddi Jagan, as prime minister. Jagan, a Marxist, sought to resolve the vast socioeconomic inequalities that had defined Guyanese society, limit the role of multinational corporations and introduce a more equitable distribution of land. One hundred and thirty-three days into his administration, the British military intervened, overthrew the democratic government, put in place a pliable interim regime, rewrote the constitution and concentrated power in the colonial governor. Subsequently, new elections were held within the framework of a more restrictive constitution. However, Jagan proceeded to win the national elections in 1956 and again in 1961. When he once more embarked on a series of measures to democratize society and increase national control over the economy, the CIA intervened to undermine his government, fanning racial animosities between Afro-Guyanese and Indo-Guyanese and resulting in the replacement of Jagan by the corrupt and despotic Forbes Burnham regime. In this case, imperial political and economic interests intervened through the use of military force and the secret police (CIA) to re-establish political control and reassert the primacy of private property interests as the fundamental factor conditioning the turn towards electoral politics. The return of elected democracy was based on a new constitution and the political, economic and military parameters of authoritarian power. The subsequent exercise of authoritarian rule by the Burnham regime was anchored in a series of anti-democratic historical events and the institutional configuration that preceded it. The Guyanese experience clearly illustrates the "instrumental" nature of democracy as far as the Anglo-American bourgeoisie was concerned. A democratic regime was overthrown when it became incompatible with imperial rule and was later restored when a pliable regime could be shoehorned into power.

Chile (1970–73)
The overthrow of the democratically elected socialist government of Salvador Allende is probably the most notorious and best known case of the local and international bourgeoisie clearly asserting its preference for a dictatorship that defended big investors over a democracy oriented towards redistributive poli-cies and socialism. The military coup of 1973 was preceded by a series of extra-parliamentary actions by the capitalist class and U.S. secret police: lockouts, boycotts, terrorist sabotage, assassination of key officials, hoarding and CIA subsidies to select mass media outlets. The failure to undercut the socialist regime's electoral support—its electoral vote actually increased between 1970 and 1973—led the bourgeoisie and U.S. corporate interests to provide whole-hearted support to a military coup. Subsequent to the coup, substantial sectors of the bourgeoisie collaborated with the military dictatorship by providing names and addresses of former socialist and communist trade union activists who had engaged in legal collective bargaining. Many were jailed, tortured, exiled or assassinated. The U.S. government, working with major multina-tional corporations, organized and financed the destabilization program, col-laborated closely with the military coup-makers and provided a detailed list of democratic activists of the overthrown regime to the newly formed Chilean secret police. After the coup, the U.S. government, which had opposed international financing of the democratically elected regime, approved a massive flow of financial resources to the military dictatorship.

In the mid-1980s, as the Chilean economy went into a deep depression (from 1982 to 1983 it shrank 15 percent, resulting in an official unemployment rate of 26 percent), and as mass unrest spread throughout the country, challenging the regime, the U.S., in alliance with sectors of the bourgeoisie, called for a return to elections within the framework of the authoritarian constitution of 1980 established by the dictatorship. U.S. envoy Robert Gelbard intervened in the process, successfully divided the opposition, convinced the dictatorship to hold a referendum and secured the acquiescence of the Socialists and Christian Democrats to the basic contours of the Pinochet socio-economic order. Following the referendum and the consolidation of the free market model, both the capitalist class and the U.S. supported a reintroduction of elections and Pinochet's promise to "teach the world a lesson in democracy." The electoral system served to legitimate the political leadership and to deepen free market policies within the institutional parameters of an authoritarian state, including the continuation of Pinochet as the commander-in-chief of the armed forces for a full decade after the first election and the institution of a non-elected security council to oversee and protect the security of the state. During the new electoral decade, military leaders frequently issued *pronunciamentos* which effectively cut off legislative discussion and judicial or executive action on matters pertaining to the military's violation of human rights, its budget, appointments, etc. The concentration of wealth and the vast inequalities that emerged under the military regime remain intact, as does the absence of any serious legislative initiatives regarding redistribution of land, income or taxation. In effect, the bourgeoisie and the U.S. reintroduced democracy in response to popular pressure, but under conditions that guaranteed the dominance of capitalist property interests in shaping institutional power, constitutional rules and the role and position of the military.

Guatemala (1950–54)
In 1950, Guatemalans democratically elected Jacob Arbenz to the Presidency. He ran as a moderate nationalist-populist, interested in curbing the excessive power of the U.S.-owned United Fruit Company and in extending social rights to trade unionists. In 1954 the CIA, in alliance with sectors of the Guatemalan army, landlords and big business interests, overthrew the government and established a military regime that jailed, tortured and killed many democratic activists. Over the next three decades the U.S. government and its corporate business supporters trained, armed and organized the Guatemalan army. The result was the killing of close to 200,000 Guatemalans, one of the worst bloodlettings in Latin America in which the U.S. military and the CIA have been found to be complicit. Fraudulent elections were periodically convened that systematically excluded opposition to the socio-economic elite and its U.S.-based corporate-military allies. A prolonged popular and guerrilla struggle re-emerged in the early 1960s and continued to the mid-1990s. At this point, Washington backed members of the Guatemalan elite who sought to open some electoral space for the guerrilla commanders. A peace accord was brokered and supported by this elite and Washington. It disarmed the guerrillas, preserved the

socio-economic status quo, gave impunity to the military for its crimes against humanity and allowed the ex-commanders and their followers to organize political parties and present candidates for elections. Thus the reintroduction of free elections by the bourgeoisie was conditioned by the guerrilla commanders' acceptance of the abolition of Arbenz's progressive legislation and the continued existence of military and paramilitary forces within an essentially authoritarian state. The primacy of property in this democratic transition is so clear that many human rights organizations and mass or class organizations formed by peasants and indigenous peoples have rejected or sharply criticized the authoritarian and elitist nature of the political and economic system. In the meantime, clauses in the peace accord designed to safeguard even elementary rights have been inoperative: paramilitary forces still operate, assassinating activists and even bishops who speak out on human rights abuses. U.S. President Clinton and Secretary of State Albright declared the Hemispheric Summit in Santiago, Chile, in 1990 to be a great victory for democracy and free markets, less than two weeks before the military-supported murder by *paras* (paramilitary forces) of the bishop in Guatemala City and only a few days before the leading human rights lawyer in Bogota, Colombia, was assassinated.

Iran (1954
Muhammad Mossadegh was the elected prime minister of Iran in the early 1950s. A nationalist who sought to curb the excessive dependence of Iran on foreign-owned (mainly Anglo-American) oil companies, he was overthrown in a coup largely organized and financed by the CIA. He was replaced by the Shah Pahlavi, who catered to U.S. business and kept Iranian national sentiments in check through the operation of a vast secret police apparatus, the infamous SAVAK. Washington provided military and secret police training as well as arms and financial assistance for over a quarter of a century.

As in Guatemala, the scope and longevity of U.S. support of dictatorship over democracy suggests that this action was not an aberration or the product of a conservative presidency but was based on a fundamental strategy of U.S. policy—to put capitalist property interests above democratic values and institutions whenever the two are in conflict. The unified response of foreign investors indicates the ready willingness to resort to authoritarianism that accompanies the pursuit of private profits. However, lack of commitment to democratic institutions when popular mandates challenge capitalist prerogatives does not preclude capitalist support for liberal-democratic politicians in altered circumstances. When the Shah was overthrown and his secret police and armed forces dismantled, Washington shifted gears and backed liberal politicians against nationalist Islamic politicians and Marxists. In the new context, after the main pillars of dictatorship had collapsed, Washington and Anglo-American business interests promoted liberal democratic politicians amenable to foreign investors as a way to conserve their privileged interests in the economy.

Thus both dictatorship and democracy are viewed in instrumental terms, and relations between capitalism and democracy are *contextually as well as structurally defined*. While capitalism prioritizes its property interests in defining its political preferences, the way it realizes its economic interests varies with the possibilities in each context. Historically speaking, capitalism has no permanent relations with democracy (or dictatorships for that matter). What defines capitalism is the prevalence and persistence of economic interests.

Haiti (1991 and 1994) and Nicaragua (1984 and 1989)

In the late 1980s a mass popular movement, the Lavalas, forced the corrupt and elitist dictatorship in Haiti to hold elections. After many years of supporting the Duvalier family dictatorship, Washington opted to support a former World Bank official in the electoral campaign of 1991 against the populist priest Bertram Aristide. Washington exerted intense pressure on Aristide to withdraw from the election. Self-designated electoral observer ex-President Carter warned Aristide that his electoral victory would provoke a "bloodbath" and massacre. Disregarding Carter's admonitions, Aristide continued his electoral campaign and managed to receive over two-thirds of the votes. Upon taking office, he immediately began to implement his populist and democratic reform agenda while seeking to curb the absolute power and privilege of the corrupt military. Appalled by this turn of events, Washington developed covert ties with the military, secret police and paramilitary forces, and in less than a year Aristide was overthrown. Although President Bush publicly condemned the coup, in fact Washington developed a working relationship with the new regime.

Washington's support for the coup in Haiti and the subsequent regime seemed to contradict its support for democratic transitions elsewhere in Latin America at the time. This paradox can be explained by the fact that in Haiti the regime sought to put in place nationalist and redistributive policies in the transition, while elsewhere in Latin America the new electoral regimes that came to power deepened and gave greater scope to foreign and domestic investors and were very partial to Washington's "free market/free trade" agenda.

The underlying antidemocratic animus that informs Washington and overseas business groups whenever investor interests are at stake was also visible in the case of Nicaragua. In 1984 the revolutionary regime there held free and competitive elections vouched for by impartial observers from Europe and Latin America. Washington, however, rejected the electoral victory of the Sandinistas and, because the winning party opposed Washington's economic agenda, chose to prosecute a proxy war through a CIA-directed mercenary army.

The important point is that during a decade in which Washington ostensibly embraced democratic transitions, it failed to do so in cases where democratic regimes challenged the absolute power of foreign and domestic investors.

This predominance of property interests in defining capitalism's relation to democracy was reinforced by subsequent events in Haiti and Nicaragua. After the coup of 1991, tens of thousands of Haitians fled the dictatorship and economic hardships and headed for the Florida mainland. Clinton developed a dual strategy of pressuring the military to allow a return to electoral politics and pressuring Aristide to renounce his reform agenda in favour of a U.S.-designed "free market" program. Through a military invasion and intense pressure, Washington was able to impose its own version of democratic transition, one that marginalized the masses, displaced the military rulers and privileged private property.

A similar process took place in Nicaragua in 1989 when the right-wing pro-Washington candidate Violeta Chamorro defeated the Sandinistas. Washington ended its support for the mercenary army and recognized these elections as democratic.

We have only touched on the issue, but the evidence is fairly decisive. With the elimination of all political regimes that seek to impose constraints on capital in the hemisphere, Washington and its big business partners could proclaim their support of democracy and the close link between free elections and free markets.

Germany (1933), Italy (1920s) and Spain (1936)

The linkage with democracy also can be examined in advanced capitalist countries. The near economic collapse, massive unemployment and the existence of powerful Socialist and Communist parties and trade unions within the democratic political system presented a serious challenge to the capitalist class in Germany (and elsewhere). On the one hand, the Socialists, who had much earlier surrendered their revolutionary agenda, pressured the capitalist class for concessions and retained a potential veto on the more severe economic austerity measures. On the other hand, although they constituted a minority, the Communists were beginning to attract young unemployed workers and were increasingly leading large marches and demonstrations that called the capitalist system into question. Together the two parties represented nearly 20 million voters, although they never formed a unified bloc.

The Nazi rise to power was financed in part by German capitalists who saw in Hitler a bulwark against Bolshevism. When the Nazis took full power and systematically destroyed the Socialist and Communist parties and trade unions, the capitalist class openly collaborated with the state and was the principal beneficiary. Capitalist employers provided names and other information on trade union militants to the Nazi secret police, while taking advantage of the new regime to rid themselves of previous power-sharing and collective bargaining agreements with workers. The German capitalist class preferred direct access to the Nazi political elite over the more circuitous and difficult task of engaging in elections with uncertain results. While the capitalist class turned to Nazi authoritarianism, the German Socialist parliamentary leaders continued to pursue tactics of accommodation, even with the emerging new order led by Hitler. The Communists, meanwhile, believed that the victory of Nazism was a temporary outcome that would create conditions for their proximate ascendancy.

The point is that both left-wing parties failed to recognize the "instrumental" conception of democracy held by the bourgeoisie. The Socialists, as a matter of principle, and the Communists, because of tactical considerations, assumed that the electoral and constitutional order provided the basis for any changes in the configuration of political power. As was the case for Allende in Chile, belief in the democratic political order explains why the Socialists and Communists did not activate the tens of thousands of working-class militia and use their well-stocked armories to fight Hitler's takeover. Hitler, of course, had no such reservations, and the bourgeoisie had no serious qualms about backing his violent repression of their class enemies.

Similar experiences of bourgeois support for violent resistance against popular electoral outcomes took place in Italy in the 1920s and shortly after the Popular Front victory in Spain in 1936. While many members of the Left perceived democracy as "good in itself" and confined themselves within the norms of constitutionality and the customary rules of the electoral game, the bourgeoisie looked at the same rules and norms as instruments to be supported or discarded according to their strategic interests. The failure of the Left to develop a more realistic view of the class parameters of democratic rules and to put their class interests into the strategic centre of their political calculations hindered countermeasures that might have prevented the success of bourgeois authoritarianism. Likewise, the return of capitalist democracy, which followed a period of prolonged authoritarian rule, in each case incorporated the institutional configurations of power and prerogatives of capital that had been established during the dictatorial period.

A whole mythology is created by theorists of democratic transitions to justify labelling the hybrid regime democratic when in fact it combines democratic rules and undisputed bourgeois state power. The pre-authoritarian past in which the Left was powerful, property relations were challenged and conflict was over basic issues of class inequality is labelled by publicists and academic apologists of the current transitions as "chaotic," "crisis-wracked" and "dominated by extremists of the right and left." This demonic image of the past obscures the fact that the essential element in the demise of democracy was the bourgeois rejection of the rules of the democratic game. In contrast, the newly established democracy under bourgeois hegemony is given a "classless" character, while the rules of the game and political procedures governing electoral competition and political alternation are described as "good in themselves," as if they existed without reference to the larger historical patterns and broader class interests they serve.

United States (1877)
The instrumental nature of democracy has been an historical norm throughout the capitalist world that has frequently led to the reversal of cumulative gains achieved by the working class and other oppressed groups. This is particularly true in historic moments when exploited social classes in different regions converge into a national movement to challenge capitalist hegemony. A case in point is the U.S. in the post–Civil War period.

Following the U.S. Civil War (1861–65), the former slaves began to exercise their democratic rights under the protective eye of the federal army. They began to organize politically and seek social and economic rights, including the redistribution of plantation land. In the North, rapid industrialization created a new working class that was highly exploited and concentrated in large industries. In the West, farmers began to question the power and authority of private transportation and financial monopolies. Each region represented a distinct set of social interests and yet faced a common political adversary—a legislature and executive controlled by big business. The convergence of these regional class interests could have seriously altered the balance of power in the nation. But the Compromise of 1877 undercut at least one leg in this potential alliance by restoring the power of plantation capital and accommodating its regional dominance in exchange for national backing of Northern industrial capital. The result was a massive reversal of the democratic rights of former slaves through a reign of terror. Paramilitary groups such as the KKK, backed by local and state authorities, secured the power of the former landowners and commercial interests. In turn, the Southern elite backed Northern industrial capital's legislation restricting the role of labour and repressing trade unions.

The point is that democratic rules were applied to the electoral competition between elites, North and South, and, through laws and terror, excluded the majoritarian Blacks in many Southern states. Constitutional forms and political compromise were selectively applied and sanctioned among the more powerful political actors in the system. The withdrawal of federal troops provided greater opportunities for Southern political elites to seek their own benefit and exclude the Black majority.

The myth of the continuity of democracy could be propagated, and public debate and electoral processes could proceed on the basis of a racially selective definition of citizenship. The bourgeois instrumental view of democracy not only leads to a more restricted view of democracy or its abandonment, but also to redefinitions of rules and procedures to accommodate new strategic alliances.

Conclusion
The notion that there are "rules of the game" and procedures that govern political participation in democracies overlooks the overarching importance of capitalist property relations and interests. Historical experience provides us

with a wide range of examples in which democratic procedures were jettisoned by the capitalist class when they provided a vehicle for popular challenges to property rights. The notion expounded by liberal democratic political theorists that "democracy is a good in itself" is not a useful analytical postulate because it assumes that one of the major contestants for power shares these values. As we have seen, this has frequently not been the case for the capitalist class. On the other hand, those of the Left who have embraced this concept have laboured at a decided disadvantage, confining themselves to constitutional norms and practices that are ultimately ineffective in dealing with the violent and subversive practices of their local and international capitalist adversaries. While there is nothing theoretically objectionable about establishing norms and procedures for democracy and arguing that they are "good in themselves" independent of outcomes, one is also obliged to identify the social actors who are willing to accept those rules irrespective of their political outcome. Hence it is irresponsible for social scientists to lecture the Left about the intrinsic value of democracy and its procedures under capitalist hegemony while ignoring historical data that demonstrates that, when the tables are turned, the capitalist class is likely to resort to antidemocratic practices.

The point is that capitalist democracy does not exist independently of class interests and class conflict. To argue that it is "good" is a relative judgement based on the degree of capitalist tolerance of opposition. Tolerance is not extended to shifts in state power. Democracy and democratic procedures function best under conditions where there is uncontested capitalist hegemony, or (theoretically) where workers are able to consolidate a new state free of capitalist and imperial subversion. In the first case, democratic functioning is directly related to marginal challenges to property in a system where capitalists, through political elites, can elaborate strategic policies favouring their interests and investments. In the second case, democratic rules provide alternation and competition among formerly exploited social classes and groups who do not derive their status, income and political influence from owning property. In a workers' democracy, competition and conflict take place within the parameters of public and small-scale private ownership.

The notion that democracy and capitalism are in constant conflict over-looks the long periods of time and extended regions of the world, particularly since World War II, where capitalist regimes have introduced or restored democratic procedures. The idea that there is a "subversive content" to democracy implies that voting, democratic freedoms and political competition contain the seeds for radical change. This has not held up in numerous cases, particularly in the U.S. and Europe. The most serious challenges to authoritarian rulers and elite-dominated capitalist democracies has taken place in extra-parliamentary struggles such as the summer of 1968 in France, the hot fall in Italy of 1969 and the mass struggles against the free market in Latin America during the 1990s. The so-called "radical content" of democratic politics comes from extra-parliamentary activity, which precedes electoral advances of the

Left. To think otherwise is to ascribe to elections an independent influence apart from the hegemony exercised by capitalism over the ensemble of social forces. The electoral process is "modified" and extended by social action, and it is precisely the extension and deepening of political engagement by counterhegemonic classes that results in the capitalist class's rejection of democratic rules, procedures and democratic institutions.

The apparent stability of capitalist democracy and the democratic rules of the game in the contemporary world can in part be ascribed to a strategic retreat by the Left from any serious challenge to capitalist property. It is crucial to understand the historical sequence that has preceded this accommodation and the role that repression, terror and illegality have played to encourage this accommodation to capitalist hegemony. The sequence has involved challenges by the Left to property within democratic politics, capitalist reaction, the reign of repressive regimes, the return to democracy and the acceptance of capitalist hegemony. What is crucial in this sequence is the middle factor—the role of capitalist violence and repression in altering the Left's political values and orientation. The disciplining of the Left, the forceful recognition that democracy has limits under capitalism, is subsequently "internalized" in their political ideology. This strategic weakness and accommodation is then converted into a virtue—the idea of "democracy as a good in itself." However, this vague formula obscures the substantive democratic politics of the Left in the past, the bourgeoisie's instrumental view of democracy and the Left's accommodation to violent forces it cannot overcome and has often failed to understand.

Chapter 7

Cooperation for Development

The language of politics is intimately related to the politics of language. Concepts and phrases that have one meaning take on another according to the political uses and context to which they are attached. This use and abuse of the language of politics is nowhere as evident as in the arena of North-South relations. Concepts such as "development," "justice" and "cooperation" frequently have been associated with particular ideological agendas and not infrequently obscure the nature and content of political-economic relations and processes rather than illuminating them. The abuse of political language is especially associated with the domination of imperial powers over Third World countries, especially in the post-colonial world where overt political control is no longer acceptable to democratic publics. A particularly egregious example of political obscurantism and the use of language to provide a positive image for ugly realities concerns the transition to capitalism in the ex-USSR. Western academics, journalists and politicians describe the private pillage of the Russian economy by foreign investors and Mafia-capitalists that has lead to a catastrophic collapse of the economy as "economic reform." Yeltsin's shelling of the Russian Parliament and his dictatorial and arbitrary rule was described as "defending democracy." Perversion of political language also occurs when victims are accused of the crimes committed against them by their executioners. In this chapter, we begin by criticizing the contemporary imperial uses of the concepts "cooperation," "development" and "justice" and then proceed to a discussion of the same terms from the perspective of national and social liberation.

Cooperation for What, with Whom and under What Conditions?

Most European, North American and Japanese foreign aid agencies (and most of their non-governmental organizations) speak of cooperation between the North and South. Yet most of their "aid" is tied to purchases of goods produced by the donor countries at prices often higher than market figures. Moreover, "aid" is tied to favourable investment and trading arrangements with the donor countries' TNCs. In order to provide aid, these agencies demand access to strategic raw materials, free entry into domestic markets and the elimination of social regulations. In other words, "cooperation" means subordination of the aid recipient to the donor, the reproduction of imperial relations under another name. Cooperation within unequal relations of power and economic exploitation merely reinforces and deepens injustice; it does not represent financial aid to transform backward and exploitative structures. Social assistance channelled via NGOs to ameliorate poverty is conditioned on the acceptance of neoliberal macroeconomic policies and structures. Within the neoliberal politico-economic context, "cooperation for the alleviation of poverty" is in reality a means to perpetuate the conditions that create poverty. Thus we have the paradox: more poverty assistance is accompanied by greater poverty.

Development: Who Owns What, Where and How?

The neoliberal development paradigm that is dominant today is based on highly concentrated private ownership of property, banks and trading networks. "Development" is measured in terms of the growth of exports controlled by major agro-business and manufacturing corporations. The massive dislocation and bankruptcy of peasants caused by imports and land concentration are merely called a "social cost" of "developmental progress." Large-scale unemployment caused by massive transfers of profits, interest payments and royalties to overseas bank accounts is described as temporary pain on the road to progress. Economists praise the massive influx of portfolio investments, ignoring the rapid flight of capital in time of crisis. "Development" is a highly class-biased concept. Indicators used to measure rates of capital accumulation, foreign trade and elite financial flows are all related to the performance (and benefits) of a very distinct and limited ruling-class group. The use of aggregate statistics to measure "development," such as per capita income based on gross national product, obscures the enormous inequalities in classes, regions, and ethnic and gender groups within the "nation." Neoliberal development theory's emphasis on the free market obscures the nature of the (foreign or domestic) market for which commodities are produced and the classes that consume. Neoliberal development theory does not tell us anything about the essential class relations that structure the economy and direct the benefits of development. In sum, "development" as defined by neoliberalism is a growth of injustice.

Justice: In the Eye of the Beholder

In the eyes of the dominant classes, "justice" is equated with the freedom to trade. For neoliberal ideologues, multinational agrobusinesses should have the same ability to sell corn in the Mexican market as a poor Indian peasant from Chiapas. "Equal justice" thus allows corporations to profit and peasants to starve. Justice is equated with the "right" of private corporations to buy public enterprises, fire workers and raise prices.

Privatization and the transformation of all relations into market relations is described by free marketers as the basis for creating a "competitive world" in which the most efficient and competent will be "justly rewarded." Efficiency is not measured by numbers of productive workers but by lower costs and higher profits. The free market image of reality is a gross distortion of the institutional context and social consequences of privatization and free market operations. The only beneficiaries of privatization are big private investors who proceed to charge exorbitant rates for public services, reduce employment and eliminate public accountability for strategic economic decisions.

In sum, what is justice for the few is injustice for the many. This suggests that there are no "universal" standards of justice or universally accepted criteria for defining cooperation and development. There are only class definitions. Each concept is put into concrete terms according to the socio-economic interests of the antagonistic classes.

An Alternative View

If we start from the assumption that the present world has been defined by the antagonistic and conflictual relations of an increasingly polarized international economy, we can envision an alternative set of conditions and relations that would produce cooperation, development and justice.

The historical and contemporary record of cooperation between the major imperial powers (the U.S., Germany, Japan) and the international financial institutions has been based on the imposition of political-economic policies that reinforce unequal relations. Genuine cooperation is based on equality, not the "formal" equality of two "sovereign states" but a substantive equality where the strategic socio-economic interests of the majority of producers in the Third World countries are given equal weight. These interests are a living wage for workers, not just investment opportunities for multinational corporation; land reform for peasants and food production for the urban poor, and not just incentives for agro-business. When these interests are given equal value, they become a basis for cooperation.

However, at the level of government-to-government relations this form of cooperation is impossible to realize because the governments of the North are imperial governments whose concept of cooperation is precisely to promote favourable relations for corporate profits, not to redress the inequities produced by corporations. Therefore, meaningful cooperation can only take place at the subnational level: between popular movements in the North who confront the same corporate exploitation as do peasants and workers in the South. Such movement-to-movement cooperation requires a demarcation between "movements" dominated by privileged and corrupt leaders and those which respond to the real needs of their members, decided via democratic representation and assemblies in which women and racial minorities are adequately represented. Too often, international cooperation has created privileged professionals in the North and corrupt bureaucrats in the South, all in the name of "international solidarity."

Development?

Even in some official circles, measuring development by Gross National Product (GNP) has been called into question. Instead of measuring aggregate quantities of goods and services, critics have devised quality of life indicators, measuring life expectancy, child mortality rates, caloric intake, educational and literary levels, etc. The elaboration of quality of life indicators is a step forward, but it is not enough. First of all, quality of life indicators cannot be understood apart from the quality of the social relations of production and the quality of state-class structural relations. In devising indicators of development, it is not only important to look at socio-economic outcomes, but also at the socio-political and economic structures and processes that produce those outcomes. This is important because favourable results in one historical moment can be reversed by the advent of a different regime. The case of the ex-USSR is a good example. The positive social indicators in the former USSR for health and education have been reversed with the ascendancy of neoliberal regimes. A similar process has taken place in Latin America, Asia and elsewhere. The issue is the sustainability of quality of life indicators, which is rooted in the class nature and democratic accountability of the political regime. Looking only at quality of life indicators only provides us with a concise and transient "photograph" of development, rather than a larger and long-term understanding of the trajectory of development and its structural roots.

Finally, "quality of life indicators" need to be refined by looking at target groups, because of great variations according to class, gender and race. While "average" quality of life indicators may show substantial improvement, in many cases these improvements have not been evenly distributed. Urban middle class males in India have longer and healthier lives than rural peasant women, so using quality of life averages only obscures fundamental social differences. The same can be said for environmental degradation. Some classes may cause environmental degradation, but other classes may be adversely affected. Timber companies strip the forests and hills of trees, but the poor peasants living on the flood plains suffer from this the most.

The larger international political issue is the style of development: "development from below" versus "development from above," and its corollary, "development from within" versus "development from without."

"Development from below" implies that the main actors and beneficiaries are the direct producers, not the current owners of the means of production.

Fundamental justice is based on the principle that social cooperation in production (embedded in the current social division of labour) should be expressed in social ownership of the means of production. The fact that imperial corporations based in Europe, North American and Japan have created gigantic networks of producers—in effect bringing millions of workers, peasants and farmers under a common organization—creates the objective conditions of shared exploitation with which to create international solidarity and cooperation.

Development from below is today more feasible than ever, thanks to the expansion of computers and information systems that universalize access to new technologies and market opportunities. The fundamental element in development from below is the democratization of the workplace via workers' and engineers' councils across international boundaries. The movements to create development from below are premised on capturing the strategic heights of the economy, not simply establishing small and isolated self-help projects in a sea of neoliberal corporations. The concept of cooperation takes on a new and revolutionary meaning when linked with movements for development from below, because it means providing aid to struggles not just against poverty but also against the institutional structures and relations that produce poverty.

Cooperation for transformation—revolution—thus recognizes that the people in struggle are at the centre of decision-making and that aid is directed at strengthening the capability of organized exploited classes to establish their own independent economies and egalitarian class structures by which they can create their own development model.

"Development from below" will most likely be accompanied by a strategy of "development to the inside." This does not mean autarky, but a significant shift of ownership, production, trade and credit to expand food production and basic necessities for the impoverished people of the "internal market." External trade will continue, as will international cooperation, but it will be subordinated to development of the internal market, which means agrarian reform and the partial transformation of export agriculture to food production for local consumption. It also means the creation of trade, communication and transportation networks that link complementary producers (in farming, industry and mining) from different regions into a national market—not into export enclaves linked to overseas markets. Cooperation in the "development to the inside" model would involve transferring know-how, technology and financial assistance to facilitate the growth of institutions with a primary commitment to local innovation and publicly oriented entrepreneurial skills that can create new and more attractive products that reflect consumer preferences.

Development "from below" and "from inside," however, do not exist in an international vacuum. Efforts to subvert the neoliberal and imperial "globalization" model require international cooperation at the political, economic and cultural level. Recent history teaches us that experiments with "development from below" evoke violent opposition, particularly from Washington and, to a lesser degree, Europe and Japan. The recent experiences in Chile under Allende, the Sandinistas in Nicaragua and earlier in Cuba suggest that efforts by imperial powers to reimpose models of "development from above and the outside" can be resisted through national popular movements and international cooperation from below. Strategic cooperation would involve extending the transformations and creating new sites for development from below in as many countries as possible to create a systemic alternative. Short of systemic transformation, cooperation could entail a variety of national and sectoral activities that create political-economic foreign policies "parallel" to the official policy of the government. The key to international cooperation is recognizing that the key element is relating to political-economic transformative movements. This means rejecting cooperation in the form of small projects designed by external donors that simply adapt to the neoliberal macroeconomy.

Positive cooperation does not mean rejecting reforms or projects per se. It means that international cooperation should fund "projects" and support "reforms" that are organized and directed by popular movements in order to build mass support to transform the macro-political economy.

An example of positive cooperation to fulfill popular aspirations for justice would be the funding of co-operatives developed by the Brazilian Rural Landless Workers Movement. These co-operatives are the products of a democratic movement of landless farm workers who have occupied large landed estates, resisted state and paramilitary repression and begun to produce enough to feed their families and take to market in adjoining towns. International cooperation which consults the leaders of co-operatives about the priorities of the producers, resists "imposing" conditions (political, economic or social) and provides the appropriate financial aid or requested technical assistance on a specific project would be an example of "cooperation for development as the fulfillment of justice." The relation would be reciprocal and equal: the donors would discuss from positions of equality, and the agenda would be set by the "host" institutions. The donor would evaluate the feasibility of financing and realizing the project, and the movement or co-operative would discuss and present a workable physical and financial plan and expected goals and benefi- ciaries. The project would immediately benefit the co-operative, and the success of the co-op would strengthen the national organization (the MST). Success in turn would encourage other landless workers to join the movement and engage in land occupations. In effect, international cooperation would meet immediate economic needs through the specific project and contribute to building a national movement intent on transforming the social system.

Cooperation in this example is clearly between groups which share a common set of values and interests and have a common idea of what "develop- ment" and "justice" entail. There are possibilities of misunderstandings and personal clashes, but these are not structural contradictions such as occur when states and TNCs speak of cooperation.

The development of an ideology that identifies the principal causes of conflict, underdevelopment and injustice is a prerequisite for the creation of an ambience of cooperation and a common understanding of development and justice. In the present world, to help superimpose "cooperation" between unequal states whereby imperial countries and corporations intervene and condition aid to maximize exploitation is to become an accomplice to injustice.

Marxism creatively applied to contemporary conditions provides us with conceptual tools to understand the concentration and centralization of power and capital, the growing social polarization between classes, and the exploita- tive social and property relations that influence state policy to benefit the rich at the expense of the poor on a global scale. However, while Marxism provides some general ideas about cooperation, development and justice, it provides no blueprint. The concrete practices of movements and struggles provide us with models and examples of cooperation, and contemporary critical social scientists and activist-theorists are elaborating more accurate measures of quality of life. Justice and ethical issues are being discussed jointly by Marxist, radical theologians and democrats who measure the progress of human beings not simply by possession of material goods, as important as they are, but also in terms of increased ability to love, care for others and share a common life in which individuality, creativity and privacy are compatible with active participation in community.

Chapter 8

NGOs in the Service of Imperialism

Throughout history, ruling classes representing small minorities have depended on a coercive state apparatus and social institutions to defend their power, profits and privileges. In the past, particularly in the Third World, imperial ruling classes financed and supported overseas and domestic religious institutions to control exploited people and deflect their discontent into religious and communal rivalries and conflicts.

Although these practices continue today, in more recent decades a new social institution has emerged that provides the same function of control and ideological mystification—the self-described "non-governmental organizations." Today there are at least 50,000 NGOs in the Third World receiving in total more than $10 billion in funding from international financial institutions, European, U.S. and Japanese governmental agencies and local governments. The managers of the biggest NGOs manage million-dollar budgets and receive salaries and perks that are comparable to those of corporate CEOs. They jet to international conferences, confer with top business and financial directors and make policy decisions that affect—in the great majority of cases, adversely—millions of people, especially the poor, women and informal-sector workers.

The NGOs are significant worldwide political and social actors that operate in rural and urban sites of Asia, Latin America and Africa, and are frequently linked in dependent roles with their principal donors in Europe, the U.S. and Japan. It is symptomatic of the pervasiveness of the NGOs and their economic and political power over the so-called "progressive world" that there have been few systematic Left critiques of their negative impact. In a large part this failure is due to the success of the NGOs in displacing and destroying the organized leftist movements and co-opting their intellectual strategists and organizational leaders.

Today most Left movement and popular spokespeople focus their criticism on the IMF, the World Bank, multinational corporations, private banks, etc., who fix the macroeconomic agenda for the pillage of the Third World. This is an important task. However, the assault on the industrial base, independence and living standards of the Third World takes place on both the macroeconomic and the micro-socio-political levels. The egregious effects of structural adjustment policies on waged and salaried workers, peasants and small national businesspeople generate potential national popular discontent. And that is where the NGOs come into the picture, to mystify and deflect that discontent away from direct attacks on corporate/banking power structures and profits and towards local micro-projects, apolitical "grass roots" self-exploitation and "popular education" that avoids class analysis of imperialism and capitalist profit-taking.

The NGOs worldwide have become the latest vehicle for upward mobility for the ambitious educated classes. Academics, journalists and professionals have abandoned earlier interests in poorly rewarded leftist movements for a lucrative career managing an NGO, bringing with them their organizational and rhetorical skills and a certain populist vocabulary. Today, thousands of NGO directors drive $40,000 four-wheel-drive sports utility vehicles from their fashionable suburban homes or apartments to their well-furnished offices and building complexes, leaving the children and domestic chores in the hands of servants and their yards to be tended by gardeners. They are more familiar with and spend more time at the overseas sites of their international conferences on poverty (Washington, Bangkok, Tokyo, Brussels, Rome, etc.) than the muddy villages of their own country. They are more adept at writing up new proposals to bring in hard currency for "deserving professionals" than risking a rap on the head from police attacking a demonstration of underpaid rural school teachers. NGO leaders are a new class not based on property ownership or government resources but derived from imperial funding and their own capacity to control significant popular groups. The NGO leaders can be conceived of as a kind of neo-comprador group that doesn't produce any useful commodity but does function to produce services for the donor countries, trading in domestic poverty for individual perks.

The formal claims used by NGO directors to justify their positions—that they fight poverty, inequality, etc.—are self-serving and specious. There is a direct relation between the growth of NGOs and the decline of living standards: the proliferation of NGOs has not reduced structural unemployment or massive displacements of peasants, nor provided livable wage levels for the growing army of informal workers. What NGOs have done is provide a thin stratum of professionals with income in hard currency who are able to escape the ravages of the neoliberal economy that affects their country and people and to climb within the existing social class structure.

This reality contrasts with the image that NGO functionaries have of themselves. According to their press releases and public discourses, they represent a "third way" between "authoritarian statism" and "savage market capitalism": they describe themselves as the vanguard of "civil society" operating in the interstices of the "global economy." The common purpose that most resounds at NGO conferences is "alternative development."

The phrase-mongering about "civil society" is an exercise in vacuity. "Civil society" is not a unitary virtuous entity—it is made of classes probably more profoundly divided than ever in this century. Most of the greatest injustices against workers are committed by the wealthy bankers in civil society who squeeze out exorbitant interest payments on internal debt; by landlords who throw peasants off the land; and by industrial capitalists who exhaust workers at starvation wages in sweatshops. By talking about "civil society," NGOers obscure the profound class division, class exploitation and class struggle that polarizes contemporary "civil society." Although analytically useless and obfuscating, the concept of "civil society" facilitates NGO collaboration with capitalists who finance their institutes and allow them to orient their projects and followers into subordinate relations with the big business interests that direct the neoliberal economies. In addition, not infrequently the NGOers' "civil society" rhetoric is a ploy to attack comprehensive public programs and state institutions that deliver social services. The NGOers side with big business's "anti-statist" rhetoric—one in the name of "civil society," the other in the name of the "market"—to reallocate state resources. The capitalists' "anti-statism" is used to increase public funds to subsidize exports and financial bailouts, while the NGOers try to grab a junior share via "subcontracts" to deliver inferior services to fewer recipients.

Contrary to the NGOers' image of themselves as innovative grass roots leaders, they are in reality grass roots reactionaries who complement the work of the IMF by pushing privatization "from below" and demobilizing popular movements, thus undermining resistance.

The ubiquitous NGOs thus present the Left with a serious challenge that requires critical political analysis of their origins, structure and ideology.

Origin, Structure and Ideology of the NGOs

NGOs appear to have a contradictory role in politics. On the one hand, they criticize dictatorships and human rights violations. On the other hand, they compete with radical socio-political movements, attempting to channel popular movements into collaborative relations with dominant neoliberal elites. In reality, these political orientations are not so contradictory as they appear.

Surveying the growth and proliferation of NGOs over the past quarter of a century, we find that NGOs emerged in three sets of circumstances. They emerged, first of all, as a safe haven during dictatorships where dissident intellectuals could pursue the issue of human rights violations and organize "survival strategies" for victims of harsh austerity programs. These humanitarian NGOs, however, were careful not to denounce U.S. and European complicity in local human rights violations or question emerging "free market" policies that impoverished the masses. Thus the NGOers were strategically placed as "democrats" who would be available as political replacements for local ruling classes and imperial policy-makers when repressive rulers began to be seriously challenged by popular mass movements. Western funding of the NGOs as critics was like buying insurance in case the incumbent reactionaries faltered. This was the case with the "critical" NGOs that appeared during the Marcos regime in the Philippines, the Pinochet regime in Chile, the Park dictatorship in Korea, etc.

The real mushrooming of NGOS has occurred in times of rising mass movements that challenge imperial hegemony. The growth of radical socio-political movements and struggles has provided a lucrative commodity which ex-radical and pseudo-popular intellectuals have been able to sell to interested, concerned and well-financed private and public foundations closely tied with European and U.S. TNCs and governments. The funders have been interested in social science intelligence like the "propensity for violence in urban slum areas" (an NGO project in Chile during the mass uprisings of 1983–86), the capacity of NGOers to raid popular communities and direct energy towards self-help projects instead of social transformations, and the introduction of class-collaborationist rhetoric packaged as "new identity discourses" that would discredit and isolate revolutionary activists.

Popular revolts loosened the purse strings of overseas agencies, and millions of dollars poured into Indonesia, Thailand and Peru in the seventies; into Nicaragua, Chile and the Philippines in the eighties; and into El Salvador, Guatemala and Korea in the nineties. The NGOers were essentially there to "put out the fires." Under the guise of constructive projects, they argued against engaging in ideological movements, thus effectively using foreign funds to recruit local leaders, send them to overseas conferences and encourage local groups to adapt to the reality of neoliberalism.

As outside money became available, NGOs proliferated, dividing communities into warring fiefdoms fighting for pieces of the action. Each "grass roots activist" cornered a new segment of the poor (women, young people from minorities, etc.) to set up a new NGO and take the pilgrimage to Amsterdam, Stockholm, etc. to "market" their project, activity or constituency and finance their centre—and their careers.

The third circumstance in which NGOs have multiplied has been during the frequent and deepening economic crises provoked by free market capitalism. Intellectuals, academics and professionals saw jobs disappear or salaries decline as budget cuts took hold, so a second job became a necessity. NGOs became a job placement agency, and consultancies became a safety net for potentially downwardly mobile intellectuals willing to spout the civil society–free market alternative development line and carry on collaborative policies with neoliberal regimes and international financial institutions. When millions lose their jobs and poverty spreads to significant portions of the population, NGOs engage in preventative action: they focus on "survival strategies," not general strikes; and they organize soup kitchens, not mass demonstrations against food hoarders, neoliberal regimes or U.S. imperialism.

NGOs may have initially had a vaguely "progressive" tincture during so-called "democratic transitions" when the old order was crumbling, corrupt rulers were losing control and popular struggles were advancing. The NGOs become the vehicle for *transactions* between old regimes and conservative electoral politicians. The NGOs used their grass roots rhetoric, organizational resources and status as "democratic" human rights advocates to channel popular support behind politicians and parties that confined the transition to legal-political reforms, not socio-economic changes. NGOs demobilized the populace and fragmented the movements. In every country that experienced an "electoral transaction" in the 1980s and 1990s, from Chile to the Philippines to South Korea and beyond, NGOs have played an important role in rounding up votes for regimes which continued or even deepened the socio-economic status quo. In exchange, many ex-NGOers ended up running government agencies or even becoming government ministers in portfolios with popular-sounding titles (women rights, citizen participation, popular power, etc.).

The reactionary political role of NGOs has been built into the very structures upon which they are organized.

NGO Structures: Internally Elitist and Externally Servile

In reality NGOs are not "non-governmental" organizations. They receive funds from overseas governments, work as private subcontractors for local governments and/or are subsidized by corporate-funded private foundations with close working relations with the state. Frequently they openly collaborate with governmental agencies at home or overseas. Their programs are not account-able to local people but to overseas donors who "review" and "oversee" the performance of the NGOs according to their own criteria and interests. NGO officials are self-appointed and one of their key tasks is to design proposals that will secure funding. In many cases this requires NGO leaders to find out the issues that most interest Western funding elites and to shape proposals accordingly. Thus, in the 1980s, NGO funds were available to study and provide political proposals on "governability" and "democratic transitions," reflecting the con-cerns of the imperialist powers that the fall of dictatorships would not lead to "ungovernability"—namely, to mass movements that might deepen the strug-gle and transform the social system. The NGOs, despite their democratic, grass roots rhetoric, are hierarchical—with the director in total control of projects, hiring and firing, as well as of deciding who gets their way paid to international conferences. The "grass roots" are essentially the objects of this hierarchy; rarely do they see the money that "their" NGO shovels in, nor do they get to travel abroad or draw the salaries and perks of their "grass roots" leaders. More important, none of these decisions are ever voted on. At best, after the deals have been cooked by the director and the overseas funders, the NGO staff will call a meeting of "grass roots activists" for the poor to approve the project. In most cases the NGOs are not even membership organizations but a self-appointed elite which, under the pretence of being "resource people" for popular movements, in fact, competes with and undermines them. In this sense, NGOs undermine democracy by taking social programs and public debate out of the hands of the local people and their elected natural leaders and creating dependence on non-elected overseas officials and their anointed local officials.

NGOs foster a new type of cultural and economic colonialism—under the guise of a new internationalism. Hundreds of individuals sit in front of high-powered PCs exchanging manifestos, proposals and invitations to international conferences with each other. They then meet in well-furnished conference halls to discuss the latest struggles and offerings with their "social base"—the paid staff—who then pass on the proposals to the "masses" through flyers and "bulletins." When overseas funders show up, they are taken on "exposure tours" to showcase projects where the poor are helping themselves and to talk with successful micro-entrepreneurs (omitting the majority, who fail the first year).

The way this new colonialism works is not difficult to decipher. Projects are designed based on the guidelines and priorities of the imperial centres and their institutions. They are then "sold" to the communities. Evaluations are done by and for the imperial institutions. Shifts of funding priorities or bad evaluations result in the dumping of groups, communities, farmers and co-operatives. Everybody is increasingly disciplined to comply with the donors' demands and their project evaluators. The NGO directors, as the new viceroys, supervise the proper use of funds and ensure conformity with the goals, values and ideology of the donors.

NGOs versus Radical Socio-Political Movements

NGOs emphasize projects, not movements. They "mobilize" people to produce at the margins, not to struggle to control the basic means of production and wealth. They focus on the technical and financial-assistance aspects of projects, not on structural conditions that shape the everyday lives of people. The NGOs co-opt the language of the Left—"popular power," "empowerment," "gender equality," "sustainable development," "bottom-up leadership," etc. The problem is that this language is linked to a framework of collaboration with donors and government agencies committed to non-confrontational politics. The local nature of NGO activity means that "empowerment" never goes beyond influencing small areas of social life with limited resources, always within conditions permitted by the neoliberal state and macroeconomy.

The NGOs and their professional staff directly compete with socio-political movements for influence among the poor, women, racially excluded, etc. Their ideology and practices divert attention away from the sources of and solutions to poverty (looking downward and inward, instead of upward and outward). To speak of *microenterprises*, instead of the end of exploitation by overseas banks, as the solution to poverty is based on the false notion that the main problem is one of individual initiative rather than of transference of income overseas. The NGOs' "aid" affects small sectors of the population, setting up competition between communities for scarce resources, generating insidious distinctions and inter- and intra-community rivalries, and undermining class solidarity. The same is true among professionals: each sets up their NGO to solicit overseas funds. They compete by presenting proposals closer to the liking of the overseas donors, for lower prices, while claiming to speak for more followers. The net effect is a proliferation of NGOs that fragment poor communities into sectoral and subsectoral groupings unable to see the larger social picture that afflicts them and even less able to unite in struggle against the system.

Recent experience also demonstrates that foreign donors finance projects during "crises"—political and social challenges to the status quo. Once the movements have ebbed, they shift funding to NGO/regime "collaboration," fitting NGO projects into the neoliberal agenda. Economic development compatible with the "free market" rather than social organization for social change becomes the dominant item on the funding agenda.

The structure and nature of NGOs, with their "apolitical" posture and their focus on self-help, depoliticize and demobilize the poor. They reinforce the electoral processes encouraged by the neoliberal parties and mass media. Political education about the nature of imperialism, the class basis of neoliberalism and the class struggle between exporters and temporary workers are avoided. Instead the NGOs discuss "the excluded," the "powerless," "extreme poverty" and "gender or racial discrimination," without moving beyond the superficial symptoms to engage the social system that has produced these conditions. Incorporating the poor into the neoliberal economy through purely "private voluntary action," the NGOs create a political world where the appearance of solidarity and social action cloaks a conservative conformity with the international and national power structure.

It is no coincidence that, as NGOs have become dominant in certain regions, independent class political action has declined and neoliberalism has gone uncontested. The bottom line is that the growth of NGOs coincides with increased funding from neoliberals and the deepening of poverty everywhere. Despite its claims of many local successes, the overall power of neoliberalism stands unchallenged and the NGOs increasingly search for niches in the interstices of power.

The problem of formulating alternatives has been hindered in another way. Many of the former leaders of guerrilla and social movements, trade unions and popular women's organizations have been co-opted by the NGOs. The offer is tempting: higher pay (occasionally in hard currency), prestige and recognition by overseas donors, conferences and networks abroad, office staff and relative security from repression. In contrast, socio-political movements offer few material benefits but greater respect and independence and, more importantly, the freedom to challenge the political and economic system. The NGOs and their overseas banking supporters (the Inter-American Bank, the Asian Bank, the World Bank) publish newsletters featuring the success stories of micro-enterprises and other self-help projects, without mentioning the high rates of failure as popular consumption declines, low-price imports flood the market and interest rates spiral—as in the case of Brazil and Indonesia in the 1990s.

Even the "successes" affect only a small fraction of the total poor and succeed only to the degree that others cannot enter into the same market. The propaganda value of individual micro-enterprise success, however, is important in fostering the illusion that neoliberalism is a popular phenomenon. Frequent violent mass outbursts in regions of micro-enterprise promotion suggest that their ideology is not hegemonic and the NGOs have not yet displaced independent class movements.

NGO ideology depends heavily on essentialist identity politics, engaging in a rather dishonest polemic with radical movements that are based on class analysis. They start from the false assumption that class analysis is "reductionist," overlooking the extensive debates and discussions within Marxism on issues of race, ethnicity and gender equality and avoiding the more serious criticism that identities themselves are clearly and profoundly divided by class differences. Take, for example, the Chilean or Indian feminist living in a plush suburb and drawing a salary fifteen to twenty times that of her domestic servant who works six days a week. Class differences within gender determine housing, living standards, health, educational opportunities and who appropriates surplus value. Yet the great majority of NGOs operate on the basis of identity politics and argue that this is the basic point of departure for the new, post-modern politics. Identity politics does not challenge the male-dominated elite world of IMF privatization, multinational corporations and local landlords. Rather, it focuses on "patriarchy" in the household, family violence, divorce, family planning, etc. In other words, it fights for gender equality within the micro-world of exploited peoples in which the exploited and impoverished male worker or peasant emerges as the main villain. While no one should support gender exploitation or discrimination at any level, the feminist NGOs do a gross disservice to working women by subordinating them to the greater exploitation of sweatshops which benefit upper-class men *and* women, rent-collecting male and female landlords, and CEOs of both sexes. The reason the feminist NGOs ignore the "big picture" and focus on local issues and personal politics is because billions of dollars flow annually in that direction. If feminist NGOs began to engage in land occupations with men and women landless workers in Brazil, Indonesia, Thailand or the Philippines, or if they joined in general strikes of mainly female low-paid rural school teachers against structural adjustment policies, the NGO spigot would be turned off by their imperial donors. Better to beat up on the local patriarch scratching out an existence in an isolated village in Luzon.

Class Solidarity versus NGO Solidarity with Foreign Donors
The word "solidarity" has been so abused that in many contexts it has lost meaning. The term "solidarity" for NGOers includes foreign aid channelled to any designated "impoverished" group. "Research" or "popular education" of the poor by professionals is called "solidarity." In many ways the hierarchical structures and the forms of transmission of "aid" and "training" resemble 19th-century charity, and the promoters are not very different from Christian missionaries.

NGOers emphasize "self-help" in attacking the "paternalism and dependence" of the state. In this competition among NGOs to capture the victims of neoliberalism, they receive important subsidies from their counterparts in Europe and the U.S. The self-help ideology emphasizes the replacement of public employees with volunteers and upwardly mobile professionals contracted on a temporary basis. The basic philosophy of the NGOs is to transform "solidarity" into collaboration and subordination to the macroeconomy of neoliberalism by focusing attention away from the state resources of the wealthy classes and towards the *self-exploitation of the poor*.

In contrast, Marxism emphasizes class solidarity *within* the class and the solidarity of oppressed groups (women, people of colour) *against* their foreign and domestic exploiters. The major focus is *not* on the donations that divide classes and pacify small groups for a limited time. The Marxist concept of solidarity focuses on the common action of the same members of the class, sharing their common economic predicament and struggling for collective improvement. It involves intellectuals who write and speak for the social movements in struggle and who are committed to sharing the same political consequences. The concept of solidarity is linked to "organic" intellectuals who are basically part of the movement, the resource people providing analysis and education for class struggle and taking the same political risks in direct action. In contrast, the NGOers are embedded in the world of institutions, academic seminars, foreign foundations and international conferences that speak a language understood only by those "initiated" into the subjectivist cult of essentialist identity. Marxists view solidarity as sharing the risks of class political movements, not as being outside commentators who raise questions and defend nothing. The main object for the NGOers is "getting" foreign funding for their "project." The main issue for Marxists is the *process* of political struggle and education in securing social transformation. The movement was everything, a means of raising consciousness of the need for societal change and to construct political power in the service of improving conditions for the great majority. For NGOers, "solidarity" is divorced from the general objective of liberation. It is merely a way of bringing people together to attend a job retraining seminar or to build a latrine. For Marxists, the solidarity of a collective struggle contains the seeds of the future democratic collectivist society. This larger vision or its absence is what gives the different conceptions of solidarity their distinct meanings.

Class Struggle and Cooperation

NGOers frequently write of the "cooperation" of everyone, near and far, without delving too profoundly into the price and conditions for securing the cooperation of neoliberal regimes and overseas funding agencies. Class struggle is viewed as an atavism to a past that no longer exists. Today we are told "the poor" are intent on building a new life. They are fed up with traditional politics, ideologies and politicians. So far, so good. The problem is that the NGOers are less forthcoming in describing their own roles as mediators and brokers, hustling funds from overseas. Concentration of income and the growth of inequalities are greater than ever, after years of preaching cooperation, micro-enterprises and self-help. Today banks like the World Bank fund the export agro-businesses that exploit and poison millions of farm labourers while providing funds to finance microprojects. The role of the NGOs in the microprojects is to neutralize political opposition at the bottom while neoliberalism is promoted at the top. The ideology of cooperation links the poor *through the NGOs* to the neoliberals at the top.

Intellectually the NGOs are intellectual policemen who define "acceptable" research, distribute research funds and filter out topics and perspectives that project a class analysis and struggle perspective. Marxists are excluded from the conferences and stigmatized as "ideologues," while NGOers present themselves as "social scientists." Control of intellectual fashion, publications, conferences and research funds provides post-Marxists with an important power base, but one ultimately dependent on avoiding conflict with their external funding patrons.

Critical Marxist intellectuals draw their strength from the fact that their ideas resonate with evolving social realities. The polarization of classes and the violent confrontations are growing, as their theories would predict. It is from this perspective that Marxists are tactically weak while strategically strong *vis-à-vis* the NGOs.

Alternative NGOs

One could argue that there are a great many different types of NGOs and that many do criticize and organize against adjustment policies, the IMF, debt payments, etc. and that it is unfair to lump them all in the same bag. There is a grain of truth in this, but this position belies a more fundamental issue. Most peasant leaders from Asia and Latin America that we have spoken to complain bitterly of the divisive and elitist roles that even the "progressive" NGOs play: the NGOs want to subordinate the peasant leaders to their organizations and to lead and speak for the poor. They do not accept subordinate roles. Progressive NGOs use peasants and the poor for their research projects and benefit from their publication. Nothing comes back to the movements, not even copies of the studies done in their name! Moreover, peasant leaders ask why the NGOs never risk their necks after their educational seminars? Why do they not study the rich and powerful? Why us?

Even conceding that within "progressive NGOs" there are minorities that function as "resource" people to radical socio-political movements, the fact is that the people receive only a tiny fraction of the funds that go to the NGO. Furthermore, the great mass of NGOs fit the description outlined above. It is up to the few exceptions to prove otherwise. A major step forward for "progressive NGOs" is to systematically criticize and critique the ties of their colleagues with imperialism and its local clients, their ideology of adaptation to neoliberalism, and their authoritarian and elitist structures. Then it would be useful for them to tell their Western counterpart NGOs to get out of the foundation/government networks and go back to organizing and educating their own people in Europe and North America to form socio-political movements that can challenge the dominant regimes and parties that serve the banks and the TNCs.

In other words, the NGOs should stop being NGOs and convert themselves into members of socio-political movements. That is the best way to avoid being lumped with the tens of thousands of NGOs that feed at the donors' trough.

Conclusion: Towards a Theory of NGOs

In structural terms the proliferation of NGOs reflects the emergence of a new petit bourgeoisie as distinct from the "old" shopkeepers, free professionals and the "new" public employee groups. This subcontracted sector is closer to the earlier "comprador" bourgeoisie insofar as it produces no tangible commodities but serves to link imperial enterprises with local petty commodity producers engaged in micro-enterprises. This new petit bourgeoisie—at least its "middle-age variants"—is marked by the fact that many are ex-Marxists who bring a "popular rhetoric" and in some cases an elitist, "vanguardist" conception to their organizations. Situated without property or a fixed position in the state apparatus, this new class depends heavily on external funding agencies to reproduce itself. Given its popular constituency, however, it has to combine an anti-Marxist and anti-statist appeal with populist rhetoric—hence the concoction of the "third way" and "civil society" notions, which are sufficiently ambiguous to cover both bases. This new petit bourgeoisie thrives on international gatherings as a main prop of its existence, lacking solid organic support within the country. "Globalist" rhetoric provides a cover for a kind of ersatz "internationalism" devoid of anti-imperialist commitments. In short, this new petit bourgeoisie forms the "radical wing" of the neoliberal establishment.

Politically the NGOs fit into the new thinking of imperialist strategists. While the IMF, World Bank and TNCs work with domestic elites at the top to pillage the economy, the NGOs engage in a complementary activity at the bottom, neutralizing and fragmenting the burgeoning discontent that results from the savaging of the economy. Just as imperialism engages in a two-pronged macro- and microstrategy of exploitation and containment, radical movements must develop a two-pronged anti-imperialist strategy.

The NGOs have co-opted most of those who used to be the "free floating" intellectuals who would abandon their class origins and join popular movements. The result is a temporary gap between the profound crises of capitalism (depressions in Asia and Latin America, collapse in the ex-USSR) and the absence of significant organized revolutionary movements—with the exception of Brazil, Colombia and perhaps South Korea. The fundamental question is whether a new generation of organic intellectuals can emerge from these radical social movements, avoid the NGO temptation and become integral members of the next revolutionary wave.

Chapter 9

The U.S. Empire and Narco-Capitalism

Throughout the history of imperial expansion, spokesmen for empires have sought to justify the conquest of peoples and exploitation of resources by citing "lofty principles." In the 19th century, the English described the pillage of Asia and Africa as part of the "White man's burden" to bring civilization to the "dark peoples." The French argued that *their* conquest was motivated by a desire to bring the fruits of French culture to backward societies.

In the 20th century, with the rise of U.S. imperial conquests, particularly in the Western Hemisphere, a similar "high moral tone" was adopted to justify U.S. military intervention in defense of its bankers in Santa Domingo, banana companies in Central America and oil monopolies in Mexico. These interventions were justified as "defending order and stability" and "protecting the lives of American citizens." With the advent of the Mexican Revolution, President Woodrow Wilson justified U.S. imperial intervention in the name of "democracy" and "order." After the Russian Revolution, Washington devised a new pretext for intervention—"anti-Communism" and the "Red menace." With the end of the Cold War and the demise of Soviet Communism, Washington turned towards the "narcotic threat" to justify its intervention and control of security policies and officials in Latin America.

The question arises: Why does Washington have to hide the real economic, political and military motivations for its interventions behind high moral principles? Basically, it is because the U.S. is an imperial democracy and moral rhetoric is used to sway or neutralize domestic public opinion. While U.S. foreign policy is largely directed towards serving the TNCs, politicians who apply that policy require votes. Hence the double discourse of U.S. policy: the practical pursuit of domination for the economic elite and the moralistic rhetoric used to secure legitimacy from the electorate. Like all imperialist powers, Washington presents its violent interventions as measures intended to defend "national security." Thus the financial and political support of the mercenary, terrorist Contras in Nicaragua and the genocidal militaries in Guatemala and El Salvador was justified on grounds of "national security"—as if poor Indians and peasants were capable of threatening an invasion of the U.S. Of course, the reality was different. The peoples and nations of Central America were not only threatened but also assaulted by Washington's interventionist policies. The end of the Cold War was a signal for Washington to intensify its empire-building project. The Gulf War, the invasion of Panama, the little war in Somalia, the expansion of NATO into Eastern Europe and the projection of a "New World Order" under U.S. hegemony were all part of this effort to create a global empire.

Of course, European and Japanese competitors did not easily accept subordination to the U.S. And in Latin America, major socio-political struggles erupted in defiance of the attempt to impose a New World Order based on an aggressive capitalism called "neoliberalism." In Colombia, Mexico and Peru, peasant-guerrilla movements were active; in Bolivia, Paraguay, Ecuador and Brazil, significant peasant movements emerged. In Venezuela and Argentina, urban uprisings and trade union strikes gained popular support. The threat from below to the U.S.-backed neoliberal elite consensus led Washington to seek a new ideology to support its intervention through the military and police. The "fight against narco-trafficking" has served Washington's empire-building purposes. First, it has disguised Washington's repressive and exploitative policies behind a high moral purpose, and thus domestic public opinion has been neutralized. Second, the fight against narco-traffickers has allowed Washington to penetrate the internal security forces of Latin America and establish its own political agenda. Third, the "narco-traffic war" has allowed Washington to have direct access to the society in order to push its economic and counter-insurgency agenda. By focusing the fight against narco-traffic towards Latin America and towards the countryside, Washington has been able to aim blows against real or potential social revolutionary movements. If Washington's leaders were truly serious about drug-trafficking issues, it would instead focus internally, on the large international banks that launder most of the drug money; they would arrest corrupt police who take drug bribes; they would invest more in anti-drug education; and they would provide decent jobs for the low-paid, marginal groups of workers who become drug dealers. The decision to look overseas and downward, instead of inward and upward, is a political choice, an imperial requirement.

Any objective analysis of drug trafficking would have to conclude that the issue is essentially a "market," or "demand," problem. Fundamentally it is an internal problem of the U.S. and its government, society, economy and cultural system. While that demand exists there will be a supply. The problem is deeply rooted in U.S. society, a fragmented social environment in which drug-induced escapism often becomes a way of life. The lack of meaningful employment, social solidarity and political mechanisms to connect personal malaise with public expression have led many U.S. citizens to seek and use drugs.

The "externalization" of the drug problem has a double value for Washington: it deflects a deep critique of U.S. society and economy, and it provides a pretext for the continuous manipulation of Latin politics, politicians and military officials.

The most intrusive method is the issue of "certification." Washington presumes the power to evaluate, judge and punish regimes according to its criteria of compliance in the war against drugs. Those officials who are most responsive to Washington's directives are "certified," but those who reject

Washington's intrusion are labelled "uncooperative" or stigmatized as "drug collaborators." The "drug war" directed from Washington fortifies U.S. imperial claims of "extra-territoriality," thus violating the legitimate national boundaries of Latin countries. The application of the Helms-Burton law is another expression of the claim to "extra-territoriality." Washington regards U.S. law as the law of the planet.

The drug war orchestrated from Washington thus goes beyond "neocolonialism" towards a return to colonial domination.

The U.S. and the New Colonialism

The attempt by the U.S. government to make its own legislation the supreme law of the planet reflects the growing centrality of imperial interests in defining its foreign policy. This imposition comes in the context of de facto U.S. penetration of the higher echelons of the executive, military and intelligence apparatuses of Latin American states. While most commentators have criticized the financial controls exercised by U.S. banks, particularly through the debt crisis, and other writers cite the pervasive influence exercised by the U.S. through its shared power in the World Bank and IMF, few analysts have combined these powerful economic levers with the organized Latin American military forces under U.S. command, a goal set by Washington in the 1960s and 1970s but unattainable until the 1990s. In Mexico, Bolivia and Colombia, the U.S. ambassadors and State Department routinely dictate which military officials and cabinet ministers are "acceptable" (certified) and which are to be dismissed as non-cooperative; and, as a matter of routine, Latin executive officials comply with U.S. demands. In all of these countries, U.S. blacklists result in potential appointees to public office being withdrawn, officers being retired and a quickening of the implementation of U.S. policies, whether towards drug eradication, repression of coca-producing peasants or expeditious payment of debt service.

The strengthening of U.S. control over Latin American internal security affairs is paralleled by Washington's pressure on Latin governments to strengthen their repressive internal police and military forces. Even at the tactical level, FBI and U.S. DEA officials direct investigations and demand that Latin officials provide intelligence. U.S. officials also oversee operations. A visit to Chapare disabuses any observer of the sovereignty of the Bolivian state. Even everyday operational activities are overseen by the dozen or so DEA officials stationed there. In Chapare and in the Upper Husallaga Valley of Peru, DEA officials make no effort to disguise who is in charge of directing operations. And most generals and presidents are very conscious of the fact that being labelled by the U.S. as a "drug trafficker" could cost them their position. The formidable influence at the presidential level is evident in the eagerness of President Samper to intensify eradication of peasant crops in Colombia and of Mexico's president to make debt payments in advance despite the deepening impoverishment of millions of his fellow citizens.

Washington's "war on drugs" is directed towards increasing U.S. power in Latin America. The use of drug money laundered through U.S. banks finances Washington's trade imbalances, while the drug war increases Washington's general influence over economic policy, allowing U.S.-based TNCs to buy Latin American public enterprises at scandalously low prices and to penetrate markets. All the major, lucrative publicly owned petroleum companies are on the selling block—in Brazil, Mexico, Venezuela, Bolivia, etc. *Maquiladores* and other cheap labour zones are becoming emblematic of Washington's economic strategy for Latin America's "export growth." Between 1983 and 1993, U.S. media services exports increased by 138 percent compared to total service exports, which grew 90 percent. U.S. media goods exports increased 201 percent, while total goods exports increased 110 percent. U.S. corporations are active in real estate as well as retail outlets and shopping malls. U.S.-sponsored militarization is directed at safeguarding the pillage of Latin America. The New Imperialism is not "neocolonial" in form; it is direct executive control exercised through a routine command structure via Latin American executive officials evaluated according to U.S. criteria of responsibility and effectiveness.

The New Imperialism attempts to strengthen its global position through a more intensified exploitation of the Latin economies. In the process, it has established two new vehicles for containing unrest: an ideology and an organizational network. The New Imperialism promotes the ideology of "globalization" and the network of non-profit NGOs. The ideology mystifies intellectuals into submission before the "inevitable wave of the future," while the organizational network provides intellectuals with a means to dismantle the national welfare state.

Nonetheless, the scope and depth of imperial penetration continue to undermine an ever-widening circle of social classes—bankrupt medium and small businesspeople, downwardly mobile public employees, displaced peasants, and temporary or low-paid factory workers. Even some intellectuals have begun to revive the notion of imperialism as a central concept for analysis and politics. But this latter move is tentative and confined to very limited circles. The centrepiece of opposition to U.S. imperial ambitions is located in the countryside: in the Landless Workers Movement (MST) in Brazil; the Zapatistas in Chiapas, the Revolutionary Popular Army (EPR) in Guerrero and the peasant movements in Oaxaca in Mexico. The most significant opposition however, is found in Colombia. The influence of FARC, with its twenty thousand guerrillas, extends over six hundred of the twelve hundred municipalities of the country.

The reason the U.S. has concentrated its anti-drug campaign in Colombia is because Washington is fearful that this Latin American nation could become the second Vietnam. Washington's demand that President Samper wage an all-out anti-drug war is related to the growing influence of FARC among the peasantry and its growing proximity to the capital city of Bogota. After thirty years of struggle, FARC has consolidated its base and is now capable of cutting highways only forty miles from the capital.

Thus Washington's anti-drug war is deeply intertwined with its counter-revolutionary politics: its military aid is mainly directed towards destroying peasant links to the FARC. By eradicating coca, promoting cheap imports and repressing peasant organizations, the U.S. and the Colombian military hope to drive the peasantry out of the countryside and isolate the guerrillas. The results of this policy have been contradictory; while some peasants flee from the violence of the paramilitary forces, others join the guerrillas. Washington's policy of polarizing Colombian society has a very profound and destructive effect on its social fabric.

The expansion of the new peasant movements is intimately related to internal transformations of the peasantry (politically, culturally and economically) and their dialectical resistance to the deepening encroachment of imperial demands. The "peasantry" today are market-oriented and also see themselves as workers. Access to credit, markets and technical aid for small producers is linked to their increasing class conditions as wage workers. The displacement of self-taught or formally educated peasants linked to modern urban centres creates a new peasantry with modern organizational and media skills that can link agricultural activities with urban styles of class combat.

It would be a serious mistake to dismiss contemporary peasant movements as the last gasp of rebellion before they disappear from the map. The persistence and rootedness of the peasantry, and the increasing displacement of urban workers, high urban crime and decline of social services has narrowed the gap between countryside and city. As movements realize land takeovers and build communities, there could be a stabilization if not reversal of the rural-to-urban migration. There is no inherent historical logic that compels the demographic change—in large part it is a political question. The core regions affected by imperial penetration are the countryside via the subordination of the state to imperial obligations: interest payments, the repression of coca farmers, and the subsidization of agro-export conglomerates all are state-directed.

The fundamental dynamics of resistance arise with the "end products" of imperial state exploitation. And it is at that end of the chain that the reverse process of transformation is occurring.

The process of empire-building is not a result of conjunctural events or particular politics but reflects deep structures and processes built into the productive system and profit balances of major institutions at the pinnacle of the U.S. economic system. Today, "the Empire" is flourishing as never before. Conditions for mineral appropriation, access to markets, low labour costs and gaining influence over other governments and militaries have never been better. The space for "reforms" is almost non-existent within the imperial formula of free markets, electoral regimes and military control. The opposite dialectical pole, however, is the decay of urban middle-sector mediating forces and the rapid accumulation of downwardly mobile workers and public employees moving towards direct social action. It is in this ambience of imperial excesses, unprecedented accumulation of wealth and massive degradation of labour that the new poles of social action in the countryside are gaining national political influence and prominence.

The fundamental turn from agrarian issues towards social transformation is built around the renewal of a socialist praxis that links cultural autonomy and small-scale production with control over the strategic heights of the economy. That can only become a reality when socialism becomes integrated into endogenous cultural and social practices and if basic producers are infused with the new values of gender equality and environmental compatibility. The Empire has struck and torn asunder the economic, cultural and political fabric of Latin American societies. It has assimilated a few and exploited the many.

But now the Left has struck back. From the villages of Colombia and Bolivia, and from the rural squatter settlements of Brazil, to the jungles of Mexico, a new movement is taking hold, writing its own history and practising its own theory.

Conclusion

From opposite ends of the political and economic spectrum, two dynamic forces are coming into an increasing confrontation: peasants versus the U.S. empire. The dynamic behind the U.S. empire is built around internal economic imperatives and external political-military opportunities. The expansion of the new peasant movements is centred on economic, cultural and social dynamics that have transformed "isolated peasants" into a cohesive, class-conscious and revolutionary force.

The pattern of empire-building is built around rentier extraction of interest payments, pillage of natural resources and large-scale transfer of public property to TNCs. Together these forces have put tremendous pressure on the Latin American social system to intensify the extraction of unpaid labour time from the direct producers—workers and peasants. In this process of extraction and appropriation the provinces and the rural areas have been especially hard hit, given that the local power structure is located in the cities. This intensification of exploitation has been accompanied by a penetration of cultural commodities that furthers the fragmentation and alienation of uprooted urban groups. Exploitation and fragmentation accompany the imperial-sponsored circulation of "market ideologies" through NGOs and intellectual think-tanks, driving a wedge between middle-class professionals/intellectuals and the working class. The imperial hegemonic bloc is strengthened by the "overdetermined" nature of U.S. influence on military and police institutions, largely through anti-narcotic campaigns.

U.S. empire-building is driven by the dependence of the largest U.S. TNCs on overseas profits and of the U.S. economy on favourable accounts with Latin America to compensate for deficits with Asia and Germany. The "anti-drug campaign" is at the centre of Washington's imperial project. But in Colombia it confronts a serious challenge from peasant mobilization and revolutionary guerrilla groups.

Chapter 10

The Practice of U.S. Hegemony:
Right-Wing Strategy in Latin America

Though a great deal has been written about leftist strategies over the past several decades, little attention has been given to right-wing strategies. A comprehensive survey of right-wing forms of struggle is essential for understanding the Left, because the strategies of the two antagonists are mutually interrelated. For example, the emergence of armed struggle on the left in the 1960s and 1970s was closely related to the Right's shift towards military rule and violent forms of governance.

When discussing right-wing strategy it is important to take note of several issues. First, the Right uses various forms of struggle (violent, electoral, mass protest), frequently combining them. Second, the strategies and tactics of the Right shift over time depending on circumstances. For example, it resorts to violence when losing power and becomes oriented towards elections when no serious challenge is imminent. Third, the Right has internal divisions, and its different sectors engage in different forms of struggle. Under serious threat (a challenge to capitalist property relations), they combine forces to defeat their common enemies. Fourth, right-wing strategies vary according to whether the Right exercises state power or is in opposition. In opposition it may encourage and use democratic slogans; in power it frequently resorts to repression of mass movements. Finally, it is important to analyze the international, national, class and institutional alliances of the Right, and its diverse sectors at different political conjunctures. Taking these assumptions into account, it is useful to analyze right-wing strategy as it evolved from the 1960s to the year 2000.

Right-Wing Power: An Historical Perspective
While in the 1990s right-wing politics were proactive in setting the parameters for political debate and action, this was not always the case. In the 1970s the Right was on the defensive and its policies were reactive. It engaged in a rearguard action in the face of the advance of the Left. While today the Right acts from state power against Left opposition in civil society, in the 1960s and early 1970s (with the exception of Brazil), the Right acted from "civil society" against national, popular and socialist regimes.

Contemporary class conflict has its origins in the period subsequent to World War II. After the defeat of fascism and the rising tide of anti-colonial revolutions in Asia and Africa, the advance of Communism in China and Eastern Europe and social democracy (and Communism) in Western Europe,

Latin America experienced an upsurge of Left-nationalist and populist regimes and movements. In Venezuela, Chile, Guatemala, Colombia, Argentina and Brazil, populist and social democratic governments came to power. These regimes favoured redistributing wealth, increasing social welfare and diverting resources from the landowning/mining classes to the urban-industrial complex. The Right responded by organizing a counterattack on two levels: by (1) forming civilian "democratic" coalitions and (2) fomenting military coups. The right-wing counteroffensive of the late 1940s and 1950s coincided with the U.S.-orchestrated Cold War. The Right "legitimated" its liberal export strategy and class interests under the guise of "anti-Communism."

In the Caribbean (Cuba, Dominican Republic and Haiti), Central America (Guatemala) and Latin America (Venezuela, Peru) the Right was able to unite the landowners and the mining and commercial bourgeoisie with the backing of U.S. multinational banks and businesses. The principal political instrument was military dictatorial regimes (Somoza, Duvalier, Batista, Odria, Jimenez).

In South America (Brazil, Argentina, Uruguay and Chile) the Right formed electoral alliances with the emerging industrial bourgeoisie around the banner of "developmentalism" that opened space for populists while relegating the Left to a marginal position. The Right engaged in electoral struggles based on its dominance over rural areas and its urban alliances with the bourgeoisie. The bourgeoisie-landlord alliance combined protection of industry and the stimulation of primary exports. By the end of the 1950s a second "wave" of popular mobilization took place, led by the Cuban Revolution.

The Reformist Experiment
Between 1960 and 1964 the Right divided between a populist sector that attempted to "co-opt" the reform agenda of the revolutionary Left and a "hard Right" that aligned with the military and the conservative hierarchy of the Church.

In Brazil, Chile, Peru and Venezuela the populist Right, in alliance with the U.S., pushed for agrarian reforms to divide the peasants from the radicalized working classes and urban poor. Under tutelage from the U.S., reform was combined with physical repression in the form of "counter-insurgency." The bourgeoisie combined electoral and armed struggle. Under pressure from the Left and the popular movements, the "populist sectors" of the Right began to lose control of the "reform process." Increasingly the "hard Right" began to organize paramilitary groups, mass protests and economic boycotts (disinvestment, lockouts). The "electoralist Right" increasingly abandoned its "populist alliance" and began to prepare covert armed action in alliance with the military and U.S. intelligence agencies.

The "reformist phase" of the Right ended in 1964 with the military coup in Brazil. Preceded by mass demonstrations in which it utilized its ties with the traditional Church, conservative mass media and civic associations, the Right fomented economic paralysis and socio-political polarization. In this context the "hard Right" allied with the military to launch the military coup.

The point is that the Right possesses an instrumental view of democracy. For the Right, the class character and orientation of the state determines its practice towards armed or electoral struggle.

The Brazilian Right's decision to take the road of armed struggle via a military coup set an example for the rest of Latin America. Military coups subsequently took place in Argentina (1966 and 1976), Bolivia (1971) and Chile (1973). The phase of right-wing electoral competition with the Left ended. The Right's inability to control the "reformist" process and its loss of electoral support strengthened the sectors oriented towards armed struggle. The Alliance for Progress announced by Kennedy was dead. The U.S. once again aligned itself with the "hard Right." In the ideological terms, the Right shifted from a democratic discourse to national security, from agrarian reform to export-oriented "modernization."

In countries in which the Right resorted to military rule (Brazil, Argentina, Bolivia, etc.), armed domination provoked a counter-response from the Left, and guerrilla movements emerged throughout the continent. In countries in which civilian rule continued (Chile, Uruguay), the process of social reform deepened and the Right radicalized its struggle through the business associations of civic groups, engaging in widespread economic sabotage.

Retreat and Reaction: The Right, 1970–76
The military coups of the 1960s and the reformist policies failed to stem the resurgence of popular struggles. Except in Brazil, the Right was unable to "contain" the electoral Left or limit the growing influence of extra-parliamentary movements. In Chile the Left won elections, in Argentina the nationalist populists returned to power, in Bolivia a popular assembly ruled the legislative branch, and a nationalist sector of the military ruled in Peru. The Right was temporarily in retreat.

The soft Right began to organize from the economy, through appeals to the middle class in the name of property, order, stability; organization of housewives; withdrawal of capital; and lockouts. The hard Right looked towards a definitive confrontation and began to knock on the doors of the military and accept CIA financing. The tactics varied from country to country, but the tendency towards combined legal and illegal approaches was clear. In Argentina and Chile the Right organized paramilitary groups to assassinate political opponents; business groups and professionals were organized to resist progressive labour legislation and social reforms; and constitutional norms were abused or rejected.

Specific groups were targeted. Middle-class women were organized to protest shortages or inflation induced by the economic Right but blamed on the Left. Religious groups were mobilized in the streets to protest secular changes and resist "atheistic Communism." Most important, the military and police became highly "politicized" and were encouraged to undermine the authority of the Left in government by disobeying orders and to repress popular movements.

The Hard Right in Power

The decade from 1973 to 1983 was a decade of unrestrained right-wing violence from the government and through paramilitary groups. Rightist violence reached unprecedented heights. In Central America, 350,000 people were killed and over 2.5 million went into exile. In South America (Argentina, Chile, Uruguay, Brazil, Bolivia and Peru), close to 70,000 people were killed. The Right resorted to state terror on a massive scale. Repressive policies were oriented towards disarticulating civil society, particularly the popular socio-political movements; destroying the political intellectual framework of the nationalist, populist and socialist political and intellectual leaders; and, more importantly, restructuring the economy and state.

The second phase of the rightist strategy was to reshape the economic, state and class structure to concentrate wealth in the export elites, banks and multinationals and to centralize power in the executive (military) branch of government. Accompanying these political-economic changes, the Right created a new neoliberal political-intellectual framework from which to shape economic and social policy. The combination of violent rule and "liberal reform" was first embodied in Chile under Pinochet and was followed later by military rulers in Argentina, Uruguay and Bolivia. The Right deepened its ties internationally while disarticulating civil society internally. The United States and the international financial agencies provided large flows of financial resources and economic advisory groups to consolidate right-wing regimes. Many of the key right-wing economic advisors were graduates of universities in the U.S. specializing in free market dogma (University of Chicago, Stanford, Harvard, etc.).

The Right established a wider economic opening for the TNCs and local exporters. Equally important, through privatization programs and financial concessions, the Right created a new class of Latin American billionaires linked to international markets and influential in the local economy. This international bourgeoisie formed the core of the new liberal Right, whose ideological expression was found in the globalization and modernization rhetoric.

Consolidation: The Redemocratization Debate

Once the liberal institutional-economic framework was set up and the process of accumulation and concentration was taking place, the Right debated the question of "governability." The discussion focused on forms of legitimization, rules for resolving the conflicts of interest within the ruling class and methods to contain popular unrest. The issue of governability became acute, with the return of mass struggles in Brazil (1979–85), Chile (1983–86), Argentina

(1982–83) and Bolivia (1981–84), as well as the revolutionary struggles in Central America (Guatemala and El Salvador).

The military regimes were no longer the most viable political instruments to deepen and extend the neoliberal model promoted by the Washington consensus. The Right turned towards a negotiated transition, in which an electoral system would preserve the state but leave the socio-economic class structure intact. What was crucial for the Right was the selection of appropriate interlocutors who would accept the parameters of politics established during the dictatorship and respect the impunity of the military. The Right divided the "democratic opposition," favouring its capitalist leaders and marginalizing the Left. In exchange for the Left's entry into electoral politics, the mass movements were demobilized and the Right consolidated its positions of socio-economic power.

The Free Market, Free Elections and Neo-Authoritarianism of the 1990s
The negotiated transition guaranteed the consolidation of the neoliberal socio-economic order. The Centre-Left was integrated as a marginal electoral opposition, while the Right remained dominant in the crucial institutions of political power (the presidency, the supreme court, the judiciary, the central bank, the military command and the key ministries). Controlling the heights of the political and economic order, the Right was once again willing to exercise power within the electoral system.

From the pinnacle of rigid class structures the Right controlled the mass media and financial resources to project an image of legitimacy, while practising a new style of authoritarian politics. Under the electoral facade of the 1990s the Right rules through the executive and legislates by executive decree. It guarantees the continuity of its rule by forcing through laws allowing for the re-election of the president, and it pressures and corrupts representatives and judges to approve anti-labour legislation that weakens trade unions and undermines class solidarity.

The Right engages in class warfare, strengthening the bourgeois class by privatizing key public enterprises and thus concentrating more power and economic resources in the hands of its key class supporters. The Right facilitates mergers of mass media empires, thus centralizing ideological control in the hands of right-wing capitalists. Neoliberal policies are less an "economic" strategy than a political-class strategy. Economic policies and political decrees are directed towards disarticulating the social base of the Left, and legal measures are enforced by physical repression.

In 1996 in Brazil the right-wing Cardoso regime presided over the assassination of close to fifty peasants. In Chile, rural workers' strikes were systematically repressed. In Argentina, protesting demonstrators are routinely attacked by the police and journalists are beaten and killed. Peru's Fujimori was responsible for the killing, jailing and torture of thousands of popular activists. Under the facade of elections and political civility, the Right acts with ruthless violence against popular opposition. The most striking example is Colombia where the narco-electoral politicians promote free markets, death squads and the militarization of the countryside.

In the 1990s the Right continued to apply military violence to such a degree that the social struggle could not be contained within the closed electoral arena. While in most of Latin America the Right relies on authoritarian executive decrees permitted by the legal system, it still exercises the option to use extra-judiciary force and violence to undercut opposition to the poverty and exploitation resulting from the application of "structural adjustment policies."

New Methods of Struggle: NGOs and Poverty Programs

The Right strategy to contain popular mobilization combines both traditional and new organizational weapons. State-promoted "poverty programs" and the NGOs are key instruments of social control. The poverty programs are thinly disguised "vote-buying" mechanisms that provide food and small-scale credit for survival to the poor in exchange for votes. The NGOs are in fact government-funded (European, U.S. or World Bank) private agencies made up of middle-class professionals who organize "projects" to promote "self-help" and micro-enterprises to undercut sociopolitical movements that struggle for comprehensive structural changes such as employment, public health and education.

The Right manages the macroeconomy by executive decree in collaboration with non-elected international advisors and penetrates the microeconomy of poor communities with poverty functionaries and privately funded NGOs.

The Right and the U.S. Empire

Any discussion of the Right in Latin America must take into account the U.S. imperial state and multinational banks and corporations. They play a central role in shaping the strategies and providing organized support and financing of the Latin American Right. In fact, conceptually they are an integral part of the Right.

U.S. strategy is right-wing because its intervention and articulation is in defense of policies that favour the maximization of profits and their free remittance by a small elite of banks and corporations at the expense of the income of wage earners and national growth. Washington's policies are articulated with business and financial groups of the Right against popular movements. Its free market ideology resonates with the liberal doctrines of the Latin American Right and is hostile to the redistributive policies of the Left.

Washington's policy varies with political context. During the 1950s Washington was allied with right-wing military dictators to promote "open economies." Its political allies were concentrated among mining and landowning elites. In a few countries such as Brazil, Chile and Argentina it supported "developmentalist" electoral regimes based on an alliance between multinational corporations, state enterprises and national industries.

After 1959, in the face of the Cuban Revolution and with nationalist and socialist parties on the rise, Washington tried to divide the movement by forming alliances with the liberal middle class and industrial sectors. Washington sought to win over the opposition by proposing a reformist program (the Alliance for Progress) to isolate the revolutionary Left movement of workers and peasants. President Kennedy tried to create an electoral alliance between the "reformists centre" and the military/business Right to fight a combined reform and counter-insurgency struggle.

Washington's "transition" to democracy during the 1960s, however, was not successful. As popular movements gained force, they undercut the Alliance for Progress's effort to establish a new, right-wing hegemonic bloc. Threatened by the electoral power of the Left, Washington supported military coups. U.S. state ideologues justified the new violent "turn" by inventing the national security doctrine and the notion of "modernizing militaries" trained by the U.S. Washington shifted its political support from the national state and private capitalist class to the export bourgeoisie linked with the world market.

Washington Changes Strategy: 1980 to 1997

The crisis of the military dictatorships in the 1980s, the debt problem and a growth of mass opposition led Washington to rethink its military strategy and pursue a double strategy: (1) it sought to divide the anti-dictatorial opposition by financing and advising the bourgeois-liberal sector while isolating and demobilizing the popular Left movements, and (2) it promoted a negotiated transition between the bourgeois liberals and the military that would maintain the armed forces, deepen "free market" policies and introduce elections.

Washington, through the National Endowment for Democracy, financed seminars, meetings and publications on the theme of "redemocratization." The "new democracy" embodied in the Washington consensus excluded popular consultation, agrarian reform, redistribution of income and comprehensive public social services. Instead it centralized power in the presidency as an instrument of neoliberal policy. Through funding election campaigns and training and promoting conservative trade union leaders and community groups, Washington penetrated different layers of Latin American society with its neoliberal "self-help" and "individualist" ideology.

Having divided the "democratic opposition," Washington articulated its economic and military policy through right-wing electoral parties and turned towards dividing the Left. Through conferences and overseas seminars Washington supported the so-called "moderate" sectors of the Left. By funding non-conflictual trade union bureaucrats, training seminars in free market economics and conferences for intellectuals and Centre-Left politicians, Washington divided the Left. The Centre-Left dropped its anti-imperialist program and accepted the globaloney doctrine.

Through its ideological and cultural programs, Washington was able to create new parameters of political discourse in which imperialism was replaced by "globalization," class struggle was replaced by "social pacts," and political mobilization was replaced by "governability." The articulation of the imperial Right with the Latin American Right is essential in understanding the economic integration and "globalization" of the Latin American economies. The ascendancy of neoliberalism as the dominant ideology defining the Right is precisely a product of the "international alliances" of the Latin American and the U.S. Right. The election of New Right politicians like Menem, Cardoso, Sanchez de Lozado, Sanguinetti and Zedillo reflects the joint effort by a united international Right, based on their common neoliberal program. The "redemocratization" rhetoric promoted by liberal academics and journalists dominates university and mass media debates, obscuring the continuity of power of the ruling elites and the deep intervention of Washington in Latin America's political and economic systems.

The changing forms of Washington's intervention, the shift from a military to the electoral strategy, should not distract observers from noting its continued support of elitist structures of power, concentration of wealth and authoritarian methods of rule, nor its continued use of force in Panama, Grenada and the so-called anti-drug struggle.

Washington's right-wing strategy reflects tactical flexibility and strategic rigidity. Washington had supported armed revolts against popular regimes (Brazil 1964, Chile 1973, Nicaragua 1981–90, etc.) but then supported electoral processes in the 1990s. The shift is based on elite electoral pacts that have replaced decaying military regimes challenged by mass popular movements (Central America 1975–91, Brazil 1979–86, etc.). These tactical shifts are combined with rigidity in the strategic goals of maintaining the capitalist order and, more precisely, deepening the neoliberal economic model. Political change and shifts in right-wing policy are always guided by class criteria: the class composition and orientation of the military, the central bank and the executive. Contrary to Bobbio (1990), the Right invents its own "rules of the game" to suit its class interests. Rightist rule is based not on democratic discourse but on state power. In opposition, the Right exploits popular grievances and promotes social organizations to engage in class struggle against Left governments. Once it takes state power, it marginalizes popular groups and rules by decree.

The U.S. Right uses the Latin Right in power to formulate decrees and legislation to privatize public property, lower social expenditures, decrease taxes and weaken labour legislation. In opposition, the Right engages in class struggle through boycotts, lockouts, paramilitary campaigns and flights of capital to destroy democratic regimes who legislate in favour of peasants or workers. The class analysis, class struggle and class vision of the political Right contrasts with the vague "democracy with equity" ideology of the middle-class intellectuals of the reformist centre and the reactive populist sentiments held among the masses. The Right's class analysis accounts for its successful imposition of neoliberal ideology over the political class. The absence of a class perspective on the Centre-Left undercuts efforts to build a substantive alternative.

Reflections on Right-Wing Strategy

Historical analysis tells us that right-wing strategy varies from context to context, but its political goals remains the same: absolute control of state power to promote the accumulation of private wealth in association with transnational capital. Today that takes the form of disarticulating the domestic market to deepen integration within the international market. In a period of rising working-class power under populist leadership, a sector of the Right, the "national bourgeoisie," broke off from the Liberal Right to form a conjunctural alliance. The division between a "national" and "liberal" Right, or between an "electoral" and "military" Right, was temporary.

Faced with the threat of a popular electoral victory with a socializing agenda, the different segments of the Right united, shed their electoral strategies and adopted a "militarist" position utilizing democratic freedoms to create social tensions and economic chaos as a pretext for the violent seizure of power. The embrace of violence by the Right as a method of seizing state power allowed it to establish new parameters of political debate and a new socio-economic order. Right-wing power was not "restorationist." The use of military violence was directed towards serving the class interests of the civilian economic and political elite. It was not an "institutional" reaction. The reconcentration of private wealth and the destruction of the alternative socialist vision were strategic goals that guided the Right. Violence was a way of domesticating intellectuals and professional politicians by marking the limits of mobilization and political debate.

By controlling the terms of public debate and establishing the new rules of the electoral game through violence, the Right provided a "political opening." Right-wing hegemony is expressed by the political class's assimilation and acceptance of the basic premises and economic projects of the neoliberal model. Under conditions of political hegemony the Right was prepared to reintroduce electoral competition and "democratic institutions."

As noted, the Right has been alternatively internally divided and united, depending on the larger socio-economic context. In "normal" times, when there is no immediate and large-scale challenge from below, the Right is divided between (1) liberal sectors (landlords, merchants, bankers) who, lacking popular support, depend more on the military, paramilitary and police, and (2) nationalist reformist sectors of industrialists, professionals and local merchants who are more likely to seek tactical alliances with popular sectors as long as they exercise hegemony. Over time the relation between these two sectors of the Right has changed: between the 1940s and 1970s the "national reformist" Right was in ascendancy. From the late 1970s to 2000 the "liberal" Right was in ascendance. Today's liberal Right has made the transition from a power bloc based on armed power to an "executive-centre" authoritarian electoral regime.

The "natural allies" of the "New Right" are the overseas banks, the TNCs, the World Bank and the IMF. Its strength is its capacity to influence the political leadership of the Centre-Left with its neoliberal ideology to a degree that was unprecedented in the 20th century. The Right not only rules directly from power, but its ideas of "privatization," "integration" and "structural adjustment" are practised and articulated by sectors of the Workers Party in Brazil, the Broad Front in Uruguay, the Sandinista National Liberation Front (FSLN) in Nicaragua, the Revolutionary Democratic Party (PRD) in Mexico, the Cuban Communist Party, etc. The most complete submission to the Right is found among the Chilean Socialist Party, which has moved from being the party of Socialist President Allende to embracing the economic program of General Pinochet.

The historic conflicts between the Latin American Right and the U.S. have diminished. In the past the "nationalist" and sometime democratic bourgeois Right resisted U.S. intervention, defended the domestic market and opposed U.S. backing of military coups. For example, Vargas and Peron, Arbenz and Goulart, and Velasco and Rodriguez all represented sectors of the reformist nationalist bourgeoisie.

Today the New Right, both the "productive" and "financial" sectors, has few if any conflicts with the U.S.: they share the liberal agenda, accept U.S. military penetration under the guise of fighting drugs and are heavily involved in selling off basic energy, utility and other public enterprises to U.S. TNCs. Proposals of regional "integration" are essentially mechanisms to deepen the political and economic links between Latin American billionaire investors and exporters with their U.S. counterparts. The early anti-imperialism of the Right has given way to deep integration. The most significant ideological expression of right-wing integration is the rhetoric of "globalization," a code word for subordination to imperialism.

The paradox of the current period of right-wing rule is that while economic exploitation and misery deepen, the Right will continue to play by the "democratic rules." However, if the popular movements seriously challenge the conditions of exploitation, history teaches us that the Right will most likely shift from free markets and elections to free markets and machine guns. The movement of capital among economic sectors, from manufacturing to finance to commerce means that the divisions between capital are much weaker and the unity of purpose against labour stronger. Today the division between Left and Right is essentially a class division; vertical populist alliances are a thing of the past.

Chapter 11

Socialism in an Age of Imperialism

In the not so distant past, millions of people the world over wanting to escape the tyranny and exploitation of imperialism sought the answer in the construction of a socialist society. Today, proposing a socialist alternative raises more questions than answers. These questions can be grouped into several categories. The most general counterpose new adverse "world-historic" political, economic and cultural conditions to the emergence of revolutionary movements and struggles. A second set, while accepting the negative structural features of an imperialist dominated world, questions whether, at the micro-level, a socialist subjectivity can develop. A third set have to do with whether a strategy for successful socialist revolution is viable or can be developed in the midst of a sea of imperial adversaries or in the context of a world capitalist marketplace.

These are important questions that must be addressed by those who would pose a socialist alternative to the reigning imperial power. Furthermore, they require precise answers. To simply envision a "utopian" alternative or to evoke a socialist dream will not take us very far and is unlikely to convince anyone except those who are already amongst the initiated. More important, individually conceived utopias are usually concocted by intellectuals divorced from popular struggle, and their ideas are as disconnected from the experiences and needs of the popular classes as are their everyday lives. Before embarking on a discussion of the historical possibility of a socialist transformation, it is useful to specify the most challenging questions raised by sceptics and adversaries of the socialist alternative.

The first set of questions emphasizes the new structural constraints. Is socialism possible in the age of imperialism? Can the power of giant global corporations be challenged within a particular country or does it require concerted action across countries? Can alternative forms of communication with a working-class perspective countermand the ideological power of the Euro-American-owned mass media and the sway of its propaganda over the urban and rural poor? Can a new revolutionary subjectivity be created? What are the historical lessons of previous periods of imperial expansion in relation to revolution?

The second set of questions deals with the problems of subjectivity, the absence of a socialist or revolutionary referent. The questions relevant to this questioning of revolutionary possibilities include the following. Recent decades have demonstrated that the increase of mass poverty and social inequalities in the distribution of resources has not led to revolution. Could it be that individual mobility and intra-lower-class relations of reciprocity have created alternative forms of behaviour and organization compatible with imperialism?

Can socialism be reconstructed on the basis of novel, national (or international) experiences in the face of the collapse of the USSR and the conversion of the Chinese elite to capitalism? Is the state an anachronism transcended by global actors committed to the imperial system?

The third set of questions does not deny the existence of opposition to imperialism or many of its negative manifestations but questions whether revolutionaries and socialists have an alternative strategy of consequence. The issue is whether there is a coherent socialist strategy that can reverse the now entrenched imperial configurations of socio-economic and political power. Is the neoconservative counter-revolution in thought and practice, and its neoliberal program of reforms, reversible without trauma and crises? Can socialist institutions be constructed and be viable in a sea of capitalist relations? Are socialist values compatible with the operation of world or even local markets? Can a socialist society organize the conditions for its national security and economic planning without succumbing to what Michels conceived as the "iron law of oligarchy" or the temptations and problems of bureaucratic rule— an overbureaucratized state?

These are important academic and political questions that relate to fundamental issues facing any proposition of a socialist alternative to contemporary imperialism. Yet there are answers, some more tentative than others, and despite all the scepticism, doubt and criticisms that prevail, they suggest a solid basis for the struggle for socialism as an objective and subjective possibility.

Objective Conditions for Socialism
One of the strongest objections to socialism relates to today's supposedly highly integrated economic processes—the greater development of the social division of labour. Today, we are told, more people than ever are caught up in the process of cooperation and exchange involved in the production and distribution of every sort of commodity in a system that is global in scale. It is argued that globalization—or, in our terms, imperialism—has broken down national and sectoral constraints on the circulation of commodities and capital, creating one interdependent market and productive unit. In one sense this is partially true, but in another it is patently false. The deepening of socialized production, a process by which many economic units located in a multiplicity of settings cooperate to produce on a world scale, is an historical fact in the contemporary world. But it is wrong to present this as a cooperative form of production based on a greater degree of "interdependence" or mutual dependence. This is because this cooperation in producing commodities is presided over by a distinct class of individuals with proprietary rights over the social means of production, control over strategic investment decisions and the capacity to appropriate profits. The private owners and controllers of socialized production are not interdependent with their workers and employees. The former set the conditions of work and the levels of remuneration, and they appropriate an undue share of the social product, allocating income to themselves in a highly unequal

fashion. The mechanisms of a competitive free market and present relations of "reciprocity" and "interdependency "do not allocate power, wealth, income and other resources fairly or even efficiently, and certainly not equitably. On the contrary, these and other resources, and all modalities of the social product, are allocated in a highly asymmetrical manner based on a system defined by relations of property in the means of production, power, hierarchy and exploitation.

In this context, imperialism has set in motion two distinct and opposing processes: (1) a high degree of social cooperation among producers as a means of increasing efficiency and (2) the private appropriation and concentration of the wealth that is produced. This contradiction, the growing polarity between cooperation for production and private appropriation of the collectively produced commodities, is fundamental in the process of socialist transformation. By any measure, increased efficiency, greater technological innovation and growing productivity are found in the greater development of the social division of labour, or cooperative production. The main function and collective aim of the private owners and corporate directors is the appropriation of the socially produced wealth. The growing concentration of wealth—the emergence of the billionaire class of super-rich—is based on the greater number of workers subsumed under this system of social production. Socialism is thus objectively situated within collective production, and the struggle is to extend social production in the direction of social ownership of its means and output.

The idea of social cooperation is an integral part of the global production process, but it is mediated, defended and rationalized by the dominant capitalist class, which is in a position to appropriate the lion's share of the social product in one form or another. The secret of capital accumulation is not in the genius of individual entrepreneurship, but in the vast army of workers, researchers and employees who add value to the social product and, in terms defined so well by Karl Marx in an earlier context, produce the surplus value that drives the system. Collective labour can exist and prosper without any single entrepreneur, including Bill Gates, but the billionaire class cannot accumulate wealth without cooperative labour.

However, while providing a solid point of departure in the struggle for collective ownership, uncovering the social nature of contemporary wealth and relations of exploitation—and thus encouraging a contemporary form of class-consciousness—will not by itself lead to socialism. What is required is a deep and far-reaching understanding, organization and struggle by the direct producers to resolve this contradiction. Thus the argument that the new wave of imperial expansion and extension of market relations across the world has ruled out socialist transformation can be turned on its head: the very process of incorporating more workers in more countries into the social division of labour will create the objective basis for collective action in the direction of socialism, that is, the socialization of the means of social production and a system that gives workers control over their workplaces and sites of production, communities control over their communities and the people control over the state.

A second objective basis for the construction of socialism is the increasingly centralized nature of political decision-making. Today, more than at any time in the past, a small group of non-elected officials have greater voice and power over vast numbers of people around the globe. Officials of the central banks and economic and financial ministries of the Euro-American empire and their appointees in the IMF, the World Bank, the Asian Bank, Inter-American Development Bank and other such international financial institutions make the decisions and take actions that adversely affect billions of people. These non-elected elite economic policy-makers represent and respond directly to the interests of multinational corporate and banking billionaires, an emerging international capitalist class. To a degree, these elite decision-makers have pre-empted political powers ostensibly held by elected officials of the non-hegemonic states. In other words, the world's electorate votes for officials who in turn are subordinated to non-elected economic elites that serve imperial institutions and interests. The institutional trappings of liberal democracy are put into place everywhere, but the popular electorate is, in effect, disenfranchised. Strategic decisions are made in centralized headquarters by non-elected officials who rule by decree and without popular representation, deliberation or consultation. Thus, while more and more people are subject to the rule of a centralized elite, they have less and less control over the economic and social conditions of their lives.

This divorce between electoral politics and elite dominance, between expanding benefits for the elite and deteriorating economic and social conditions for the many, establishes the objective basis for popular struggles and opens enormous opportunities for revolutionary forces to challenge the claim that capitalism and democracy are coterminous. The centralization of decision-making and power provides the objective basis for an argument that real democracy can only be achieved, or recovered, under socialism.

Imperialist Expansion and Socialist Revolution

If the contradictions of the imperialist system provide an objective basis for awareness of the need for and possibility of building a socialist alternative, past historical experience provides us with another. Imperialism is a result of the inner workings of capitalism combining with external opportunities, which are already in part artifacts of imperial policy-makers. In the past, as in the present, the expansion and conquest of overseas markets and sources of state revenues have refashioned class relations and state configurations so as to maximize imperial economic interests and strategic politico-military positions.

Within the imperialist system the increasing scale of capitalist development has separated direct producers from their means of production and resulted in exploitative labour relations and oppressive conditions for a rapidly growing and ethnically mixed proletariat. The intra- and cross-class conflicts generated by these conditions are either exploited by the ruling classes or distract attention and struggle away from issues of class-based inequalities. The political overlords in this system are accountable only to their own ruling classes, thus provoking conflicts with a range of classes and groups, from pre-imperial elites to intellectuals and wage labourers. These conflicts have led to innumerable revolts and, in some instances, to successful socialist revolution, particularly in periods of inter-imperial wars, when local ruling classes and governing elites have been weakened and discredited.

The theoretical point of these developments is clear: large and long-term imperial systems have neither inhibited revolutionary struggles nor prevented socialist revolution.

To date, socialist revolutions or experiments have been products of wars waged by workers and plebeians within the imperial countries, or by colonized or quasi-colonized people. Take the famous Paris Commune. It was an out-growth of the Franco-German War of 1870–71, between an early imperial country and an emerging one. The German military victory and the conquest of most of France set in motion a powerful popular uprising in Paris and the subsequent commune. While the Paris Commune lasted only a few months, its organization, legislation and even its mistakes served as a practical model for revolutionary theorizing by both Marx and Lenin. The first inter-imperialist World War (1914–18), with its millions of deaths, population displacement, hunger and destruction set in motion massive popular uprisings, protests and revolutions. The First World War's pursuit of imperial conquest by military means destroyed the conventional bonds between bourgeois leaders and plebeian followers and undermined the control of landlords over submissive peasants. Socialist revolutions took place in Hungary, Bavaria, Finland and Russia. Military men and workers revolted in Berlin and in the Baltic fleet. The mighty European imperial system, which dominated five continents and was sustained by massive armed force and overflowing treasuries as an impregnable bastion of capitalist power, produced massive worker and peasant uprisings and a successful socialist revolution in Russia.

In the interwar period there was a resurgence of imperialism, particularly in the emerging imperial countries of Germany and Japan, that challenged the established European countries and the U.S. in their spheres of influence and hegemonic power. The ensuing conflicts and conquests unleashed a powerful new wave of popular anti-imperialist movements in countries that were war-ravaged and hyperexploited, particularly among the millions of displaced peasants in China, Indochina and Korea. Imperial expansion and war had intensified the pillage of the land, mines and productive units, creating a vast army of revolutionary resistance and leading to socialist revolutions under the leadership of indigenous Communist parties in China, Indochina and North Korea. What began as anti-imperialist wars were converted into civil wars in which socialist forces eventually triumphed. In Europe a similar process unfolded in Yugoslavia, while in a number of other countries the anti-colonial struggle was divided between regimes that consolidated a neocolonial relation-ship and those that sought to create a mixed national-populist and non-aligned state.

Two points need to be emphasized here. In the first place it was precisely the virulent new imperialism with its powerful military machines and totalitar-ian state structures that set off the popular revolts that undermined imperial domination. Second, the old European and new U.S. imperial powers were not able to restore hegemony in several important countries (China and half of Korea and Indochina). The point is that, despite its greater firepower and manpower and the scope and depth of its economic reach, this second wave of imperialism could not prevent socialist revolutions from successfully trans-forming society. It is important to note that these revolutions succeeded despite, and not because of, any aid from the "socialist" regime and society in the USSR. Oceans of capitalist relations could not prevent social revolution.

The post–World War II period witnessed the emergence of U.S. imperial-ism on a global scale, with a worldwide network of military bases and alliances, the biggest military budget, the most advanced military technology and heavily capitalized giant enterprises geared towards expansion to conquer overseas markets (that is, the emergence of the so-called multinational corporations). While the new American empire was able to repress and defeat a number of popular revolutionary uprisings throughout the world, it was defeated in two major conflicts (China and Cuba); held to a draw in a third (Korea) and temporarily defeated in several others (Nicaragua, Angola, Mozambique, Chile, Grenada, Dominican Republic). Successful revolutions occurred pre-cisely in countries where U.S. imperial presence was most dominant: Indochina, with 500,000 U.S. troops and tens of billions of dollars of investments in regional military infrastructure. Cuba was a country with a great concentration of U.S. ownership and a major naval U.S. base (Guantanamo). The U.S. provided more military aid and advisors during the Chinese civil war than any other country during the mid- to late 1940s. And the U.S. committed hundreds of thousands of troops and billions of dollars to conquer the Korean peninsulas but had to settle for a compromise dividing the country. The point is that the deepening military and economic presence of the U.S. empire was a condition-ing factor that precipitated successful socialist revolutions and was not merely a powerful inhibitory factor.

Regarding the relation between socialist revolution and the absence or presence of the Soviet bloc, it should be noted that all the revolutions in the post–World War II period occurred despite the opposition of the Kremlin: Yugoslavia, China, Cuba and Indochina. While the Soviets provided impor-tant support once the revolutions were consummated, the fall of the USSR did not lead to the collapse of the revolution in Cuba, even as it forced Cuba to adjust its policies towards foreign capital and seek new trading partners. The initiation and success of all 20th-century socialist revolutions had less to do with the presence of the Soviet bloc and more to do with the development of class and anti-imperialist struggle and international solidarity within the country. This suggests that the absence of the USSR ("the sea of capitalism") was not a new historical impediment but rather a constant factor throughout the 20th century.

The re-emergence of mass popular struggles under socialist or, at a minimum, anti-neoliberal/anti-imperialist leadership throughout the world at the commencement of the new millennium should put to rest the notion that the triumph of Euro-American imperialism is irreversible and unquestioned. In Latin America the Revolutionary Armed Forces of Colombia (FARC), the rural Landless Workers Movement (MST) in Brazil and the brief seizure of power by an alliance of Indians, peasants and junior officers in Ecuador are high points in the resurgence of an anti-imperialist Left connected to a new wave of popular movements. In Asia similar mass popular movements based on industrial workers' unions (South Korea) and mass urban and peasant organizations have emerged in Indonesia, the Philippines and Nepal, to name a few.

Sweeping generalizations about the universal triumph of capitalism/imperialism in the wake of the demise of the USSR, as trumpeted by its defenders and echoed by demoralized sectors of the Left intelligentsia, have no empirical basis. This triumphalist ideological posture can only be sustained by the mediocrity of its advocates and, on the Left, by the desire to find a niche within the empire.

If Euro-American imperialism was indeed as triumphant as its celebrants and the demoralized ex-leftists claim, there would be no need for the empire to resort constantly to violent counter-revolutionary policies and to enlarge and deepen its military capacity for intervention. If the revolution has ended, or, as at least one leftist writer has claimed, the empire has scored a decisive historical victory, why the need to constantly arm NATO and to engage in offensive wars in the Balkans, the Gulf and the Horn of Africa? Why is NATO recruiting new clients and members and increasing military budgets and new weapons systems? Why is the U.S. increasing its military aid in Colombia and multiplying the number of military bases and FBI offices in more than thirty countries? None of these military moves are directed against attack from a particular state. The most plausible argument is grounded in the rather fragile socio-political equilibrium that exists between pro- and anti-imperialist forces throughout the world, between a still powerful empire and an emerging anti-imperialist movement with a distinct and growing anti-capitalist current.

The Subjective Conditions of Popular Revolution

A significant disjuncture currently exists between the objective conditions for socialist revolution and the form of consciousness achieved by the classes of exploited, oppressed and marginalized people. However, this disjuncture of necessity will constitute a social basis for revolutionary change. The objective conditions for such change are being generated by the capitalist development of the imperialist system itself. On this there can be little doubt, although there is much speculation as to the precise or critical conjuncture of a revolutionary situation. The problem appears to be more subjective—the formation of a revolutionary consciousness.

General development and deepening of revolutionary consciousness can occur as much after a revolutionary upheaval as before. In the final analysis, revolutionary subjectivity is not merely a reflection of the rapacious economic exploitation of expanding empires. It is an essential link between the apprehension of the objective conditions at work and the transformation of this understanding into a political program for revolutionary action. Objective conditions are necessary but insufficient to create a revolutionary social class. Capitalist development and imperial expansion displace and/or subordinate many small producers, convert peasants into landless workers and lead to a "multiplication of the proletariat." They expel wage workers from the production process, converting some into a chronically unemployed surplus population and others into an informal, self-employed urban poor. In addition, many small and medium-sized bourgeoisie are pushed into bankruptcy; in many developing countries these too swell the ranks of the working poor.

However, the ideological and political response of these adversely affected cannot be predetermined by reference to their objective situations. But a determinant of this response can be found in the availability, organizational capabilities and leadership of the competing ideological groups that appeal to the oppressed and exploited, and seek to mobilize their discontent into resistance and opposition—and revolution.

In the present circumstances there are several responses to Euro-American imperialist domination. The most conservative response finds its expression among the ethnic surrogates of Euro-American power who promote imperial appropriation and exploitation from above and the expropriation of the wealth of other ethnic groups from below (i.e., via ethnic wars of liberation that legitimate thievery of property and public assassination).

A second response is a kind of "clerical nationalism" in which former traditional elites challenge imperial domination to restore the power and prerogatives of religious and, in some cases, commercial landowning elites. In the absence of a secular Left, such religious anti-imperialists offer alternatives to decadent Western morality rather than a sustained challenge to Euro-American economic power. Not infrequently, a division of political, cultural and economic power transpires in which the religious authority controls cultural and political institutions while pro–free marketers control the economy.

A third response to imperialist domination has been taken by sectors of the petit bourgeoisie adversely affected by free trade, policies that undermine local manufacturing, debt payments that reduce credit and raise interest rates, and speculative investments that generate economic volatility and provoke bankruptcy. Their response also typifies groups of progressive professionals, NGO leaders and others interested in seeking an accommodation with imperial power—to make the best deal possible for themselves, the only "practical option." These groups can be found in the corridors of imperial power, seeking a place in the sun or at least an opportunity for dialogue, if not confrontation. They struggle for recognition or for a place at the table in the meetings of the IMF, World Bank and WTO. They argue for some regulation of capital flows, greater access to Western markets and against Western-dictated labour standards. In the current imperialist context their most radical demand has been the Tobin Tax (a tax on short-term financial transactions). The most consequential anti-imperialist, anti-systemic movements can be found in the burgeoning popular alliances formed between landless rural workers, small farmers and peasant producers, as well as urban workers. They form the modern anti-imperialist movement that links radical reform to socialism.

The multiplicity of responses to Euro-American imperialism demonstrates both the breadth of the opposition and its fragmented character. These different responses only partially reflect class positions, as most contain a variety of mass bases even though their leaders tend to come from a particular social milieu. It is clear that imperial exploitation generates a variety of political responses and agencies. Politicians evidently are not the products of economic processes; instead they are created in the field of cultural, ideological and political struggles. The political agencies most likely to succeed are those whose organizations resonate with everyday experience, provide a general rationale (no matter how flawed and irrational), seem to solve everyday problems (no matter how predatory) and create the positive image of a triumphant victim. In short, the problem today is not objective: the world's vast inequalities and the transfers of wealth from the recolonized world to the Euro-American empire are transparent. The capitalist world is largely and increasingly polarized; peasants and workers are exploited as never before; the number of impoverished grows; and above it all, directing the process, is an omnipresent, arrogant and intrusive Euro-American empire with incredible resources but few saving graces or virtues.

The problem thus is more subjective than objective, and the specific weakness is found in the opposition and critics of imperialism. Few of these critics recognize the political and economic imperatives that define the system as a whole, influenced as they are by the concepts used by their adversaries, as is evident in their adoption of the language of empire ("globalization," "economic reform," "structural adjustment", etc.).

While rightly focusing criticism on the WTO, IMF and World Bank and on the problems of speculative capital, poverty, etc., the NGOs have no organized base among the workers and peasants, the direct producers of the world's wealth. Having no organic link to these classes and their situations, the NGOs generally do without a class analysis of the problems faced by the many and are therefore unable to offer effective solutions predicated on substantive social change.

Many intellectuals, including critical *pensadores*, have adopted a pessimistic view of the world, inflating the power of the empire and the reputation of its apologists while berating the Left (and those who have the audacity to engage in the anti-imperialist struggle) for not sufficiently fathoming the depths of their defeat and adapting to the new realities, i.e., finding a realistic niche in the system where they can rub elbows with the "New Right"—Social Democrats turned social imperialists. Lacking a world view, this genre of intellectuals makes use of the dominant paradigm, provides only a measure of abstract criticism, and traces this paradigm's ascendancy and projects its future continuance while exposing its excesses and offering unsolicited palliatives in a "realist"-servile manner to the powers that be.

The traditional trade unions, with some notable exceptions, have adapted to the exigencies of neoliberal policies and the demands of the economic conglomerates. Top trade union officials have adopted a position *vis-à-vis* the state similar to the relationship between monarchs and nobles: they pledge fealty to the neoliberal order in exchange for control over their fiefdom. Nevertheless, significant minorities of rank-and-file workers inside and outside of the official labour confederations have engaged in numerous unauthorized militant actions and have frequently joined with other leftist anti-corporate social movements in massive opposition to the WTO, World Bank and IMF and their corporate extensions overseas.

A significant minority of intellectuals and students have elaborated anti-corporate, anti-globalization programs to match and inspire their direct-action politics. Because the historic parties of the Left (Communists) and Centre-Left have moved towards embracing neoliberalism (Blair's "Third Way" being the clearest example), the new anti-imperialist, anti-corporate groups have created their own international networks, their own movement-style political organization and innovative forms of direct action that have included land occupations in Paraguay and Brazil, general strikes and popular uprisings in Ecuador and Bolivia, factory occupations in South Korea, massive civilly disobedient demonstrations in London, Seattle, Washington and Amsterdam and major guerrilla struggles in Colombia. Intellectuals are active in the anti–foreign debt movements, in progressive anti-globalization NGOs and in attacking neoliberal economic models.

The rising tide of extra-parliamentary opposition to imperial domination (mislabelled "globalization") has introduced a new factor into the political equation: a subjective link between exploitative objective conditions and popular social transformation. New movements working towards a new society through their multi- or single-issue politics confront several important challenges in fashioning a new socialist society. For economy of space, we list them in abbreviated form: (1) the international division of labour, (2) dependence on external markets and finance, (3) heavy debt payments, (4) overseas migration (the imperially induced emigration of skilled labour), (5) upper- and middle-class dependency on imported consumer goods, (6) party and trade union apparatuses tied to the status quo, (7) hostile mass media linked to conglomerates and transmitting pro-imperial propaganda, (8) possible economic embargoes and military threats, (9) a tyranny of the doctrine of the

"inevitability of globalization," (10) capital flight, and (11) surrogate mercenary, ethnic or military revolts.

To construct a new socialist society it is incumbent on practitioners to
anticipate possible adverse scenarios in order to prepare responses. Socialism
must be seen as an integral change based on transformations in the economic,
cultural and political spheres and based on an understanding of the multidi-
mensional domination of imperialism. It is difficult to push a hostile state
apparatus towards a policy of economic transformation or introduce social
changes under conditions where the mass media exhort excessive consumer
demand, military rebellion, etc.

While recognizing the profound challenges that Euro-American imperialism represents to a socialist transformation, socialists possess several strategic
political assets. In the first place, information technologies (IT) provide enormous possibilities to collect information on sourcing alternative markets,
competitive conflicts between imperial powers or unused resources within the
country, as well as to inform and register popular demands. The new technologies can gather enormous amounts of information and provide a wider public
with the costs and benefits of alternative paradigms and policies. IT is not a
substitute for democratic policy-making but rather a tool that enables the
populace to register their wants via a wealth of data, facilitating optimal
decisions. An essential precondition for democracy with IT is a new, appropri-
ately configured state. The state plays a pivotal role by providing the terrain for
popular participation, debate and formulation of a program that moves from a
neo-imperial to a socialist economy.

New state configurations presuppose several strategic changes in society
and economy. First and foremost, the principal social base of political support
must be transformed from passive to active: the mass of the exploited, excluded
and displaced populace must be mobilized, organized and provided with
channels for deliberation, consultation and effective decision-making. An
economic strategy must be fashioned that makes the social base of the regime
the prime beneficiary in order to demonstrate that the revolution is by and for
the people and not an ideological subterfuge for upwardly mobile intellectuals.

Along these lines, the second strategic change involves reordering production, investment, lending and market priorities to stimulate the employment,
income and production of the mass base. This is essential to move towards the
new economy and consolidate political support. Interrelated with such change
and the introduction of new production priorities is the need to redistribute
income and land in order to break the power of landlords and conglomerates
and enhance the position of the working and petty producers.

Finally the state is pivotal in reordering budget priorities related to
taxation and expenditures—ending imperial corporate export subsidies and
increasing social expenditures for universal health care, public housing, education and pensions. To avoid a fiscal crisis, tax rates should become more
progressive on income, profits and property.

These socio-economic changes are strategically important to strengthen the capacity of the democratic socialist state to confront the inevitably subversive intentions of the imperial corporate opposition. That opposition will first express itself as a crisis of investor confidence—a scare tactic designed to cower the regime into reneging on its policies. This requires the state to be resolute and make tactical moves compatible with its strategic goals. Essentially the state's preventive action can be three-pronged. First, economic shock policies, modelled on the IMF, only with the beneficiaries and losers inverted: freezing bank accounts, profits and other assets; price controls on essentials; freezing all employment. This can be followed by structural adjustment policies from below: bankrupt or economically troubled enterprises would be intervened in, their debts restructured and their administrations reorganized, introducing worker and technical employee control. These policies can be part of a more extensive package of economic reforms that would emphasize broadening and deepening the domestic market, selective closing of the economy to monopolistic conglomerates and fostering entrepreneurship within socialized, cooperative medium and small private firms. These economic reforms would combine a democratically formulated national plan with decentralized and autonomous public, co-op and private firms coordinated by the national legislative assembly and executive.

These policies will most likely provoke opposition from pro-imperial quarters, leading to a crisis in the transitional economy. Thus a crisis management strategy is required. Several lines of action can be followed simultaneously. First, policy must be directed towards guaranteeing basic necessities for the mass social base. Second, austerity policies must be applied to the rich, both foreign and domestic. The country can take TNCs hostage in order to bargain. The choice must be posed: cooperation or expropriation. It should be pointed out that disinvestment is a two-edged sword. Hurting the popular economy can be presented as a one-shot deal: once investors leave, there is no coming back. Third, the regime must substitute new factors of production to replace capital flight. This requires mobilizing unused resources—the unemployed and underemployed, fallow lands, animal transport for short distances, indigenous technology, etc.—to produce commodities to extend and deepen the domestic economy and sustain exports. Through IT data bases, policy-makers can redeploy unused resources to meet basic needs in the micro- and macro-economy.

Towards a Socialist Transition
There are two basic fallacies regarding socialist transformations. One relates to the notion of "delinking" related to the ideas of "self-reliance" and "building socialism in one country." The other relates to the more recent idea of "market socialism," the notion that market-driven forces can create the material basis for socialism. Both conceptions contain grains of truth, but in their underlying logics are very harmful to the construction of socialism.

First, the cause of developing socialist productive forces delinked from world production leads to costly, inefficient and ultimately prolonged periods of harsh "accumulation." In most cases, delinking is just not feasible without giving up essential products necessary for consumption and production. Only under harsh wartime conditions or in periods of boycott or states of siege does it make sense to try to make a virtue of necessity by appealing for "self-reliance" and sacrifice and encouraging the idea that despite a harsh external setting the revolutionary population can produce and survive. Such was the case when the U.S. and the ex-USSR encircled Mao's China and restricted its external trade relations. But it would be an egregious error to convert special circumstances into a model of development.

The second erroneous approach is the Dengist idea that market forces, private ownership, free trade and foreign investment directed by the Communist Party can become driving forces towards the construction of socialism. The ascendancy of market forces has transformed the Chinese labour force in a global reserve army of cheap labour; it has converted the cadres and leaders of the Party in businesspeople who plunder the state for private gain, destroy the environment and produce ecological disasters. In a word, it is the market that directs the Party and its leaders, and not vice versa. The result is the worst-case scenario where the authoritarian political structures of Communism are combined with the brutal socio-economic injustices of capitalism and a catastrophic degradation of the environment. That is the operative meaning of "market socialism."

The construction of socialism should be approached in a different way. First of all, the working class has created a vast body of "world knowledge" over time. The revolutionary regime must link up with this world knowledge to avoid the cruel and costly earlier stages of development in which this knowledge was created. The revolution must also link up with world centres of know-how as a necessary step to increase local capacity to advance the forces of production and democratize its relations. But this external linkage must take place under conditions that, in addition, increase the internal capacity to deepen the domestic market and serve popular needs.

Second, economic exchanges—"market relations," both external and internal—can only have a progressive function if they are subordinated to a democratic regime based on direct popular representation in territorial and in productive units. Assembly-style democracy is not only a strong deterrent to bureaucratic distortions but also serves as an essential control mechanism over the content and direction of market exchanges.

The current fragmentation and dissolution of production is a result of the "enclave nature" of export strategy, where key production units specialized in specific commodities serve the international strategies of overseas and domestic investor elites. The socialist strategy focuses on the creation or reconstruction of essential links between domestic economic sectors. The socialist economy resembles a grid rather than the hub and spokes of a wheel model that is characteristic of imperially-dominated export economies.

The current overseas economic package that combines foreign invest-ment, control and management decision-making with technology transfers (when they occur) must be disaggregated under socialism. The capturing of technology without the inconvenient encumbrances of foreign dictates and outrageous CEO salaries and foreign ownership is possible because of the plethora of technologically knowledgeable individuals and enterprises that can be contracted and paid to transfer know-how. This form of "dependence" is temporary and has less possibility of reperpetuating itself. Learning from borrowing becomes the basis for adaptation to local needs and development of autonomous innovative capacities. Breaking the tyranny of globalization requires a rejection of ownership and control and a selective acquisition of knowledge and products that produce dynamic growth. Thus the parasitical and exploitative structures of globalization (imperialism) need to be differen-tiated from creative and productive factors.

This process of rejection and acquisition poses one of the most important challenges to any transition from neoliberal capitalism to socialism. It is the challenge of managing the inherent contradiction between internal socialist relations and external participation in the capitalist marketplace. This requires not only democratic control over economic processes but also, more fundamen-tally, the ideological and cultural education of working people in values of solidarity, cooperation and equality. This educational process can only have credibility if the values articulated reflect the behaviour and practices of the leadership and cadres. The sorry feature of socialism in the ex-USSR was the dissociation of the ideas expressed by leaders and their actual practices, which led to disillusion, cynicism, distrust and a fatal attraction for globalist propa-ganda.

A fundamental appeal of constructing a socialist power bloc to transform society, and a primary task on assuming power, is the creation of socio-economic linkages between domestic needs (and "latent demands") and the reorganiza-tion of the productive system. The existing export strategy is a product of inequalities: the labour force is seen as a cost, not as consumers (demand). Hunger salaries and labour impoverishment fuel high profits in overseas markets. The socialist transformation recognizes the enormous potentialities of the domestic market based on equalized property, income, education and health. It recognizes the tremendous potential in utilizing unused or underused labour.

The turn inward is essential, but the external linkages to overseas markets and knowledge remain a key factor for providing earnings and techniques to complement domestic revitalization of the economy. What is crucial, however, is that external exchanges do not continue to substitute for local production and local centres of technical knowledge creation.

Essential to any socialist undertaking is a profound agrarian reform that includes the redistribution of land and transfer of property ownership, along with a reorientation of credits, technical assistance, marketing and transport to facilitate food production for mass consumption at affordable prices while providing a livable income for rural producers. Whatever the particular ownership patterns—and there are too many variables to provide general blueprints—the agrarian reform should encompass agro-industrial complexes and related employment. Thus the production of "inputs" and industrial "processing" become part of the agrarian transformation. Practical experience and the negative lessons of the ex-USSR teach us that agriculture requires a decentralized organization in which direct producers make basic decisions in consultation with technical advisors to integrate exchanges between regions, sectors and classes.

The transition from a globalized imperial export strategy towards an integrated domestic economy requires the integration of regions and production and consumption into a unified whole, substantively recreating the nation and reorienting the state away from the imperial aspirations of export and financial elites.

The Role of the State in Building Socialism

A necessary precondition for socialist transformation is a fundamental political change in the state. Contrary to the unreflective musings of both rightist and leftist globalist theorists, the state has played a powerful role in formulating the strategies of globalization, allocating economic resources to "global actors," bailing out elite losers and re-enforcing the policing of globalist victims and opponents. To argue that the state has been weakened is to mistakenly identify the state with the welfare state; it is to confuse the apologetic pronouncements of the globalist ideologues who lament their impotence when faced with "global pressures" with the reality of their active collaboration with state institutions.

The state and nation become the central units for reconstructing a new internationalist socialist order. Popular movements in civil society are in basic conflict with the ruling classes over who controls the state and the nature of the socio-economic project. Once again ex-leftist ideologues disorient popular movements by pointing to conflicts between "the state" and "civil society" rather than examining how the most willful and cruel exploitation occurs within civil society between landowners, bankers and financiers on the one hand and landless peasants, indebted small producers and unemployed workers on the other. So let us move beyond the intellectual posturing of repentant ex-leftists seeking merit points from their new paymasters to practical measures that can move the popular movement from political power to a socialist transformation.

In this regard we can learn from the transition strategies engineered earlier by neoliberal globalists. Key to the implementation of a new socialist economy is an immediate shock therapy for the ruling class. Profits should be drastically reduced, bank accounts and financial holdings frozen, overseas payments suspended and a moratorium on debt payments implemented. This shock therapy has political and economic value: it disorganizes and disorients the ruling class and prevents hoarding, capital flight and the provocation of hyperinflation. More important, it involves strong state intervention to re-structure the economy and reconfigure state budgets and institutions. The purpose is to open the economy for domestic production and to offer credit and investment for expanding production and exchanges at the national, regional and local level. Shock therapy will predictably evoke protests and dire cries of injustice and arbitrariness. But quick and resolute action in following up the shock therapy with substantive new investments and credits towards the domestic market can generate more than sufficient support for sustaining the regime. Shock therapy, rationally applied, means renegotiations with former globalist patrons and partners, not repudiation. It does not spell rupture but rather a reordering of priorities and relations to favour the new forces of the domestic market.

The second phase in the transition involves economic reconversion: the shift from hyperspecialization in single commodities and limited activity in the industrial assembly plants to diversified production, a better balance between local consumption and export production, and greater investment in educa-tion, research, health and productivity. Economic reconversion requires a shift in investments, employment and income policy. It requires a structural adjust-ment program from below. Essentially this means the redistribution of land, income and credits; the breakup of private monopolies; reform of the tax system; realistic assessments based on market values of property; rigorous enforcement of tax collection (with severe sanctions for chronic evasion); protection of emerging industries; and opening of trade for commodities that don't compete with local producers. Financial controls will eliminate specula-tive activity, and state planning can redirect investments towards human capital formation, employment-generating public works and inter-regional production.

To avoid inflation and stabilize the economy, a tight monetary policy will need to be put in place. Monetarism from below means the elimination of state bailouts of billion-dollar debts created by mismanagement, swindles or specu-lation by the private sector; the elimination of low-interest (subsidized) loans and cheap credits to exporters; and elimination of tax abatements for multina-tional corporations in so-called free trade zones. The gains in state revenues and savings can fund alliterative socio-economic activity and prevent the need to resort to the printing of money.

There are significant differences between a socialist and a neoliberal program of structural adjustment. Socialization of the means of production would replace privatization as the key to increasing efficiency, competitiveness and productivity. Socialization would include extending transport and commu-nication networks to further inter-regional exchanges, thus revitalizing provin-cial enterprises, markets, units and agents of production. This means that "cost-benefit" analysis would be based on regional or national measures rather than on the narrow balance sheets of a particular enterprise. For example, train service to rural areas could result in "losses" to the railroad but might also increase production and consumption in the regional economy. The net outcome calculated on the basis of larger units over time provides a clearer and more appropriate (socialist) criteria for measuring cost-effectiveness. Likewise, public investments that employ the unemployed and increase output provide another measure of efficient utilization of human capital. In terms of competitiveness, what is determinant is the recognition that economies are about nurturing people—an elementary and basic point. Socialized enterprises that produce staple food items are far more competitive in meeting basic needs than their counterparts in the export model who ignore them. In meeting basic food needs, socialized production is more responsive to and more able and willing to meet "popular market demand."

Socialization of economic enterprises is necessary but not sufficient to create a viable socialist economy. What is required is a plan of industrial reconversion and "productive transformation"—to use the language of ECLAC— with the "equity" (a fair and socially just distribution of the fruits of development) that ECLAC calls for but is unable to design or deliver because of its commitment to capitalism and its institutions (private ownership of the means of production, markets, wage labour, etc.). Outcomes related to production or the distribution of benefits and costs should be based on popular participation, not the decision-making power of impersonal corporate bureaucrats or vested interests. Among other things, this means closing or reconverting luxury-producing and -importing enterprises and substituting enterprises that produce quality goods for mass domestic consumption. Working people as consumers will need to play a vital role in the decision-making process to avoid the shabby output of the ex-Communist states.

Industrial conversion (productive transformation with equity) also requires a balance between domestic and overseas production. Export earnings will continue to be important to finance vital inputs to the dynamic domestic growth model. What is crucial here is the reinvestment of surplus export earnings in the development of the internal market, not their transfer overseas or into speculative activity as is the case today.

Crucial to the structural adjustment model from below is the modernization of the state. The state in the export model is largely made up of regulators who fashion rules and allocate resources to satisfy overseas investors and traders, drawing on domestic resources and providing little information to local producers about the decision-making process. This elite process is fraught with corruption as is evident in bailouts and privatization scandals.

In rejecting the neoliberal model there is no going back towards the centralized bureaucratic state that stifled popular democracy, blocked innovations and produced gross inefficiencies. The modernization of the state means the decentralization of administrations of state allocations and their redistribution to local recipients in civil society able to vote on their own priorities. It means the redeployment of political appointees from useless bureaucratic functions to productive work. State reform means the relocation of health workers to the neighbourhoods, agronomists to the countryside and teachers to the overcrowded popular urban schools.

Socialism means rural schools—extending schools to the whole population. It means balancing consumption with production: balancing workers' rights with obligations to increase productivity and observe workplace discipline. It means that the working class, consumers, women and ethnic minorities are included in production and consumption decisions.

Consumers and citizens need to play a key role in directing state and economic institutions so as to avoid another "dictatorship *over* the proletariat" or overabundance of cheap and unneeded consumer goods.

Probably the most basic and novel feature of the new socialism will be the key role that workers, consumers and ecologists will play in the review and evaluation, and hiring and firing of managers. Avoidance of a privileged bureaucracy in public economic enterprises rests in an active role for direct producers and consumers in fundamental decision-making. Thus, under the new socialism, self-managers at the state, regional and local level are the alternatives to the private export elites of the globalized economy and the state bureaucrats of the past.

The key role of direct producers also involves responsibilities, a recognition that in the transition some workers may still retain "habits and practices" of work harmful to production and the creation of quality goods. Guaranteed lifetime employment is not viable; periodical peer evaluations of performance of quality and quantity of services should be the norm. Chronic offenders should be fired, abusive bureaucrats called to account, and public utilities managers and workers made accountable for unacceptable delays. Local, decentralized organization allows friends, neighbours and citizens to take decisions into their own hands to provide repair to telephone lines, etc. Absentee teachers should receive "absentee salaries" and answer to parents, students and others. Professors who recycle outdated lectures on yellowing note cards should be evaluated and advised to upgrade their courses or face dismissal.

The new socialism is based on workers' and peoples' control of their workplaces and communities, of the important conditions and decisions that affect their lives. It means the end of double and dishonest discourse. Personal lifestyles should be in accord with public discourse. Intellectuals cannot critique neoliberalism and then engage in frenzied consumption of imported consumer goods. One cannot preach equality up to the doorstop of one's household and then practice authoritarian (patriarchal) politics within the family. The new socialism recognizes the complexity of the contradictions in the transition—foremost the need to democratize gender, ethnic and race relations, a key element in the transition from globalism to a new socialism.

Consolidating the Transition:
The Politics of a Post-Imperialist Regime

The emergence of a free socialist and cooperative society cannot be derived from a preconceived model. It will involve a mixture of conscious intent and contingencies based on the behaviours, attitudes and economic and political performances of key social actors and classes. For example, the transition might begin with a model of co-participation of capital and labour, but under circumstances of disinvestment might evolve from a system of workers' control to a process of expropriation and restructuring and, ultimately, self-management. In turn, a decentralized self-management system might be modified to a degree that national social priorities are embraced or rejected, and self-enrichment, leading to new inequalities, informs the decisions of self-managers. Selective state intervention in the forms of taxes and redistributive policies might be legislated to avoid a development of gross regional and sectoral inequalities.

While the new socialist regime might provide wide latitude to forms of property, certain strategic sectors such as banking, foreign trade, telecommunications, natural resources, transportation, infrastructure and health care should be publicly owned and under popular oversight. The public sector should combine entrepreneurship and popular accountability. The old, narrow, profit-oriented form of entrepreneurship can be restructured to make innovation, management and research more responsive to the creation of national capabilities. New flexible management styles would be introduced, adapting to workers, family and environmental and consumer needs. IT should provide program matrix flows to facilitate the new management style.

One of the key areas for the new leadership is the problem of political corruption and illicit earnings. Overpricing by privatized firms will require price controls over basic commodities such as pharmaceuticals, water, grain, transportation, etc. This can be combined with free pricing in luxury goods, subject to steep import duties and personal property taxes. The new regime should investigate and seize assets illegally transferred into overseas accounts. It should seize the domestic assets and overseas holdings of drug, prostitution and contraband capitalists and their financial accomplices.

Control over the state requires the dismissal or arrest of high officials who are corrupt or engage in behaviour prejudicial to the popular classes, such as repression leading to loss of life. This will involve the creation of new military, judicial and central banking institutions. A new state structure would have to be formed compatible with a democratic socialist regime and economy. A new national security policy would also have to be elaborated to ensure the security of citizens and the nation from imperial intervention and subversion. This would require popular organization and new legal codes that bar imperial financing and the promotion of client candidates.

Local and regional assemblies (in the style of the state of Rio Grande de Sol in southern Brazil) should debate and resolve budgeting allocations for social, economic and cultural projects.

Annual workplace assemblies should meet to debate and decide on new investment projects as well as local community priorities in consultation with community groups. Workplace committees should be elected to oversee production in association with engineering, marketing and management committees on the basis of 50/50 representation. Short-term economic policy should be directed towards retaining external trading relations while moving as rapidly as feasible towards diversifying markets, the composition of exports and creditors, while deepening the domestic market. A moratorium on debt payments should be put into effect, and loans secured by corrupt politicians and private loans by enterprises for non-productive purposes should be repudiated. Payments should be renegotiated and postponed until the economy stabilizes. Any punitive or overtly politically hostile measures by lenders could lead to debt repudiation. Tax loopholes would be closed and transfer pricing by corporations would be punished. Strategic sectors of the economy would be socialized and paid with long-term bonds with deferred payments in order to recapitalize and modernize the enterprises. The economic capacity of the state would be modernized to increase its expertise and capacity for economic administration and to upgrade its efficiency in detecting tax evasion and regulating occupational health and working conditions. Import-substitution production would be deepened and accompanied by developing continuing education in political solidarity and technological innovation. Domestic markets must be an essential priority in the nation-building process.

Imperialism and free market policies have disarticulated the peasant economy and bankrupted provincial industries in countries such as Argentina, leading to massive depopulation of the interior. For imperialism the "nation" is the urban and mining enclaves and the administrative centres which enforce the free market agenda and promote foreign takeovers. The nation as a political-geographic entity is an empty formality. The task of a socialist regime would be to recreate the nation by reconstructing the markets and productive units of the interior of the countries via credit, public transport grids that link complementary productive sectors of the provinces, and social infrastructure.

National security involves consolidation of nation building and the popular social base of the regime. Raising the nutritional level of the population requires a major commitment towards investment in food self-sufficiency. This would require the promotion of local producer co-ops and family enterprises. Local production of popular consumer goods has a multiplier effect, leading to extended reproduction and a vibrant domestic market.

The efficiency of socialized production, distribution, transportation, telecommunications and IT should be measured by the degree to which it stimulates growth of income, production and living standards for the social economy; low cost state inputs may result in enterprise deficits but also in societal surpluses—in terms of general living standards and the expansion of productive networks in provincial economies. A calculus of social profits is the best measure of efficiency in a socialist or socialized economy.

Conclusion

By understanding its historical and structural limitations and underlying class ideology, it is possible to escape the tyranny of "globalism." Alternatives are not disembodied utopias "imagined" by individuals sitting in front of their computers, browsing the internet and probing cyberspace. Alternatives grow out of past and present experiences and the opportunities that emerge from the failures and crises of the "new economic model." The construction of a socialist alternative will require a long and hard struggle, the concerted collective action of the most diverse groups in society and the mobilization of their forces of opposition and resistance.

By focusing on social relations and the state as the building blocks of global empires, we can escape the prison of globalist thinking and enter the realm of political and social action. The inversion of the policies of globalist ideologues leads to the formulation of an alternative strategy in which social mobilization and state power provide a new class content to the shock treatments, industrial reconversions and structural adjustments of the neoliberal model. The new socialism learns not only from its capitalist adversaries about how to turn the table, but it also learns from the mistakes of the old socialism. It is more inclusive, drawing all parts of society into a collective project of economic and social development that is both equitable and sustainable. It will possess a greater sensibility to the notions of freedom at the workplace and on the farms. It will have a greater appreciation of the consequential discourse that integrates personal values and public practice.

The dynamics of globalization in Asia, the ex-USSR, Africa and Latin America are creating tremendous hardships but also provide an historic opportunity to transcend capitalism. It would be a failure of nerve of historic proportions to settle for anything less than a new socialist society, the new nation as an integral whole, a new culture of participants and not spectators, and a new internationalism of equals.

Bibliography

Abel, Christopher, and Colin Lewis (1993). *Welfare, Poverty and Development in Latin America*. London: Macmillan.

Aglietta, M (1982). "World Capitalism in the 1980s." *New Left Review* 136 (Nov.-Dec.): 5-41.

Anderson, Perry (1979). *Lineages of the Absolutist State*. London: Verso,

Barnet, Richard, and John Cavenagh (1994). *Global Dreams: Imperial Corporations and the New World Order*. New York: Simon & Schuster.

Bealey, F.W (1993). "Capitalism and Democracy." *European Journal of Political Research* 23 (2): 203-23.

_____ (1988). *Democracy in the Contemporary State*. Oxford: Oxford University Press.

Bello, Walden (1994). *Dark Victory: United States, Structural Adjustment and Global Poverty*. London: Pluto Press.

Bergsten, Fred, and Randall Henning (1996). *Global Economic Leadership and the Group of Seven*. Washington, D.C.: Institute for International Economics.

Bienefeld, Manfred (1995). "Assessing Current Development Trends: Reflections on Keith Griffin's 'Global Prospects for Development and Human Security.'" *Canadian Journal of Development Studies* 16 (3).

Blackburn, Robin (1998). The Making of New World Slavery: From the Baroque to the Modern, 1492-1800. London/New York: Verso.

Bobbio, Norberto (1990). *Liberalism and Democracy*. London: Verso.

Borón, Atilio (1981). "Latin America: Between Hobbes and Friedman." *New Left Review* 130 (Nov.-Dec.): 45-66.

Bowles, Samuel, and Herbert Gintis (1990). "Rethinking Marxism and Liberalism from a Radical Democratic Perspective." *Rethinking Marxism* 3 (3/4): 37-43.

_____ (1986). *Democracy and Capitalism*. New York: Basic Books.

Burbach, Roger (1994). "Roots of the Postmodern Rebellion in Chiapas." *New Left Review* 205.

Cammack, Paul (1997). *Capitalism and Democracy in the Third World*. London: Leicester University.

Castañeda, Jorge (1993). *Utopia Unarmed*. New York: Vintage.

CEPAL (Comision Economica para America Latina). 1998a. Economic Survey of Latin America, 1997-1998.

CEPAL (Comision Economica para America Latina). 1998b. La inversion extranjera en America Latina. Also available in English as ECLAC (Economic Commission for Latin America) 1998. Foreign Investment in Latin America.

Chossudovsky, Michel (1999). "Brazil's IMF Sponsored Economic Disaster." chossudosky@pop3.sprint.ca (Janauary 27).

_____ (1997). *The Globalization of Poverty*. London: Zed, Penang: Third World Network.

Dahl, R.A. (1971). *Polyarchy*. New Haven: Yale University Press.

Davis, Mike (1984). "The Political Economy of Late-Imperial America." *New Left Review* 143 (Jan.-Feb.).

Deinger, Klaus, and Lyn Squire (1997). "Economic Growth and Income Inequality: Reexamining the Links." *Finance & Development* 34 (1).

Diamond, L. (1992). "Economic Development and Democracy Reconsidered." *American Behavioral Scientist* 35 (4/5): 450-99.

ECLAC (1991). "Internacionalización y regionalizacion de la economia mundial: sus consecuencias para América Latina." September. Santiago de Chile: CEPAL.
_____ (1998a). *Balance preliminar de las economias de América Latina y el Caribe*. Santiago.
_____ (1998b). *Estudio economico de América Latina y el Caribe*. Santiago.
_____ (1998c). Foreign Investment in Latin America and the Caribbean (*La inversión extranjera en América latina y el Caribe: Informe 1997*). Santiago.
_____ (1998d). *Panorama preliminar de las economias de America Latina y el Caribe*. Santiago.
_____ (1990). *Productive Transformation with Equity*. Santiago.
Fields, G.S., and A.B. Newton (1997). Changing Labor Market Conditions and Income Distribution in Brazil, Costa Rica and Venezuela." In S. Edwards and N. Lustig (eds.), *Labor Markets in Latin America*. Washington, D.C.: Brookings Institute.
Financial Times (1999). "Global 500." January 28.
Fitch, Robert (1996). *The Assasination of New York*. London: Verso.
Follari, Roberto (1992). "Dominación y legitimación democrática en América latina." *Sociologica* 7 (19): 109-18.
Friedman, Jeffrey (1990). "The New Consensus II: The Democratic Welfare State." *Critical Review* 4 (4): 633-708.
Friedman, Milton (1982). *Capitalism and Freedom*. Chicago: University of Chicago Press.
Friedman, Milton, and Rose Friedman (1980). *Free to Choose*. Harmondsworth: Penguin.
Fukuyama, Francis (1991). *The End of History and the Last Man*. London: Hamish Hamilton.
Griffin, Keith (1995). "Global Prospects for Development and Human Security." *Canadian Journal of Development Studies* 16 (3).
Griffin, Keith, and Rahman Khan (1992). *Globalization and the Developing World*. Geneva: UNRISD.
Huntington, Samuel (1991). *The Third Wave: Democratization in the Late Twentieth Century*. Norman: University of Oklahama Press.
_____ (1984). "Will More Countries Become Democratic?" *Political Science Quarterly* 2: 193-218.
Inkeles, A. (1990). "The Effects of Democracy on Economic Growth and Inequality: A Review." *Studies in Comarative International Development* 25 (1): 126-57.
International Labour Organization (ILO) (1996). *World Employment, 1996*. Geneva: ILO.
International Monetary Fund (IMF) (1995). *International Capital Markets: Development, Prospects, and Policy Issues*. Washington: IMF.
Johnson, P. (1980). *The Recovery of Freedom*. Oxford: Blackwell.
Kapstein, Ethan (1996). "Workers and the World Economy." *Foreign Affairs* 75, (3).
Landes, D.S. (1966). *The Rise of Capitalism*. London: Macmillan.
Leftwich, Adrian (1993). "Governance, Democracy and Development in the Third World." *Third World Quarterly* 14 (3): 605-24.
Leiva, Fernando, and James Petras, with Henry Veltmeyer (1994). *Democracy and Poverty in Chile*. Boulder, Colo.: Westview Press.
Levitt, Kari (1990). "Debt, Adjustment and Development: Looking to the 1990s." *Economic and Political Weekly* July 21: 1585-94.
Lindblom, C.E. (1977). *Politics and Markets*. New York: Basic Books.

Lipietz, Alain (1989). "The Debt Problem: European Integration and the New Phase of the World Crisis" *New Left Review* 178 (Nov.-Dec.).

_____ (1987). *Mirages and Miracles: The Crisis of Global Fordism.* London: Verso.

_____ (1982). "Towards Global Fordism." *New Left Review* 13 (March-April).

Lustig, Nora, ed. (1995). *Coping with Austerity: Poverty and Inequality in Latin America.* Washington, D.C.: Brookings Institution.

Magdoff, Harry (1992). *Globalisation: To What End?* New York: Monthly Review Press.

_____ (1969). *The Age of Imperialism.* New York: Monthly Review.

Marglin, Stephen, and Juliet Schor (1990). *The Golden Age of Capitalism: Reinterpreting the Postwar Experience.* Oxford: Clarendon Press.

Martin, Hans-Peter, and Harold Schumann (1997). *The Global Trap.* London: Zed.

McMichael, Philip (1996). *Development and Change: A Global Perspective.* Thousand Oaks, Calif: Pine Gorge Press.

Mead, Walter (1991). *The Low Wage Challenge to Global Growth.* Washington, D.C.: Economic Policy Institute.

Meiksins Wood, Ellen (1995). *Democracy Against Capitalism: Renewing Historical Materialism.* Cambridge: Cambridge University Press.

Morley, Samuel (1995). "Structural Adjustment and Determinants of Poverty in Latin America." In Nora Lustig, ed.

Morris, Morley, and Chris McGillion (1997). "'Disobedient' Generals and the Politics of Redemocratization: The Clinton Administration and Haiti." *Political Science Quarterly* 112 (3): 363-84.

Nelson, J. (1989). *Fragile Coalitions: The Politics of Economic Adjustment.* New Brunswick, N.J.: Transaction Books.

Novak, M. (1982). *The Spirit of Democratic Capitalism.* New York: Simon & Schuster.

O'Donnell, G. (1973). *Modernization and Bureaucratic-Authoritarianism: Studies in South American Politics.* Berkeley: University of California.

O'Donnell, Guillermo, Philippe Schmitter and Lawrence Whitehead (1986). *Transition from Authoritarian Rule: Prospects for Democracy.* Baltimore: Johns Hopkins University Press.

OECD (1994). *The OECD Jobs Study: Facts, Analysis, Strategies.* Paris: OECD.

Offe, Claus (1983). "Competitive Party Democracy and the Keynesian Welfare State: Sources of Stability and Change." *Dados* 26 (1): 29-51.

Offe, Claus, and John Keene, eds. (1984). *Contradictions of the Welfare State.* London: Hutchinson.

Omae, Kenichi (1990). *The Borderless World: Power and Strategy in the Interlinked World Economy.* New York: Harper Business.

Overloop, Norbert Van (1993). "Democracy and Liberty: For Whom?" *Contradictions* 73 (Jan.): 87-105.

Patel, Surendra (1993). "Taming of Capitalism: The Historic Compromise." S.V. Desai Memorial Lecture, Ahmedabad. *Mainstream.* New Delhi.

_____ (1992). "In Tribute to the Golden Age of the South's Development." *World Development* 20 (5).

Petras, James, and Howard Brill (1985). "The Tyranny of Globalism." IDS working paper no. 85-3. Halifax: Saint Mary's University.

Philip, George (1993). "The New Economic Liberalism and Democracy in Latin America: Friends or Enemies?" *Third World Quarterly* 14 (3): 555-72.

Przeworski, Adam (1991). *Democracy and the Market: Political and Economic Reforms in Eastern Europe and Latin America.* Cambridge: Cambridge University Press.

_____ (1986). *Capitalism and Social Democracy*. Cambridge: Cambridge University Press.

Robinson, M. (1993). "Will Political Conditionality Work?" *IDS Bulletin* 24 (1): 58-66.

Robinson, William (1996). "Globalization: Nine Theses on our Epoch." *Montelibre Monthly* March/April.

Rostow, W.W (1960). *The Stages of Economic Growth*. Canbridge: Cambridge University Press.

Sau, Ranjit (1996). "On the Making of the Next Century." *Economic and Political Weekly* 31 (April 6): 14.

Schumpeter, J.A. (1941). *Capitalism, Socialism and Democracy*. London: Allen & Unwin.

Shapiro, Svi (1990). *Between Capitalism and Democracy: Educational Policy and the Crisis of the Welfare State*. New York: Bergin and Garvey.

South Centre (1997a). *Foreign Direct Investment, Development and the New Global Economic Policy*. Geneva.

_____ (1997b). *South Letter* 3-4 (29).

_____ (1996). *Liberalization and Globalization: Drawing Conclusions for Development*.Geneva.

Stephens, Evelyne-Huber (1989). "Capitalist Development and Democracy in South America." *Politics and Society* 17 (3): 281-352.

Strange, Susan (1994). *States and Markets*. London/New York: Pinter.

Third World Guide 95/96 (1996). Montevideo: Instituto del Tercer Mundo.

UNCTAD (1994, 1997, 1998). *World Investment Report*. New York and Geneva: U.N.

UNDP (1992). *Human Development: Reports 1992*. New York: Oxford University Press.

UNIDO (1997). *Industry and Development Global Report, 1996*. Chapter one ("Globalization: Its Challenges and Opportunities for Industrial Development") in *Economia Política: Trayectorias y Perspectives* (Universidad Autónoma de Zacatecas), 12 (Marzo-Abril 1997).

UNRISD (1995). *States of Disarray: The Social Effects of Globalization*. Geneva: UNRISD.

U.S. Dept. of Commerce, Bureau of Economic Analysis (1999). *Balance of Payments. Transactions by Area* (March 4). Washington, D.C.

_____ (1994, 1999). *U.S. Direct Investment Abroad. Capital Flows*. Washington, D.C.

Varman-Schneider, Benu (1991). *Capital Flight from Developing Countries*. Boulder, Colo.: Westview Press.

Veltmeyer, Henry (1999a). "Labour and the World Economy." *Canadian Journal of Development Studies* 20, special issue.

_____ (1999b). *The Labyrinth of Latin American Development*. New Delhi: APH Publications.

Veltmeyer, Henry, and James Petras (1997). *Neoliberalism and Class Conflict in Latin America*. London: Macmillan Press, New York: St. Martin's Press.

Waters, Malcolm (1954). *Globalization*. London/New York: Routledge.

Watkins, Kevin (1995). *Oxfam Poverty Report*. Oxford: Oxfam.

Woodward, David (1992). *Debt, Adjustment and Poverty in Developing Countries*. London: Pinter Publishers/Save the Children.

World Bank (2000). *World Development Report 2000/2001: Attacking Poverty*. New York: Oxford University Press.

_____ (1988, 1990, 1991, 1993, 1995, 1997). *World Development Report*. Oxford: Oxford University Press.

_____ (1995). *World Development Report 1995: Workers in an Integrating World*. New York: Oxford University Press.

_____ (1994). *World Debt Tables, 1994/95*. Washington, D.C.: World Bank.

_____ (1992a). *Governance and Development*. Washington, D.C.: World Bank.

_____ (1992b). *World Bank Structural and Sectoral Adjustment Operations*, Report of the Operations Evaluation Department (June). Washington, D.C.: World Bank.

World Commission on Culture and Development (WCCD) (1995). *Our Creative Diversity*. Paris: UNESCO.

Index